Barenaked Ladies

Public Stunts, Private Stories

Paul Myers

A Fireside Book
Published by Simon & Schuster
New York   London   Toronto   Sydney   Singapore

Rockefeller Center
1230 Avenue of the Americas
New York, NY 10020

First Fireside edition 2003

Published by arrangement with Madrigal Press Limited

Originally published in Canada in 2001 by Madrigal Press Limited

FIRESIDE and colophon are registered trademarks
of Simon & Schuster, Inc.

For information regarding special discounts for bulk purchases,
please contact Simon & Schuster Special Sales at
1-800-456-6798 or business@simonandschuster.com

Designed by Christine Weathersbee

Manufactured in the United States of America

Library of Congress Cataloging-in-Publication Data

Myers, Paul.
    Barenaked Ladies : public stunts, private stories/Paul Myers.
—1st Fireside ed.
        p.   cm
    "A Fireside book."
    Originally published: Vancouver, BC : Madrigal Press, 2001.
    1. Barenaked Ladies. 2. Rock musicians—Canada—Biography.
    I. Title: Public stunts, private stories. II. Title.
ML421.B335M94   2003
782.42166'092'2—dc21
[B]   2003042715

10 9 8 7 6 5 4 3 2 1

ISBN 0-7432-3835-4

To Liza, my sweetheart, who never fails
to keep me amused and amazed.

Acknowledgments

The author would like to thank all da Ladies in da house: Tyler, Steven, Ed, Jimmy, and Kevin (let's not forget Andy), for letting me break into their old apartments and for sharing the private stories behind their formidable public stunts. (Now you have to write a book about me; tag, you're it.) To Fin, for making the road a better place to be. To Cathryn France, for the phone calls of encouragement and affirmation and virtual hand-holding. And lastly, to Terry McBride, who asked the musical question "Where's my book?"

Here it is.

Paul Myers
New Delhi
March 11, 2001

Contents

How to Use This Book
(Model Number 4URBNL)

System requirements: This is a book. As printware it does not require any interface with a computer whatsoever. But it is a good idea to get a very fast processor and a really fast modem. Cable versus DSL? We're not saying which is better. I mean there might be an endorsement deal in the wings, right? Anyway, good computer gear is kind of essential these days. Not for the book, mind you, it's just a good idea. And get a good color printer while you're at it.

May contain: opinions, facts, recollections (fuzzy and/or otherwise), wry turns of phrase, warm remembrances, musical jargon, references to short pants, near-death experiences, near-life experiences, births, deaths, marriages, driver's license renewals, and/or pine nuts.

Installation: This book is ready to use whenever you wish; however, in the interest of public safety, we suggest the following precautions, practices, and safeguards to maximize your enjoyment and ensure multiple readings:

1. In-store procedures: Once you have selected a copy of the book, proceed to the cash register. A financial transaction, agreed upon by you and the merchant, will transpire. At such time, you will be free to leave the store with the book, or many copies

thereof (provided that the larger resultant fee is also tendered by merchant).

2. Transportation from store to home or home of friend: Regrettably, Barenaked Ladies, their management, the author, the publisher, and all other affiliates cannot provide rides to and from place of purchase. You're on your own. We apologize for the inconvenience, but our cars are in the shop, eh.

3. Safe reading tips: The makers of *Barenaked Ladies: Public Stunts, Private Stories* suggest that the reading of this book take place in a location that has adequate lighting and ventilation. We cannot assume responsibility for asphyxia, eyestrain, or temporary or permanent blindness as a result of misuse of printed matter. A comfortable chair, such as a recliner, beanbag chair, chaise lounge, or Adirondack chair are recommended but not required. Clothing is optional, but must conform to personal comfort guidelines to be decided upon by the reader. Patrons reading in partial or total undress in a public place that is not designated for such non-attire do so at their own risk and consequence.

4. Turning of pages, sequence, and procedural notes: *Barenaked Ladies: Public Stunts, Private Stories* may be read in any sequence; some may wish to skip to the dirty parts, while others may wish to read the same page or word again and again in a repetitive, if not redundant, manner. In such instances, Barenaked Ladies, their management, the author, and all other affiliates reserve the right to sneer at and badger the reader in a judgmental and taunting fashion. When reading biographical chapters, it's recommended that readers follow sequentially (in accordance with numeric page designations contained within) to maximize retention of linear events.

5. Reader-enjoyment liability notes: This is a tricky

thing to gauge. I mean, some people are kinda, well, kinky. To put it tastefully, these people are freaky-deaky, like they got some wild stuff goin' on in their minds, dig? In deference to the wide-ranging enjoyment requirements of our audience, we have endeavored to provide content and graphical presentations to meet these needs. It is our hope that we do. We like you. You're cool. You're smart. No, really, we mean it. Hey, you're blushing. You're kinda cute when you're flustered. *Flustered*? Sure it's a word! No, I did not make it up. People say *flustered* all the time, honest. I'll admit it's a funny-looking word, but it does sort of have a certain onomatopoeical charm. Oh come on, you've heard that word before haven't you? *Onomatopoeia*! You know, words that sound like what they mean. Like *thud* or *swoosh* or *Billy Ray Cyrus*. Look, I just wanted to give you a little compliment and all I get is a lecture on how I'm showing off my vocabulary. What? Oh, come on. *Vocabulary*. It means "the words that one has at one's disposal." If you knew that, then why did you ask? Hey, where you goin'? You forgot your book. Sheesh.

1

Alcatraz, 1998
San Francisco Bay

In the '40s, singer Tony Bennett claimed, in song, to have misplaced a vital organ here. In the '80s, Starship claimed to have built this city on rock and roll, although I happen to know for a fact that this city is actually built along a fault line. And as a result, the earth below San Francisco does tend to rock and roll from time to time. There are certainly rolls, sourdough rolls served with the clam chowder you get down at Fisherman's Wharf. And smack-dab in the middle of San Francisco Bay is "the Rock," Alcatraz Island, which was once the site of the most notorious federal penitentiary in America.

Now, on this sunny evening in May 1998, Alcatraz has been taken over by a landing party of trained music-business professionals—with the emphasis on *party*. The cold, decrepit prison buildings have been rented out to Warner Bros. Records for a national meet-'n'-greet. Events like this give selected music retailers from all over the country a chance to get to know some of the Warner recording artists in an informal, though not typically prisonlike, setting. Caterers have cleaned up the mess hall and are presenting a hot and cold buffet. Cell phone–wielding reps hold cocktails and mingle in the same room where cell mates, dodging rats and cockroaches, used to dine. But tonight, there are only bartenders behind the bars. Incarceration gives way to incapacitation as the food and drinks run free. Representatives of music-store chains mix in the mess hall with Warner's outfield—the regional point people from its offices around the country. Tonight, Warner Bros., the warden as it were, will reveal its plans to execute killer promotional strategies and plot the breakout of its up-and-coming artists. Country and rap artists converge. Stetsons and dreadlocks pop up from time to time as good ol' boys and homeboys chat among themselves. Then it's over to the meet 'n' greet itself.

Along what is affectionately known as "Broadway," an infamous stretch of cell blocks that once held gangsters like Alphonse "Al" Capone, George "Machine Gun" Kelly, and Robert "Birdman of Alcatraz" Stroud, stand the most-wanted photo ops in the joint. Their names are equally colorful, their legends every bit as notorious. Reps will meet and have their pictures taken with the likes of Stephanie "Stevie" Nicks, Fleetwood Mac's shawl-bearing sorceress, and "Solitary Man"–cover guy Christopher "Chris" Isaak.

Let's pretend, then, that you're a rep at Alcatraz on this warm spring night. Get in line, for you're about to meet a band of deceptively good-natured Canadians who are guilty of forging a successful recording career. Right away, there are a few things you should know about Barenaked Ladies. They are not ladies. They are not, for the most part, naked. Their name is meant to convey childlike innocence, and they are not misogynists. Let's talk about who they are.

Both lead vocalists, Steven Page and Ed Robertson, play guitar and generally write most of the band's material. Steven has a big, almost operatic voice and a powerful range. Onstage he's not afraid to dance like a madman if the spirit takes him. Ed's vocal style can change from earnest folky to freestyle rapper at the drop of a mic. Onstage he's not afraid to get the security guards into the act by letting them play his guitar during the show.

Jim Creeggan, the tall, lanky guy with the red hair, plays a double bass that's almost as tall as he is. He's also one of the best bass players in popular music today, and, according to Steven, his bass technique is the cornerstone of the band's sound.

Beside him is Tyler Stewart. Tyler's official role in the band is "drummer." But as the other BNL members will tell you, his affable personality and sharp sense of humor are equally important to the chemistry of the group.

Kevin Hearn plays keyboards, guitars, and, with his samplers, provides a little digital mayhem to the band's sonic stew. He may seem like a choirboy (well, he *was* a choirboy), but don't be fooled. He's a musical mad scientist.

Barenaked Ladies are mainly from Scarborough, Ontario, which used to be known as a suburb of Toronto, but that's another story.

My name is Paul Myers. I first met Barenaked Ladies when I was a musician playing in the Toronto music scene with my band, the Gravelberrys. Back in 1990, we were booked into a cozy little club called Ultrasound Showbar on Queen Street West. The club was booked by Yvonne Matsell, who'd called me to ask if she could book a band she liked in the opening slot for the Gravelberrys' upcoming Monday night show. She told me that the band was called Barenaked Ladies. I wanted to snicker. With a name like that, I thought, they'd probably be some kind of frat-boy, kegger-party band. But Yvonne's question, as it happened, was not the kind that required a yes or no answer from me. It was more like "Here's your new baby brother; do you like him? Of course you do." And when the big night came, I wasn't prepared for how much fun these guys would be. I was genuinely charmed by their stage antics. Steven and Ed did something that I hadn't seen in the clubs of late: They actively engaged the audience. They worked the room. They were funny. They were good musicians. They were great entertainers.

So when they opened for us again a few months later, they brought a huge crowd with them. They were on their way.

2

Burbank, 1998

It's been . . .

The heavily compressed voice of Steven Page suddenly grabs my attention, leaping, as it does, from the tinny AM radio in the airport taxi. How portentous, I think. How exciting, I say to myself.

I've just arrived at the Burbank, California, airport. Yes, "beautiful downtown Burbank" as Gary Owens used to say on *Rowan & Martin's Laugh-In* in the late '60s. Before any of the Barenaked Ladies were born. When dinosaurs roamed the earth. The place I'm going, Universal Amphitheater, animatronic dinosaurs of the phylum Spielbergus Jurassicus, born in domesticity, still do, in fact, roam the earth. Many times daily. As do numerous other attractions such as "Indiana Jones," all of which give tourists a chance to ride the movies.

Like Harrison Ford, I'm getting frantic . . .

Coming to Hollywood through Burbank is sort of like entering a mall through the service-and-delivery entrance. No frills. No glitter. You won't find a BURBANK sign suspended in the hills. In fact, you can't even see the Hollywood sign from here. But it's a warm day, and the sky is as brown as a movie star's synthetic tan. This is the valley, the land of filmmaker Paul Thomas Anderson's *Boogie Nights* and *Magnolia*. Affluence does exist here, but it mingles casually with rusted-out cars and cheap storefronts. On this side of the valley, anything goes. As long as it still can. In Hollywood, any car older than last year's model is considered vintage and likely to be owned and/or driven by Jay Leno.

I'm not so sure about this taxi's odds of going the distance, but going I seem to be. And where I'm going is a lovely concert venue with a capacity of 6,500, which tonight will host a sold-out show by Barenaked Ladies. I'll be joining the tour here, sharing a week in the life, and bus, of the band as they take a sort of victory lap around America. Again.

Hot like wasabe when I bust rhymes . . .

Ed Robertson's rap, partially obscured by bursts of white noise and the cab dispatcher's barking, has become prophecy. Right now, Barenaked Ladies are as hot as a big wad of that spicy green Japanese condiment. They're hot like the number-one single in America. Hot like the seemingly ubiquitous rotation of their breakthrough video for "One Week" on MTV and VH1. Hot like the sight and sound of entire audiences singing along with BNL for every single syllable of every single word from every single song.

The taxi leaves me at the venue's will-call entrance. I will now be *credentialed*.

Getting one's credentials is one of the last vestiges of hierarchy in the world of rock. There are many levels of the backstage pass. Are you "preshow only," "after show only," or are you a "very important person"? It all matters in the world of backstage access. Well, bless my soul, I've been granted a pass even better than VIP, for my laminate bears the words *All Access*. The security personnel hand me my precious laminate and, after some unintelligible walkie-talking, I'm escorted to the portal of "backstage." This being Hollywood, however, a golf cart is enlisted to spare us the three-hundred-foot walk. Plane, cab, and now golf cart; that's three separate vehicles just to get me to this moment.

3

This Is Where It Starts
Parry Sound, 1988

The Barenaked Ladies' story begins at the Manitou-Wabing Sports and Arts Centre near the sleepy summer town of Parry Sound, Ontario, with the meeting of Ed Robertson and Steven Page. Every summer, the Scarborough board of education held a ten-day camp for any and all Scarborough students, boys and girls, who demonstrated an ability or interest in music.

Enter Steven Page, a witty, if brooding, seventeen-year-old high-school student with creative aspirations, who'd come up to the camp in 1987 and been impressed by the woodland retreat and its symphonic symposia. Of course, it didn't hurt that, since the camp started in June, one could skip the entire last month of school by volunteering as a counselor. And it certainly didn't hurt that during the 1987 music-camp session Steven met an "older" girl named Carolyn Ricketts. Carolyn was a music-history student at the University of Western Ontario and well on her way to getting her bachelor's and M.A. in musicology. That summer, Steven offered her an "extra" ticket to see Paul Simon's *Graceland* tour concert at Maple Leaf Gardens in Toronto—their first real date.

So it was then that in 1988, with his eighteenth birthday (June 22) approaching, Steven kicked off another camp session with added incentives. At this time in his life, the introverted young Steven had been writing songs, among other creative works, with his close friend Geoff Pounsett, whom Steven admired as much for his extroverted personality as for his kindred artistic spirit. "Geoff was the most popular guy," remembers Steven today. "He and I were always creative partners, but the teachers would rarely see that. They would never understand why he thought I was in the same league as [he was], because I wasn't the same kind of performer or didn't have the same outgoing personality."

Steven and Geoff, schoolmates at Churchill Heights in Scarborough, created their own inner world, where the only thing that mattered was the tireless pursuit of making stuff up. Incessantly inventive, they collaborated tag team–style on short stories, one-act plays, and even a couple of comic books. "I'd do two frames and pass it over, and then Geoff would add two more frames," says Steven. "Eventually we'd do whole stories during class, especially during French class. They'd be totally bizarre stories, and we even had pen names like 'S. O'Terek.' Like, there was this guy who had a giant bird named Furt who was terrorizing him. You'd write a phrase, and the next guy would read it and take it in a new direction. There was a trio of us, me, Geoff, and a guy named Andrew Torres. Andrew was the guy who seemed the most serious, but when he was funny he was funnier than anyone else. And no one else knew he was that funny except us."

But it was only Geoff who accompanied Steven to music camp in 1988, and true to form, the two could be seen wandering like alternative minstrels around the grounds daily, playing some of their decidedly original songs. Carolyn recalls one particular concert, at a faculty party, that proved pivotal in her life. "Steven sang, and I was hooked" is how Carolyn remembers it.

Steven and Geoff formed a duo with the characteristically

striking name Scary Movie Breakfast. The name came from the title of a little story that the two had written to amuse themselves during Monsieur Ceurstemont's French class in Scarborough. Surreptitiously passing a sheet of paper back and forth, they took turns writing whole stories, alternately adding sentences or paragraphs. Their stated mission was for one of them to make the other one laugh out loud in class, a mission they accomplished on a daily basis. So while they named their duo after one of their better stories, they could've just as easily taken their name from another favorite: "Aunt Hill's Monkey Works."

"Steve grew up in a house that had a piano, a set of drums, and at least one guitar lying around," remembers Geoff. "Our house had a piano, a banjo, a couple of guitars, and a mandolin." Since both boys had been studying piano and other instruments, it seemed inevitable that they would begin to experiment with the tools at hand. Even at their first public performance together, a high-school assembly with Steven on guitar and Geoff pounding away on a solitary snare drum, Steven's satirical side was in evidence as the pair ran through a humorous medley of the pop hits of the day. Albeit, in their own skewed way.

"The arrangements of the songs were misleading," recalls Geoff, "so there was a laugh of recognition when the lyrics came in. I remember we climaxed with "Venus" by Bananarama. Steve may remember the other tunes we used. We refurbished the act a couple of times, at school and at the now-legendary music camp."

So it happened, while working up an offbeat arrangement of the "Roadrunner" theme song (from the Warner Bros. cartoon), the wily pair was struck by a sixteen-ton idea: Why not write some original songs for the two to play? "Steve wrote a few tunes entirely on his own, and I think I wrote one," recalls Geoff. "Some were pretty schmaltzy, and some grasped for art. The ones we wrote together usually involved me fiddling on the guitar and Steve singing/writing a melody line and the backbone of the lyrics." Geoff remembers that although a lot of the songs were written purely to amuse themselves, the Breakfast also discovered the importance of being earnest songwriters. While Geoff describes their overall sound as being "folky-poppy," he admits that the duo conjured a wide array of sounds and styles out of the essentially acoustic instruments at hand. "We did an a cappella version of the dance tune 'Popcorn' with what I can only describe as voice-over narration: 'Popcorn. Pop, pop, pop, pop, pop.'"

Steven describes the song "Really Don't Know" as a nonsensical love song and "kind of a Nick Heyward sort of thing." Nick Heyward, the English popsmith who, while he still makes solo records, is perhaps best remembered for his work in the '80s band Haircut 100. Maybe the most significant influence Heyward had on the young Steven was the former's use of wordplay. In songs like "Love Plus One" and "Favourite Shirts (Boy Meets Girl)," deceptively catchy melodies were often packed with lyrical non sequiturs that defied logic on a literal level, but spoke evocatively on an emotional level. That's a trick that you'll find in some Barenaked Ladies songs to this day. "I really loved Nick Heyward's lyrics," Steven admits, "even in Haircut 100—and his first solo album, *North of a Miracle*, was full of lyrics that didn't make any sense. For example, 'Why oh why/Lemon fire- brigade why?'"

While Steve and Geoff devoured most of the alternative music of the '80s, they took inspiration from other sources like the Beatles, Taj Mahal, and various blues, folk, or bluegrass artists. And then there were the singer-songwriters such as Elvis Costello and Lloyd Cole, and a guy named Stephen Duffy, otherwise known as Tin Tin. "It all got mashed in there somehow," Geoff admits. "We were pop-culture and music nuts. We wore big ugly ties and baggy pants to school dances, and wool turtlenecks and jeans to perform in. We were trying to be iconoclasts, but friendly iconoclasts with a taste for the silly and the sublime."

Apart from live appearances at school and camp, Scary Movie Breakfast tried their hand at a few small acoustic-friendly clubs in downtown Toronto. Often playing open-stage nights, the two traded off on guitar, or Geoff would double on banjo while Steven assumed lead vocals.

But a misunderstanding with a nightclub manager over a canceled booking still haunts Geoff to this day. Geoff had called Jimmy Scopes, the locally legendary promoter of the also locally legendary Cabana Room of the equally locally legendary Spadina Hotel, weeks in advance to notify him that because he would be out of town with his family, the Breakfast could not be served on their previously-agreed-upon date. Geoff remembers that later an angry Scopes called up the Page residence demanding an explanation from Steven's mom. Scary Movie Breakfast, it appeared, would never play the Cabana Room again.

Geoff, however, puts it all in perspective. "I burned our bridge there, for sure, but soon after I left for university, Steve started playing with Ed, and the Cabana Room went belly up anyway. I don't think I injured Steve's career too much."

Soon Scary Movie Breakfast was history, but they did leave behind a small but crucial recorded legacy, one that clearly indicates the direction that Steven's musical career would take in the next few years. Of the duo's "two major recording sessions," Geoff says that Steven's engineering and producing techniques could be fairly straightforward one minute and highly unpredictable the next. Geoff recalls one such session, for their song "Broken-Down Mustang Blues."

"We recorded bass, drums, guitars, harmonica, piano, various percussion, and at least two vocal tracks all on a four-track with only two of us playing and only one microphone. Other songs were simpler in arrangement, though the tools were pretty rudimentary and we were learning as we were going along." Steven and Geoff made copies of these recordings and sent them to whomever they could think of. Significantly, one of the tapes wound up in the hands of Stephen Duffy.

The English songwriter had scored a hit record in the United Kingdom called "Kiss Me." Steven had heard the record while

13

listening to the Toronto alternative station CFNY, and it had left a lasting impression on him. CFNY 102.1, "the Edge," had made an impression on Toronto-area musicians, mostly due to the station's decidedly eclectic playlist of innovative new music from around the world. The world, of course, meant England and the New York new-wave bands like Talking Heads, Blondie, and the Ramones. The effect of CFNY's programming on the consciousness of a whole generation of young Toronto musicians cannot be underestimated. Suddenly, somewhat marginally known U.K. artists like Gang of Four, the Undertones, the Buzzcocks, the Slits, Lene Lovich, and Ian Dury and the Blockheads shared the Toronto radio waves with better-known new music from Thomas Dolby, Bauhaus, Siouxsie and the Banshees, Gary Numan, and Howard Jones.

So it was that, aided and abetted by a slightly skewed modern-rock radio perspective, Steven was convinced that Tin Tin was a "big group from England" regardless of their relative anonymity in North America. Somewhat fearlessly, Steven wrote a letter to Duffy expressing not only his musical admiration but offering his personal views on art and life. Duffy was impressed by Steven's courage as well as his critical candor, and could relate to Page's fan letters, having written many like them to his own heroes in the past. "I'd written to folks like the Incredible String Band and Sparks when I was a kid," says Duffy. "I wrote one to David Bowie, and Angie [Bowie] replied, so I was aware of my responsibility. I'd also followed the Clash around in the late seventies and they treated us well, letting us in for sound checks and things, so I retained my punk ideals even if my music was pants.[1]

"He [Steven] wrote me a letter shortly after the release of my first album, *The Ups and Downs*," recalls the artist formerly known as Tin Tin. "He must have been about fourteen or fifteen,

---

[1] "Pants" is U.K. slang for "rubbish" or "nonsense." Duffy is using it here in a charmingly self-deprecating way.

14

but his letter was original and he'd obviously listened to the record and he got into it. He also remarked on the bits stolen from [Beat poet Allen] Ginsberg in one song and the Beatles in another, so I wrote back."

Soon the two were pen pals. And as Steven broadened his tastes to non-pop poets such as Leonard Cohen, Duffy mutated his muse into a decidedly folky project he called the Lilac Time. Steven applauded this new direction. "When he got the first Lilac record and was into it," remembers Duffy with great relief, "I wasn't banished to the gulags of teenage embarrassment." To return the compliment, Steven sent Duffy a tape of Scary Movie Breakfast, making him one of the privileged few to own a custom dub of the extremely rare recording. "I wrote back and said it was the most entertaining tape I'd ever been sent," Duffy recollects. "At least I hope I did. It was the only tape I played to other people. There was one song with the longest whistling solo ever recorded—people wanted copies of it. Again, it was original and he obviously loved doing it. Everyone's first tapes are derivative and pretentious; it's the law. Scary Movie Breakfast didn't sound like anyone else, and it wasn't pretentious."

More tapes followed, and as he became busier, Steven's letters got shorter and turned into postcards from the road. "I found one the other day," Duffy tells me, "saying that Scary Movie Breakfast was over and he had a new band and partner and it was called Barenaked Ladies, but in brackets he wrote 'a name I detest.'"

In August of 1989 Steven went to England, where he'd finally get to meet his pop-culture pen pal face to face. Duffy was rehearsing for the Cambridge Folk Festival and invited Steven to stay with the band in a rustic, rural farmhouse located, says Duffy, "in the middle of nowhere." Travel-weary and hungover after a long transatlantic flight, Steven took the train to the countryside retreat where the Lilac Time were holed up. There to greet him off the train was Duffy. "It's a strange way to meet one of your closest friends," admits Duffy. Of course now I'm embarrassed I didn't put him up at my house, but at the time it didn't occur to me. I suppose someone else was at my place, but I just knew it would be okay."

When the Lilac Time finally got to Toronto to play the Rivoli on February 1, 1990, Duffy got a taste of Steven's world. Onstage that night, Duffy thought it would be a friendly gesture to come out for his encore sporting a Toronto Maple Leafs hockey jersey. Was he unaware that this sort of home-team-sports-jerseyism was strictly for arena-rocking heavy metalers? Or perhaps this was an ironic gesture. Nonetheless, Steven was disappointed in the ambiguity of the fashion statement, and he let his new friend know it. "Steven berated me for wearing a Maple Leafs shirt for the encore," remembers an amused Duffy. "I was supposed to be the 'waif poet,' and I was wearing a hockey shirt. But we were immediate friends, and I feel pretty much part of the extended family now."

Eventually the two became such good friends and Barenaked Ladies tapes got so much better that Duffy offered to produce Mr. Page and his partners. Not that they had a plan, per se. "I don't think we ever had any intention of me doing this," admits Duffy. "I just thought it might be a useful aside." Useful asides aside, the two remain close friends and collaborators, and the team of Page and Duffy continues to appear in the credits of every Barenaked Ladies release since *Maybe You Should Drive*.

It's a safe bet that, at the time, young Steven Page really didn't know how significant the summer of '88 would be for him. He would begin some of the most significant partnerships in his young life, including a life-altering musical acquaintance with a mutual friend of Geoff's.

4

The Special Education
of Special Ed

Enter Ed.

Lloyd Edward Elwyn Robertson, the fifth child born to Earl and Wilma Robertson, arrived in this world on October 25, 1970, in (where else?) Scarborough, Ontario. But by the time Lloyd Edward Elwyn began his education at Walter Perry Public School, he was answering to a shorter name. You can call him Ed. Everyone else does.

Papa Earl held a job at the Honeywell plant on Birchmount and Ellesmere Avenues, where he was the foreman of shipping and receiving. But by night, Earl Robertson liked to play his guitar. Early on, Ed was drawn to the sound of his father's old acoustic.

"That was why I started playing guitar," he remembers. "Dad just played around the house and at family gatherings. He had an old Harmony guitar, like a cheap-copy version of the Gibson Dove." In fact, Ed still has the guitar and keeps it under his bed. Although it's barely playable in a practical sense, he's held on to it for obvious sentimental reasons. And let's face it:

The thing still looks good even if it doesn't sound especially nice. "I kept it even though it doesn't work anymore," Robertson admits. "The neck is totally pulled away."[1]

His mom, Wilma, headed up the steno pool at Imperial Oil, (which later became Esso), out by the Don Valley Parkway and Eglinton Avenue East, just over the Scarborough border, making for an unusual domestic life. "She worked the night shift, and my dad worked the day shift," remembers Ed of his parents' conflicting schedules. "So there was always someone home with us crazy kids. It was cramped. We lived in a tiny bungalow with a hardly finished basement and one bathroom and seven people in a very small Scarborough house."

Ed was the youngest of five children, after next-to-youngest brother Bill, sister Bonnie, brother Doug, and finally sister Lynn, the eldest sibling, who is actually fifteen years older than Ed.

None of his siblings shared an interest in playing music. Ed's two brothers were hockey maniacs, in particular his brother Bill, so Ed pretty much had his own space in the Robertson household due to the wide gap in the children's ages. It's likely that this situation gave Ed the strong sense of independence that would later become important in his music career.

Ed remembers the most musical times for the Robertson clan were the family jamborees, like the annual Markham Fair in nearby Markham, Ontario. "My aunt and uncle and their kids lived up there, and they'd all show up, and it kind of composed a complete country band," Ed recalls with pride. "My uncle Robert and my dad both played guitar."

No, Uncle Robert is not that Robbie Robertson from the Band, but to young Ed, his uncle was just as influential, and besides he was way cool, too. In fact, these get-togethers probably cemented the junior Robertson's already piqued interest in getting up there and making his own joyful noise. "My uncle,"

---

[1] It still works as a prop though, and Ed says the old Harmony has been featured in many of the BNL videos, where looks count more than intonation.

Ed boasts proudly, "was the kind of guy who could throw some lead lines in there. And a family friend, this guy Keith, played the banjo while his son, Mitchell, played mandolin and Dobro. Everybody sang harmony and stuff. So, I just wanted to be a part of that whole thing." Is it really all that surprising to learn that the very first songs Ed tried to learn were by Tom T. Hall, George Jones, and, frankly, Kenny Rogers? No, I guess it's not. "Mom and dad would always sing old country-and-western ballads and sing harmonies and stuff," recalls Robertson. "I started playing guitar so I could play Kenny Rogers's 'The Gambler' or 'Coward of the County,' and really old country stuff." What Ed can't recall is just which recording artists produced the original versions of some of the other country songs he learned at home, because, in most cases, Ed never actually heard any of those original recordings. "I've never heard versions other than my mom and dad's. In fact, country flat-picking and strumming is still my main influence as a guitar player. It's still at the root of what I do."

Country may have been in his roots, but young Ed was not ready to be unplugged so soon. He formed a heavy rock band called the Rage and developed a gift for pyrotechnical fretwork that earned him the nickname "Eddie," as in Van Halen. Ed remembers well the transition from hardwood to hard rock. "When I was a kid, all I liked was country stuff," he admits. "That's what I learned on the guitar. I was country when country wasn't cool. As soon as I discovered it wasn't cool, I got into rock."

Indoctrinated by the purchase of his very first rock album, *Exit . . . Stage Left* by Toronto's Rush, Ed became a zealous Rush fan. "I loved it and then, sort of, Rush was like the only band that mattered to me," says Ed, looking back "Geddily." "I had all their albums. I made a shelf out of quarter round, nailed quarter round to my wall in two sections and had all the Rush albums up on my wall as art." He also had a huge color poster of Rush's *2112*, and frankly every Rush poster he could get his hands on.

He even had vinyl-album picture discs. But although his walls were virtually filled with Rushernalia, he did manage to retain a tiny little strip dedicated to Black Sabbath and their bat-chomping lead singer, Ozzy Osbourne.

"I got into Black Sabbath when my brother gave me *Master of Reality* for my birthday. Whatever records you get, when you're that age you play the shit out of them. You get way into it." Amped up from his new passion, it was time for Ed to go electric: a gold-and-brown Sunburst Les Paul copy made by Vantage. But soon, as he began to form little bands here and there, the fifteen-year-old outgrew the training wheels. It was time for a genuine Gibson Les Paul, the real thing. Strangely, his parents were more than obliging. "My mom took me down to Long and McQuade on Bloor Street and bought me a candy-red Les Paul Custom."

Ed first began to use his red guitar playing with the Rage, formerly called Rude Awakening. "It started as just me and the drummer, and it was that for two years. I think we only called it the Rage as we were breaking up." Ed recalls writing only two songs for Rude Awakening. One was a love song to his then girlfriend, whose name he remembers as Elina Yakimov. The only thing he can't remember is the song itself, its title, or even how it went. But he remembers the other song as a totally progressive, aggressive rock song in the tradition of his heroes Rush. Ed dubbed this genre "Young High-School Guy Prog-Rock."

"It was more like when Rush got into their pop-music phase," Ed specifies as only a true Rush aficionado would. Even down to which Rush album the genre most closely resembled. "It was more *Signals* era–influenced," he admits. Ed then details the history of his band's many monikers. "We were called Rude Awakening for ages," he explains. "And then we changed the name to Three Guys from Barrie, even though there were five guys in the band and no one was from Barrie." As the Three Guys from Barrie, the band played a lot of house parties and even won the Midland Collegiate Battle of the Bands. "We changed it to the Rage," Ed recalls, "and then we broke up. Get a shit name and you've gotta break up."

Although the Rage may have closed its doors, Ed was already contemplating his entrance into the music business. In fact, as early as the fifth grade, when he first strapped on a guitar, Ed knew what he wanted to be when he grew up. "I said, 'I'm going to be a musician.' I never understood what that meant, but our teacher at the time, Mrs. Macdonald, had her husband come in. Her husband was in a band, and they were called the Mad Cats."

Mrs. Macdonald had brought her husband in for a kind of career-day event, where students were encouraged to bring in their parents to discuss their professions and answer questions from the class. Curious Ed grilled the Mad Cat about being a professional musician, a concept that clearly appealed to his sensibilities. You'd think that being into progressive rock, especially Rush, would've made Ed dream of being a guitar hero, a sort of "Yngwie J. Robertson" tossing off lightning runs up and down the fret board of his ax. You'd think wrong, though, as Ed just wanted to play well enough to get the chords right so he could sing along. In fact, he's surprisingly humble about his technical abilities on the six-string. "I've never really been a very good guitar player, you know. For me it was always about performing. I'd learn all these Max Webster songs and stuff, but I was never interested in learning the guitar solo. I wanted to play and sing the song. I didn't want to be a hot guitar player. I just wanted to be in a band. I just wanted to play and sing, you know. I just liked the energy of that."

He admits that he never wanted to be just a guitar guy. "I remember deciding that, too, listening to music and thinking, okay, I can hear what he's doing. I know what his fingers are doing, but I just don't want to put the work in to be able to do that."

There were other things that Ed decided around this time as

well. As *Stunt* climbed the charts at the end of 1998, Ed disclosed his father's drinking problem in an interview with *Rolling Stone*'s Will Hermes. "It wasn't a flippant, offhanded comment," Ed maintains. "It was a *Rolling Stone* interview. The guy was with us for three days." Answering the simple question "Why don't you drink?" Ed replied, "Well, I saw my dad drink a lot. He was an alcoholic."

But Ed was quick to add in Earl's defense that his dad had never been mean to him and that he was always really supportive of him. "I never questioned his pride about me or his love for me," Ed remembers telling Hermes, "but I just decided that I never wanted to be that." The whole revealing exchange was quoted in the pages of the world-renowned rock magazine. "I thought it was a pretty honest, sympathetic sort of statement," says Ed of the piece, "but my dad was pretty upset. The truth is that I've considered my father's alcoholism a main motivating factor in why I turned out the way I did."

Of course my next question was "If your family was upset about the *Rolling Stone* piece, how would they feel about such details being included in a book?" "Well, it's me" is Ed's reply, without missing a beat. "It's why I am who I am, and I don't mind talking about why I am who I am. He's a great guy, he's just an alcoholic," he says candidly. "But he's well liked and he's a good guy and he's never missed a day of work in his life. He was never mean to anybody and was always really loving and supportive with the whole family. But he had a drinking problem. He just drinks too much and can't stop.

"It wasn't until getting quite a bit older," Ed adds, "that I looked back and thought, wow, we didn't really have that much. I go back now and look at school pictures, and I see myself, with ripped jeans and handed-down Daryl Sittler T-shirts with grape Kool-Aid stains on them, and I start to think about all that stuff. Like the fact that we lived in a tiny house."

Ed also credits the fact the he went to school outside his own neighborhood during the ages of fourteen and fifteen, what he jokingly refers to as the "formative drinking years," for keeping him out of the liquor cabinet. Between the half-hour bus commute and his dedication to playing guitar and video games, when's a boy got any time for teenage drinking parties? "I wasn't really hanging around with the kids in my neighborhood because I went to this gifted program over at Churchill Heights. I would take a bus for half an hour and all my friends lived, like, a forty-five-minute bus ride away, all over Scarborough. There wasn't a lot of drinking with the people I grew up with anyway. I ran with a pretty much nondrinking crowd."

Ed says that in the beginning, being gifted meant he was often stigmatized as being special. But everything was different by the time he got to Woburn Collegiate. "All those lines [of distinction] kind of blur in high school," he explains. Ed even took gifted gym, a program born out of necessity due to the fact that, as Ed recalls, most of the gifted kids were "weaklings, stereotypical pocket-protector geeks." And while he admits to having been a little more athletically endowed than some of the others, Ed passed on the offer to take the regular physical-education program, opting to remain in the gifted gym class. Better, he thought, to be a big fish in a small pond.

The whole gifted gym thing was actually new to the school. The instructor, Mr. Grigg, found it especially amusing. "Mr. Grigg, who was also the geography teacher, was a well-liked teacher and a really very funny guy," Ed recalls. "I think he'd been at Woburn since the day it opened. He thought the whole gifted gym thing was pretty funny. He was fond of saying, 'Okay, so we're smaller, but at least now everybody's smaller, so we'll play sports and we'll do this. But part of the gifted gym thing is they thought it would be a good idea if you guys did essays about sports too.'" The first essay involved going on a trip to a baseball game and then writing about the game. "I'll remember the name of the essay till the day I die," Ed recalls, laughing. "It was called 'A Symposium on the Effects of Hardwood on a Leather Sphere.'"

One of Ed's best friends at the school was a guy named Dave

Kwak. As Ed recounts the story of how they met, I start to realize that this Dave guy may be the most important link in the chain of events that led to the formation of Barenaked Ladies. "Dave came up to me in the schoolyard and said, 'Do you know anybody?' I said, 'No.' He said, 'Me neither. Do you want to be my friend?' I said, 'Okay.' So he was a good friend of mine all the way through grade school and high school. Really smart, really nice guy."

One day, in the twelfth grade, Dave told Ed about something called the Scarborough Music Camp. "He said, 'You should be going to music camp,'" Ed recalls. "'The place is, like, made for you. You need to be going there.'" But Ed almost didn't make it up there. He wasn't, as he describes it, a camp kid. He felt his independent streak wouldn't fit in among the all-for-oneism inherent in camp life. "I wasn't into the whole camp thing," Ed admits. "I knew I'd know a bunch of people because a bunch of people from Woburn went every year, but I was a very independent kid. I liked doing stuff by myself. I was never interested in team sports, never wanted to be in any sort of group-activity stuff. I always liked to play with one friend or do things by myself."

Ed told Dave about his misgivings, but Dave wasn't taking no for an answer. In fact, he told Ed that he needed to go there, and he was so adamant that he went to unusual lengths to make sure Ed went. "He actually filled out my registration form for the camp and paid my deposit," Ed explains, still in awe of Dave's commitment to the idea. "So I've always sort of credited him with the beginning of this band [BNL], because I never would've started hanging out with Steve if I hadn't gone to music camp."

Carolyn, Steve's now wife, remembers seeing Ed and Dave at camp. "Ed would stroll around the camp with his buddy Dave, and they'd sing songs all the time. I remember [the Talking Heads' song] 'Psycho Killer' the most prominently." In hindsight, Carolyn says that, at the time anyway, no one would've guessed that Steven and Ed would even get along, let alone form a long-term friendship and platinum-selling recording group. "You have to take the image of geeky Steven," she explains, "preppy and in the artsy crowd." On the other hand, there was Ed, whom Carolyn remembers as "the rocker-looking guy with the hippy and artsy crowd."

5

Steven and Ed

At the same time Ed attended Woburn, lurking in the halls was Steven Page, whom Ed knew about from the fourth grade on, but never really talked to until after high school. Steven says that he and Ed had become curious about each other back at Woburn, but hanging out in separate cliques had precluded any formal introduction. In the socially isolated atmosphere of summer camp, however, the rules of etiquette were tossed out the window. "I actually knew Steve's friend Geoff better than I knew Steve," Ed says. "He was in a science class of mine or something, and I got the Scary Movie Breakfast tape from him. I was playing in this cover band at the time and working really hard to get, you know, all the parts down for these cover songs. Then I heard this tape and went, 'These guys are actually making music and having fun and being jerks, you know?' It made me laugh, and I thought it was really cool." For fun, Ed decided to learn all the Scary Movie Breakfast songs from their tape.

Steven never thought of himself as "really cool" in those days. While not exactly a social pariah, he says that he did possess a certain chameleonlike tendency to blend into the background socially. "I don't think I ever saw myself as an outcast," Steven explains. "I was always the best friend of the most popular guy in school. I wasn't the least popular guy or anything. I remember once this guy that Ed knew from Woburn, whom I didn't know, came up to me at a show and asked me, 'So you went to Woburn, too?' And I said, 'Yeah.' And he said, 'Funny, I don't remember you.' So I asked him if he remembered Geoff Pounsett. He said, 'Yes.' Then I said, 'Did you ever look to his right?'"

Soon they would be looking to Ed's right and seeing Steven. "I ran into Steve at music camp," Ed begins, recounting the now mythic tale of their meeting. "I just sort of started playing one of the Scary Movie Breakfast songs; I think it was 'Really Don't Know' on guitar. Steven was caught off guard. 'How do you know that?' was all he could ask.

"He was really shocked and flattered that I knew it," Ed continues, recalling Steven's amused and amazed expression. Flattery will get you everywhere, and Steven was sufficiently flattered by the gesture. The two soon began to play music together, eventually becoming friends in the process. But at first, the attraction was mainly musical. Ed needed a creative foil, someone to nurture his latent songwriting ambitions and challenge his own musicality. Steven Page would do. Simple as that. "I always had a desire to play music and be involved in music," Ed explains. "And for the first time, I saw a window into the creative end of it that I hadn't really known before. I thought, 'Hey, this guy's my age and he writes songs. I could probably do that and do it with him.'

"I was overwhelmed by Steve when we started hanging out," Ed admits. "It was like, the guys I hung out with were into horror movies. I was a guy that played video games and liked to stay up all night and watch movies. I'd listened to country-and-western stuff growing up. Then I got way into Rush, and I was just sort of coming out of that. Steve was already a guy that read novels. Steve was into poetry and listened to eclectic music. He knew a lot of music. Steve would say to me, 'Oh, have you heard this Leonard Cohen record?' Well, I'd heard of him, but it never occurred to me to listen to him.'"

As Ed's listening tastes grew, so did Steven and Ed's friendship. They were now becoming interested in forming an acoustic duo together. "We started singing together just for fun, really," remembers Ed. "We were just two guys goofin' around, never thinking they were ever going to be a band."

Before the Three Guys from Barrie/the Rage, broke up, Ed had committed them to perform at a benefit concert for the Second Harvest Food Bank to be held in Nathan Phillips Square outside Toronto City Hall. A week before the event was to take place, an organizer from the food bank called Ed to remind him of the date. He'd completely forgotten, since his band wasn't even together, but the organizer told him that they were counting on him. So to honor that commitment, and with no band, Ed would have to invent one.

The Name

Ed and Steve came up with what would end up being their band moniker at a Bob Dylan concert at Toronto's CNE Stadium. "We spent the whole time yapping in the crowd because the concert was so friggin' boring," Ed recalls. "This was the tour where G. E. Smith, from the *Saturday Night Live* band, was the bandleader. It was brutal. We were way up in the grandstand and we were pretending we were rock critics and were mentioning names of bands that never existed. 'Remember that band, Colonel Ernie?' 'Oh yeah, they were awesome.' Just being goofs, just trying to make each other laugh. I don't know who said it, but someone said, 'Oh, yeah, remember Barenaked Ladies? Man, they were great. Actually, they played at Woodstock.' 'Yeah, yeah, but they went on before tape was rolling, so everybody forgot about them.'"

"So when I got that call from the food bank a couple of days later, I said, 'Yeah, we're still on, but the name of the band is Barenaked Ladies now,'" says Ed. "Ed suddenly called me," recalls Steve, "and said, 'Do you want to do this gig? Because my band's broken up,' and I said I'd love to do something, and he said 'Great, because I already booked us; we're called Barenaked Ladies.' I'd just turned eighteen, and I remember thinking, 'Well that's a cool name because it'll keep us alternative and we'll never hit the mainstream.' I remember thinking it was like the Jazz Butcher—even though they were pop, they could never be mainstream with a name like that. It [the name *Barenaked Ladies*] made us laugh and reminded us of when we were eight years old and would look at the women's underwear section of the Sears catalog."

Ed says that the name, for him, is far from sexist or misogynist, but rather conjures up childlike naïveté. "It's supposed to be kids' language; it implies children's excitement. It summed up a lot of what we thought the band was about. There's nothing sexist about Barenaked Ladies. We're always very careful to see it's not interpreted that way." "When Ed got us our first gig," Steven says, "he told them we were called Barenaked Ladies, and after that there was no backing out. Because if we changed our name, how would the seven people that were there find us again?"

The food-bank benefit, as it turns out, was actually a battle of the bands. Ed and Steven got to City Hall early and crammed to learn songs—any song—to play. "We just showed up early at Nathan Phillips Square under the pedestrian ramp, which takes you up to the next level," Ed recalls. "I taught Steve some chords for the choruses of things so we could strum along. We sort of hunkered down in there and worked out stuff. It was like, 'You know that Janet Jackson song? Okay, I know that.'"

Regrettably, despite their valiant last-minute attempt, Ed and Steven had to face the facts. It was definitely a case of too little, too late. Undaunted, the two went back to the show's organizers with a unique proposition. "We told them that we couldn't really enter because we didn't have enough stuff, but we would go on while they were changing over between bands," Ed recalls. "They said that would be fine, so we went on while they were switching over, and we were, like, totally the hit. Everyone was loving it because we couldn't even keep straight faces. We were laughing. We couldn't believe we were onstage singing songs that neither of us knew. And we'd get to a chorus and we'd make it up when we didn't know it, then the next time we got to the chorus, we'd sing it in harmony even though we just made it up."

Clearly, it sounds like the guys were having too much fun— likewise the audience, who wouldn't let them leave. "Every time we'd get offstage," recalls Ed, "we'd go back under the ramp and work out three more songs to play. Then we'd go back on the stage in between the next bands."

Musician Tony Kenny, from a popular Toronto rockabilly band called the Razorbacks, was one of the contest's celebrity judges. Kenny witnessed the crowd's enthusiastic reaction and came over to congratulate the guys after the show. He had a proposition of his own for the infant duo. "He said, 'You guys are great!'" relates Ed. "I told him, 'No, we're shit,' but then he said, 'We're doing a round at the Horseshoe this week, and I'd like you guys to open for us.'"

According to Ed, accepting the gig at the Horseshoe Tavern was, in hindsight, one of a handful of deciding moments in Barenaked Ladies' history. "We probably wouldn't have ever done another gig," reckons Ed. "The food-bank benefit would've been our first and last. We had no intentions of doing it again."

6

Sound Check:
Corky and the Juice Pigs,
Part One
Toronto, 1990

You can tell a lot about a band by their sound
check. For those of you who are curious about this tour-time ritual, the sound check is generally the first time in the day, usually
late afternoon, that the band members actually get to pick up
their instruments and play music. The crew has generally been
out in the hall setting up as early as 9:00 A.M., rigging up the
speakers and lighting trusses and placing the band's equipment
in designated positions on the stage. Backdrops, set pieces, and
props are put up as well. Stage technicians have gone about
plugging in amplifiers and playing the various guitars.

The lighting director has directed his lighting crew, setting
up and changing any bulbs that've burned out or been broken in
transit. So by 4:00 the stage is ready for the sound engineer to get
an idea of just what the band will sound like in the room. (Even
arenas are frequently called "rooms" in rockspeak.)

And so it is that the band is needed to play a few songs in the
empty venue, enabling the master of the mix to adjust and fur-

ther fine-tune the sound levels. Since these levels can change from night to night, depending on the size of the venue, it's in everyone's best interest, the crew and band alike, to go through this process. And most important, this process makes it easier for the fans, who've paid their hard-earned, or hard-borrowed, money to actually hear the band they've come out to see.

However, it's safe to say that in 1990, Ed and Steven were not thinking this far ahead—or even this strategically. But for better or worse, they were now officially a dynamic duo called Barenaked Ladies. For the first year of the band, they went out onstage, just two guys with acoustic guitars, two voices, and thirty minutes of material. The trouble was, they kept booking gigs where they were required to play forty-five minutes of material. Not that there was anything wrong with that. They simply became adept at improvisation, which probably has a lot to do with the way the band sounds today.

"We'd spread out the songs we knew over the three sets and just fill space with stuff," Ed recalls. "That was kind of the essence of the band in the beginning, the fact that we didn't care about anything. We'd get onstage and just strum and sing whatever came into our heads. It was fun." But when they began touring campus pubs, like the Elbow Room at the University of Western Ontario, they were suddenly required to come up with not one, but two, sets. And each set had to be an hour and a half in length. Here's how they pulled that one off:

"For the first set, we'd play everything we knew," Ed recalls. "So our second set would always be a bullshit set. We'd just play. We'd have a request sheet, and for the next set we'd play requests. We'd tell people, 'We don't know any other songs than what we're playing now, so write down anything you want to hear, and we'll just make it up.'"

Okay, Ed, but what if I'd requested, say, Don McLean's "American Pie"? "We'd just make up the verses and just sing the actual chorus, every time making up thirty verses that were complete bullshit," he responds. Soon Steve and Ed were making up songs on the spot so often that they were actually getting quite good at it. The spontaneous part of their set became a featured attraction.

I remember seeing them play at Sneaky Dee's one chilled November night in Toronto. Steven had just sung what I thought was a very respectful rendition of Madonna's "Material Girl." Then, without missing a beat, he and Ed segued seamlessly into what I believed to be a song they'd written themselves. In hindsight, I suppose you can't blame me for being unaware that the "song," which I vaguely recall as an ode to floppy nacho chips and flaccid burritos (Sneaky Dee's served Mexican food), was totally made up.

Ed admits that spontaneous combustion became their addiction. "We've so often gotten onstage and played off the top of our heads something that people think we've written, something that turns into a pop song but is so retarded, you know, a pop song about walnuts or whatever. Often people will ask us when we wrote that song, and we have to tell them, 'Well, it just happened.'" But it wasn't until much later in the band's career that they attempted to take any of their improvs and make real songs out of them. And when they did, one of them became their biggest hit in America.

"For some reason," Ed tries to explain, "it was just the realm of improv, and it came and went and never became anything. It was always just live for that moment. It wasn't until we wrote 'One Week' that any of that stuff made it onto a real record, because it was written as a freestyle. But it was just the kind of stuff we do all the time."

Among the first covers that they actually knew the real words for were the old music-camp faves "Psycho Killer," "Wishing Well" by Terence Trent D'Arby, Johnny Cash's "I Still Miss Someone," and a couple of songs by another dynamic duo, Scotland's the Proclaimers. Both Ed and Steve felt an immediate kinship with the Proclaimers. Beyond the fact that they were twin Buddy Holly look-alikes with impenetrably thick Scottish accents, they were likewise two guys rocking out with acoustic guitars.

Steven discovered the first Proclaimers record, and, as he says, "I fell in love with it. It was perfect for us because it was exactly what we were. Two guys with acoustic guitars, singing in harmony. They had all the energy of punk rock—but just with acoustic guitars and voices."

"That was the first tape Steve ever gave me when I went up to his house to do music with him," remembers Ed. "He'd sent me home with a cassette of their album *This Is the Story.* Steven lived up in Richmond Hill. I remember putting the tape in my tape deck as I was pulling onto the Don Valley Parkway off Highway 7. I totally remember the moment, just hearing this loud, crazy acoustic guitar and these screaming Scottish guys, and I thought that it was the best thing I'd ever heard."

Steven and Ed went to see the Proclaimers live in concert at Toronto's legendary El Mocambo nightclub. That night, they discovered another local artist they would soon become fans of and friends with, Kurt Swinghammer. "The place was just packed," says Steven of the "Elmo" show. "Kurt Swinghammer was opening for them [the Proclaimers], and we'd never seen him before. He just blew us away. I think maybe the audience wasn't really listening or something. But I'll never forget what he said onstage that night. He said, 'I'm playing over at C'est What on Monday, and even if one percent of you come to my show, then I'll know this was a success.' So of course, Ed and Steven trudged out to C'est What on the following Monday to get another listen to Swinghammer's set.

"We loved it, so he became another guy that we'd go see all the time," says Steven of Swinghammer. "Oh, my, what a guitar player. We learned a lot from him. Just the twists and turns melodically and chordwise, plus the lyrical stuff. If you listen to stuff like "Blame It on Me," you know, I feel that Ed's guitar part is really influenced by Kurt Swinghammer." But soon, a local group would prove to have an even greater influence on the fledgling duo.

While attending the Just for Laughs Festival in Montreal, Ed saw a musical comedy trio busking on the street that he thought was hilarious. This trio, known as Corky and the Juice Pigs, featured the high-speed, high-energy, and high-maintenance guerrilla comedy stylings of Sean Cullen, Greg Neale, and guitarist Phil Nichol. Back in Toronto, Ed saw a poster for an upcoming Corky and the Juice Pigs appearance at the Siboney Club in Toronto's Kensington Market area. Now it was his turn to drag Steven along to a show. "We went and we just died," remembers Steven of their inaugural Juice Pig event. "I'd never laughed so hard in my life. I was crying, I was choking, I thought I was going to throw up, I was laughing so hard. We just loved them. We went to see them every time they played after that. It didn't matter where, we'd find out and just go there. We drove to London, Ontario, one night to see them play at Western, because we just had to see them."

I caught up with Juice Pig Sean Cullen on the phone from his new location, an apartment in the San Fernando Valley, near the Burbank Airport just north of Hollywood, California. "When I first met Steven and Ed," Cullen begins, "the Juice Pigs had been touring for a while. I don't really know how they heard about us, but one night they just showed up at one of our shows at the Spoke at the University of Western Ontario. It was quite early on in their career, and in ours, too, actually. They gave us this tape and said, 'You guys are great; here's our tape. Maybe we could open for you guys sometime.'"

That tape was a collection of songs called *Buck Naked*, which was recorded in Ed's basement in 1989. (While Ed figures about 500 copies of the tape were distributed, Steven puts the number closer to 150 copies.) "We didn't hear from them [the Juice Pigs] for a long time," Steven recollects. "One of the guys had it [the *Buck Naked* tape] somewhere but couldn't find it for a while."

"We listened to the tape and we quite liked it," Cullen tells me. "My favorite thing on it was a version of Terence Trent D'Arby's 'Wishing Well' that they'd done with a cheap little tiny

Casio keyboard." So eventually, Barenaked Ladies were asked to open some college dates for their new heroes. For Ed and Steve, it was not only a dream gig, but also proved to be a great learning experience for the neophyte performers.

Steven admits that he and Ed probably learned most of their comedy skills from the radical trio. "Sure, there was definitely an original spark in what we did," Steven qualifies, "but we learned everything in our early days from watching those guys. What they did that was so amazing was that they had a set that was just 'bang, bang, bang, bang!' Rapid-fire comedy."

But there was also a musical element to the Juice Pig equation—yet another reason to believe that they were BNL's kindred spirits. "Phil played the acoustic guitar like a punk rocker," says Steven, "and I think he was the fastest acoustic-guitar player I'd ever seen. And I was always intimidated by Sean Cullen, at first, because he's just so remarkably funny. I mean, he's one of the funniest guys and he's also very kindhearted and one of the sweetest people out there. He's so brilliant. I wish him all the success, like I just think he should be huge. He should be the new Robin Williams, because I know he has it in him to act, do all kinds of characters, to have compassion and sensitivity in what he plays but to also be ridiculously funny. He's so quick-witted."

After a few local and regional dates together, Corky and the Juice Pigs decided to invite Barenaked Ladies to open for them on a national tour of Canadian universities. The thinking was that Barenaked Ladies mixed music with comedy, while Corky and the Juice Pigs mixed comedy with music. Two great tastes that taste great together. Did Ed and Steve feel like running off with their new friends? What do you think? "We were like, yes, of course we do," Steven recalls of the relatively short time it took them to decide the matter. "We were both still in university. I guess I was in my third year, and Ed was in his first—also at York. And that was it."

But before Steven could go off on tour, Mr. and Mrs. Page had to be persuaded to let Steven drop his studies and join the circus. "Their [the Juice Pigs'] manager at the time, John King, had to come over to my parents' house and try and convince them to let me do this thing," remembers Steven. "I was nineteen and still living at home. And I was going to have to take a lot of time off from university and so on."

While he liked his courses at York, Steven was rather annoyed with having to live at home and commute to college. "I graduated high school when I was sixteen," Steven says. "My parents wouldn't let me go away to university because I was so young. They just didn't want me to go away, so I ended up going to a commuter school, which meant I didn't get any of that 'university life thing.' You know, where you're supposed to go away and go and get loaded and puke and roll out of the dorm room and go to school. I had three years where I really resented that. So when the opportunity came to go on the road with Corky and the Juice Pigs, I thought, 'This is my chance to do something.'"

"So they went with us," says Cullen. "It was quite fun. We went out west to Vancouver, and then we went out east and we did a lot of shows closer to home in Ontario." "What we ended up doing," says Steven, "was traveling in the same van with them to do these shows with them. It was a great environment to be in. We'd get in the van, and we'd laugh and just sing all the time. We had a great time with those guys."

Steven likes to describe BNL's early sound as a cross between the Proclaimers and Corky and the Juice Pigs. "Although," he remembers, "we used to joke that we were a cross between Simon and Garfunkel and Ernie and Bert." "I think they had mixed reviews," offers Cullen, "because our audience was more of a comedy audience and they expected more of that sort of thing from the opening act. And I remember one time we played this all-girl college, Mount Allison, I believe it was, and they requested that Barenaked Ladies change their name for the day, because it wasn't considered politically correct. It was a weird tour. The shows were up and down; our crowd either loved them or hated them."

"I think that's the case for most bands starting out," offers Steven. "But it was very odd, you know, being a music group and opening for a comedy group on comedy night at a university. And there we are, when the audience is expecting to see comedy. So that's where a lot of our schtick came from in our show, just to keep the audience's attention."

"I think speed was our big thing," says Cullen, cutting back in. "Just pelting the audience with a million things at once. You can't lose them that way. And I think that was impressed upon them." Steven agrees that of the many lessons he and Ed learned from witnessing the Juice Pigs' show night after night, one of the most crucial concerned audience participation. "We learned," he says, "how to keep an audience involved—how to make your set flow. Their energy level was just so high and we had to match that with just two guys on stage with acoustic guitars. You're in a situation where people are there to actually watch what's going on onstage, which is what happens at a comedy show, and the audience is actively participating while you're up there doing a forty-five-minute set. It was a challenge."

The Canadian tour pressed on, in segments, for about four months. Over the course of some forty-plus shows, Ed and Steve honed their performance skills. "They started out just being kids," remembers Cullen, "but I think that during that time they learned that it's hard work, it's a business. I remember when they played, Ed would wear a red fez, and Steven would wear a kind of beanie hat, like Jughead would wear. They both wore shorts, in fact they looked like little boys. Which I suppose, at the time, they were. I think they were only like seventeen or eighteen years old. That became their look, and I think they carried it on for quite a while."

But Cullen also has vivid memories of those few nights when the audience just didn't get the Barenaked Ladies schtick at all. And on those nights, Steven was transformed, like the

Incredible Hulk, into the Incredibly Angry Young Man. "I think Steven was generally the more mercurial of the two," says eyewitness Cullen. "Steve would get personally offended by a hostile or indifferent crowd reception. He tended to take it much more personally than Ed, who would just let it roll off his back."

Steven admits that, as a child, he was something of a perfectionist and therefore prone to being, shall we say, rather temperamental. "I was a pretty sensitive, emotional kid, I guess," Steven confesses. "I was the kind of kid who, in art class, if my drawing didn't come out exactly the way I'd pictured it in my head, I'd just tear it up."

"One night," says Cullen, "I can't remember where this was, they'd just finished one of their songs when all of a sudden, Steven just started jumping up and down really hard, screaming at the top of his lungs for no apparent reason. He just seemed really angry, and people were not enjoying it."

Steven didn't exactly enjoy much of their first taste of Halifax, Nova Scotia. Much of his feelings were documented in the lyrics of "Hello City," a caustic and cautionary tale that opens the band's 1992 debut release, *Gordon*.

I think this harbour town is waist deep and sinking fast . . .

"When we were in Halifax," Steven begins, "we played at this bar called the Lower Deck, where they have mostly Celtic music, being as there are mostly sailors in there, drinking."

The sun didn't shine on Barrington Street . . .

"We stayed at this place called the Carlton Hotel, on Barrington Street, which was upstairs from this metal bar called Rosa's. It's no longer there, but it was a total flophouse."

The doom and gloom of the hotel room . . .

"The room that Ed and I shared had four beds. One of them was up against the wall, and another had a mattress falling through its frame. There was a bathtub with no shower. It was just gross."

Climb down three flights of stairs to the streetlights and the bar fights / We're just taking in the sights . . .

"Halifax on a weekend, you can't go anywhere without seeing somebody bleeding somewhere. To get to the street from our terrible room, you had to walk down three or four flights of stairs and then step over some bleeding body. We were young, none of us were real drinkers, Ed didn't drink at all, and the whole drink culture of Halifax was just shocking to us."

I wish this seaside beer hall would just sink into the bay . . .

"So we were playing at the Lower Deck, this sailor's watering hole, and no one would pay attention. I remember taking a picture from the stage, and when I got the pictures back, there was nobody looking at the camera."

Hello city, you've found an enemy in me . . .

"I remember thinking, 'I hate this place, I hate this place.'"

Maybe I caught you at a bad time / Maybe I should call you back next week . . .

"We've actually had great times there since, but that's because we learned the 'when in Rome' axiom. You know the expression, 'do as the Romans do'? So 'when in Halifax,' we learned to 'do as the Haligonians do,' which in this case means drinking and bleeding."

I hope tomorrow that I wake up in my own bed . . .

Soon Steven would wake up in his own bed, but not for a few days yet. And as the emotional roller-coaster ride of the Juice Pigs' eastern Canadian tour wound down, they found themselves in Miramichi, New Brunswick. "One of the last dates on the [first leg of the] tour was at a place called the Miramichi

Tavern," Cullen recalls. "There was one of those mobile signs on wheels, you know, where you put the plastic letters on it? It said BARENAKED LADIES PIZZA AND WINGS NINETY-NINE CENTS."

Finally, Ed and Steve could go home for a short while to assess the plusses and minuses of the first leg of their first-ever tour. Overall, the plusses outweighed the minuses, and they agreed to return for the western leg of the college tour. But, being as they were home for Christmas, they booked themselves a little holiday gig at the Last Temptation, the scene of their one and only Toronto club show before commencing the next stint on the Juice Pigs' tour.

The Last Temptation of Christmastime, Oh Yeah

"We were in the middle of the Corky tour," recalls Steven, "and between the eastern and western legs, we booked another show at the Last Temptation for a couple of days after Christmas." "Mitch Potter [an entertainment columnist from the *Toronto Star*] came to the very first Last Temptation gig," says Ed, "and we actually got a little write-up in the *Star* as being cool."

Knowing that at Christmas break a lot of their friends would be home from university, Ed and Steve wanted to make this particular evening a little different. They hit upon the idea to invite a couple of their old pals from music camp to sit in with them for a few songs. "We thought, 'Let's get Jim and Andy Creeggan from music camp to come up and play with us, and we'll look like a real band, at least for one set anyway,'" Steve recalls. "There'd be bass and congas—Andy played congas then—and of course Ed and I."

The four of them put off rehearsing until the night before the show, when they finally managed to get together in Ed's parents' basement. The quartet crammed and jammed until five o'clock the next morning. Ed had a good feeling about the Creeggans, if only because they managed to knock off all the songs in short order, at the last minute. In fact, Ed was nothing short of amazed at the brothers' musicality. "The thing that amazed me about Jim and Andy right away was their incredible ability to pick up things and remember them," Ed recalls. "They learned all of the songs, back to back, for a whole hour-and-a-quarter-long set, in one evening and didn't forget anything—including all of the shots and pushes. They just picked up musical notions so quickly and easily."

So on show night, a few hours after their only rehearsal, Ed and Steven took to the stage and played one set as a duo. Then it was time to make history. After a short break they called up Jim and Andy. Suddenly, all the songs had a full, rich sound, the grooves were anchored, and everybody was blown away. Perhaps no one was more blown away than Ed and Steve themselves. "We just kind of looked at each other and said, 'That's it.'" Steven recognizes this as a turning point in the band's evolution. "That's what this band was supposed to sound like. There was no turning back."

Although he admits to being a little confused by how good it was sounding, Ed nonetheless knew that they were on to something with this lineup. "It was supposed to be just that one time," Ed explains, "because Barenaked Ladies was just me and Steve. It wasn't these Creeggan guys. They were just going to play with us for one night. But we just liked it so much and had so much fun having the extra harmony and rhythm and bass to it, I remember thinking, 'Okay, this is Barenaked Ladies now.'"

And although Steven and Ed went ahead with their original plan to finish the rest of the Juice Pigs tour without the Creeggans, they were now quite sure about who BNL was.

7

Scarborough, 1988

Enter the Creeggans.

Lurking at the very same Scarborough summer music camp, during that very same summer, at the very same time as Steven was clearing away his Scary Movie Breakfast dishes and contemplating becoming Barenaked with Ed, were two very musical siblings: Jim Creeggan, born on February 12, 1970, and his younger brother, Andy, born a year later on July 4, 1971. They lived in the wilds of deepest, darkest "Scarberia," at the outskirts of town, where lions and tigers roamed free. Honestly. You see, the Creeggans lived just south of Toronto's cageless Metro Zoo. Their house was near both Lake Ontario and the Rouge River, which meant summers at the beach and skating on the frozen river in the winter. In fact, the young Creeggans almost became paddlers, not musicians.

"We always had a canoe," recalls Andy, "and we'd go on little trips here and there all the time in the summer. Finally, this would've been like grade six to grade eight or something like that, we decided to go to this canoe school/day camp, which was run by a canoe club." There, the Creeggans became involved with racing and something called War Canoe. Being strong paddlers, they were urged to race kayaks and enter regattas along the Rouge River.

Back on dry land, Jim's lanky frame and strong legs made a him natural track-and-field runner. Indeed, he was probably more interested in setting track records than recording tracks. With his parallel development in both running and music, Jim actually managed to excel in both. "In grades one and two," boasts humble Jim, uncharacteristically, "I was really fast. I was taller than most kids, and I came in first quite a bit up until grade nine. It was kind of a funny point because I was doing both at the same time, like playing music in the symphony orchestra and running track and being really successful at both. I was enjoying being the only bass player in the school and the fastest guy in the school."

But fate stepped in, and Jim the track star was faced with a heartbreaking running injury. "I tore my hamstring in grade nine," recalls Creeggan. "I couldn't run anymore. I ended up taking up the electric bass really intensely, practicing and taking lessons from a guy named Rob Wolanski who lived down the street. That was where I first got into listening to the bass and taking it off records and stuff."

That's not to say that the accident wasn't traumatic for the young runner. He'd suddenly lost his identity, and it'd be three long years before he could run again. But instead of dwelling on his situation, Jim did something really important, from a survival standpoint. He focused on his musical gifts and became even more obsessed with the bass. "I don't think there was even an uncomfortable period," Jim remembers. "I just kept on forging ahead with this new avenue. It was already set up and ready to go. It was already there in my hands, and everything went into it. And, I got into firecrackers and made lots of models."

Jim's running career was also threatened by his frequent bouts with bronchitis and various allergies. He now believes all of this may have had something to do with his self-described overachieving personality. "I pushed pretty hard, which tends to seize up everything—your lungs, et cetera." Jim switched into bass-playing with the same intensity that he'd approached running. "It was like, just the next thing, go, *whoosh!* It was just, look for the outlet—I'm always looking for the outlet."

Lucky for Jim, he'd been exposed to music early on. Jim played double bass in the string orchestra at Charlottetown Public School in Scarborough from grades one through six. The double bass is a very big instrument to lug around, and young Jim got to know the joys of carrying the darn thing everywhere. Yet it was also something he could show off to other kids. "I probably carried it more than I played it," he admits. "I always thought I'd practice more, but I mainly liked carrying it, being seen with it."

In grades six, seven, and eight, Andy could often be found on the basketball court. Although Jim was always the taller of the two, Andy was considered tall for his age and developed serious hoop dreams of his own. At least until his head start, heightwise, was over. "My peak was grade eight. I was on the team that won the Ontario championships. It kind of went downhill from there, or more like I stayed in the same place and everybody else went uphill."

According to Andy, the Creeggan boys, including eldest brother, John, were constantly soaking up musical information as a result of their parents' rabid enthusiasm for music, singing at picnics and other Creeggan family occasions. Jim, however, never really thought of the Creeggans as what he would describe as a musical family. But when I remind him of certain glaringly obvious signs of domestic musical life, like a big piano plunked down in the living room, or the fact that his mom, Naida, was the neighborhood piano teacher and his paddler daddy, Burn, would dip and swing on the keys in his unique, rhythmically-challenged style as the boys scrambled to get ready for Sunday church, Jim wisely concedes that the signs of a musical life were everywhere while he was growing up. By the way,

47

Jim remembers that his dad's piano song of choice was Henry Mancini's "Moon River," revealing a true oarsman's love of water themes.

After school, the Creeggan living room was constantly ringing with the sounds of Mom's piano students bashing away at the family upright, so much of the brothers' earliest music education came in the form of example rather than formal instruction. They got their first taste of the chorales and hymns of J. S. Bach through their local Anglican church, but Jim also describes his early musical influences in the BNL newsletter, *The Ladies Room*, as "Bach being banged out by kids in my mom's after-school piano lessons juxtaposed with *Flintstones* music on the tube and the weekly church-choir practice. Every Wednesday night, the hallelujahs, the socializing, and the coffee and smoke wafted up to my bedroom, keeping me from pleasant slumber." Jim realizes that he learned a lot of the classics "through listening to the fumbly playing of kids."

With so much live music around, the boys didn't really branch out into buying records and listening to the radio for quite a while. In time, Jim would swoon to the lascivious disco bass lines of the Village People, and, of course, the Bay City Rollers offered him his earliest evidence of ulterior motives for making music: creation of mayhem and attraction of the opposite sex.

And then Jim got his first clock radio and discovered the devil's music. CILQ, or Q-107, "the mighty Q," was the place for teenage boys and their headbangin' girlfriends to get their metal. So it was that on the rare occasions that the Creeggan boys listened to Jim's new radio, brother John insisted that it be dialed in to the adolescent-friendly rock of Q-107. "John was definitely a Q-107 guy," remembers Andy of his oldest brother. "He's the one who brought in the Rush albums as well as April Wine's *The Nature of the Beast*, the one where the guy had a tiger's head and a human, guitar-playing body on the cover. I kind of just followed in line with those guys because they were into that."

During Andy's listening days, the playlist of his favorite station, CHUM-FM, was peppered with artists like Duran Duran, Corey Hart, and Toronto's own glam-pop trio du jour, Platinum Blonde. "We never went to concerts or anything like that," he says. "We didn't take a whole big interest. We weren't obsessed the way Steven was, never went downtown to shows. We were sort of doing our thing out in Scarborough in our little bubble." Andy's real music exposure came more from high-school dances at Oliver Mowatt Collegiate. "I didn't really listen to the radio that much; it was sort of all high-school-dance music, like Eddy Grant's "Electric Avenue," he says, then he sings, "We gonna rock down to Electric Avenue. . . ."

Rockin' down was a family thing, and Jim's voice hushes to a decidedly confessional tone as he comes clean about buying, and subsequently learning to play, Rush's entire *2112* album and other "Gothic-era Rush" discs. As if to prove it, Jim begins to approximate the singing voice of Rush's Geddy Lee. "We are the priests of the Temples of Syrinx!" he shrieks. An incredible simulation, really. "Andy, John, and I would play air guitar, the whole thing, you know. Andy would set up the pillows and bang them, make a lot of dust. We'd just groove on Rush, then April Wine." It was jamming along with records, particularly AC/DC's *Back in Black* album, that really got things rockin' at chez Creeggan.

Since Jim already had a feel for the mammoth proportions of the string bass, how hard could it be, he wondered, to master the relatively puny dimensions of the electric bass? "I thought if I got an electric bass," Jim reasons, "it would sound like AC/DC, big and fat. But it was just, duh! A big surprise. I never really started playing bass because I heard a great bass player. I started because I'd already started playing double bass. When I discovered that distortion was one of the key elements in the rock sound, I quickly took my stage amp and cranked everything up to the top. I had this five-dollar wah-wah pedal, and I stomped on a certain spot and it made this cool distortion sound."

Recently, Jim enjoyed stumbling across his early rock heroes rehearsing at a studio right next to Barenaked Ladies'. Nearing the hall, Jim and his band mates were more than pleasantly surprised to discover just who was making the racket. "It was AC/DC live!" Jim enthuses. "And they completely are just the best rock band, you know."

Jim's very first electric bass was a blue Vantage, an imitation of a Fender Precision bass. At the same time, Andy got his first set of Westbury drums. Wait a minute—hold the phone—didn't Andy play keyboards? What gives?

Like many fans of Barenaked Ladies, I was surprised at first to hear that Andy was a drummer early on. I was reminded of the story of Edward and Alex Van Halen—Edward started out on the drums, while Alex played guitar. One day they switched, and the rest is history.

But since the piano is such a key element in Barenaked Ladies' sound, one could almost forget that Andy's first role in the band was pounding on the conga drums. "I'd taken piano lessons from grade two on," recalls Andy. "I was just all right. I don't think I was awesome or anything. I was one of those really lazy kids who tries to pick it up by ear more than sight."

And it's true—one does have to develop one's ears to be a great musician. Sure, studying notation is extremely important, but just as a good cab driver learns the roads by driving them, map or no map, you have to know your way around intuitively as well. But to be fair, Andy was in fact rather gifted, if not perhaps just a little underachieving. "Sure, there was always potential there," he confesses, "but I was also interested in girls and sports, almost more than music. Then there was a band program at Charlottetown Public School, which we entered in grade four. Jim was a year ahead, and they alternated year to year [with] strings and band. So Jim was in the string year, and he was tall and lanky, so he got the bass. I was in the band that year."

Andy, of course, ended up on drums. The whole music class had been split into little groups and introduced to various band instruments. After a brief orientation, each student was given a kind of musical aptitude test to determine if he or she had any latent talent on a given instrument. "They took all the people who could tell when the notes were going up and when they were going down and allowed them into the band," Andy recalls. Andy passed the first test but failed what he refers to as the "God-given-talent test" because "I couldn't make anything on anything, so they just threw me on drums."

Manual labor, perhaps, but young Andy was indeed thrilled to be beating the drums—in school, no less! "I was the classical drummer guy in the music programs," he remembers. "I started with snare and bass drum, then I gradually got into it and began to really enjoy myself. By grade six, Jim had a bass, and it was time to get a drum set, you know."

As soon as they realized that nothing—even canoe racing—compared to the thrill of playing music, Jim and Andy set about forming bands. While the two have recorded three full albums as the Brothers Creeggan, they've also been members of bands with names like Tuna Straight, the Synthetics, Bobby Brown and the Scottish Accent, the Young Virtuosos, Clam, Widdershins, and Think Tank. Then there was Seeing Red, which Jim cryptically describes as "my own inner orchestra."

But of all their pre–Barenaked Ladies bands, the two were probably most in sync with each other in a band called, eventually, the Backstreet Band. No, it wasn't a boy band with five neat and tidy cute guys singing diluted soul songs. Nor was it the band that's backed the Boss for many years.

"Initially, the idea of getting a band together wasn't my doing," Jim reveals. "It was this guy named John York who got Andy and me and this other guy Rob Morin together to form the Backstreet Band. Rob was a singer, and Andy played the drums; I think he wanted to play conga. He was getting into percussion." For the next five years, the band went through a variety of membership changes (twenty alumni) not to mention shifts in style and size. "We played a lot of variety shows, like the annual Christmas variety shows. We were into that. There was a variety show after Christmas, and we'd be the pit band, or one of the pit bands. The older kids were there at the beginning. We were just sort of the young band, and then we started becoming more of a core of that sort of thing. That was a big thing."

Industriously, they even convinced their school to let them organize and perform their own lunch-hour concerts. According to Andy, one Christmas set list featured the King's "Blue Christmas" and "Santa, Bring My Baby Back to Me" in along with the requisite "Blue Suede Shoes" and "(Let Me Be Your) Teddy Bear."

"We also did a lot of swinglike stuff, although we weren't aware that there was anything called swing," Andy admits. Then there was the inevitable clash with their friends in the Orgasm Spasm, a punk-rock band. "[Backstreet Band was] kind of like this fifties-retro eighties thing," Jim continues. "The Stray Cats type of thing, only more like Elvis. Even though their band [the Orgasm Spasm] was into punk, we were all friends. I remember we did a double bill at lunch hour with them. It was awesome, man. I remember their bass player, Vako Karhunen, who sat beside me in class, calling out to his band mates 'Okay, do ya wanna play "Killer Force"?' I couldn't forget that, man."

The Backstreet Band's musical style continually evolved almost as much as their name did. "It was originally called the Back Street Basement Boogie Blues Band," Jim says. "Then we discovered that they couldn't say it on the school announcements, so we just shortened it."

Gradually, as certain members of the band came and went, they began to stretch out and experiment stylistically. "We got into the Blues Brothers and did a lot of that sort of stuff," says Andy. "We even did a bit of Simon and Garfunkel." Jim remembers playing popular tunes of the day like "You Can Call Me Al" and "Diamonds on the Soles of Her Shoes" from Paul Simon's *Graceland* album. He also vouches for Andy's admission of their brief infatuation with the Blues Brothers, complete with older brother, John, introducing the band in his best Elwood Blues voice as they laid down the signature Memphis rhythm-and-blues beat.

Inevitably, they began writing songs of their own. "Jim got his bass and this little tiny stage amp," says Andy. "We just started jamming and Jim stepped on his incredible stomp box, charged his amp up to ten and did this cool little double-stop thing on the bass. One of the first songs to come up was "Fast Love," this awful, awful song. We'd trade verses and put on these awful gruff voices."

And now, for the first time anywhere, Andy Creeggan shares the lyrical wisdom of "Fast Love."

> *Cruisin' down the highway in a four by four*
> *Just seen a sight*
> *That I've never seen before·*
> *She was a dressed in red, black and white*
> *C'mon, c'mon baby*
> *Letsa have it tonight*

"And the whole band," Andy recalls, "would yell out 'fast love' on the chorus." When I suggest that this sounds like Cab Calloway meets Bachman-Turner Overdrive, it appears that I'm at least partly correct.

"We were listening to the Guess Who. One of the albums we had was *The Best of the Guess Who*, the one where they're all standing in the water. The only song I really remember is 'Bus Rider.' This was the kind of awful, awful teenage song we never, ever played live in front of anybody, but we recorded it."

The Backstreet Band continued to change guitar players the way most people change guitar strings, (or the way Spinal Tap changed drummers). Their next guitar player, for a brief stint anyway, was one Gino Trino. Although he played an electric guitar, Trino was decidedly more of a classical-guitar player. "He was a really nice guy and he was into it," Jim remembers, "but he held down three jobs and had just graduated from high school, so it was hard finding practice time. So we needed a new guy." The search for Trino's replacement ended the day that Andy told Jim about a great guitar player he knew. His name was Eddie Robertson.

It was the June after grade eleven for Andy and grade twelve for Jim. Andy had met up with Ed at the now-famous Scarborough Summer Music Camp. So how did Andy end up getting Ed into the Backstreet Band? "Okay," Andy begins, "this was the deal. I kind of knew all the percussionists in the city that were sort of into doing music-camp stuff, Scarborough groups and stuff like that. Suddenly, there was this name, Ed Robertson, in the best band, right, playing percussion. Well, who the hell's this? That's gutsy for someone to come in in grade twelve and be that good. So I already had a big question mark about this guy. Then there he was, this charming guy, who carried his guitar with him all over the place."

Additionally appealing to both Creeggans was the fact that Ed was also into Rush and could even play a lot of Neil Peart's drum parts. Wait a minute, I thought you said that Ed was a guitar player. "He wasn't the actual drummer in his band," Andy clarifies, "but he'd taken the time to learn some of the grooves and some of the stuff, not 'to a T' like some people we know, but he can play drums awesomely."

According to Andy, Ed had a mild legacy around their small world. "He was in the best band and I'd never heard of him, right? So we hit it off like crazy. We were constantly getting in trouble for talking. Talking about Neil Peart and grooving and stuff. I was just so thrilled about this guy, Eddie Robertson."

"Ed really connected with us on things like Rush," recalls Jim. "Andy just knew that Ed had it." Andy remembers his initial pitch to Ed: "You gotta meet my brother, you gotta meet Jim. We'll get you in the Backstreet Band." His salesmanship worked. "All through [Jim and Ed's] grade thirteen and my grade twelve year, Ed played in the Backstreet Band. Actually, we have a laminated Backstreet Band poster—Dad's got it above his desk." (When Barenaked Ladies went to high school, Ontario students were required to complete grade thirteen if they wanted to continue on to postsecondary studies.)

At music camp, Andy and Ed played together in the orchestra. "Andy and I were sort of the hot percussion players, so we split the job in half," recalls Ed. "He would play snare, and I would play bass drum. Then we would alternate, and he'd play bass drum while I played the snare."

Jim and Andy's Backstreet Band (Version 6.0) with Ed on board, had by now featured a horn section for more than two years, and Ed's arrival brought the head count to nine musicians. For a while, this nine-piece horned behemoth took on some rather odd gigs. One trip to Ottawa had them playing for a river-rafting party, ostensibly because Eric, their trumpet player, was a rafting guide. And Jim, a member of the cross-country ski team, would compete during the day only to join up with the band that night to play the ski tournament–dance party.

With Ed in the band, the Backstreet Band's sound became decidedly more rocking. However, they retained their eclecticism, leaping from funk fusion directly into the flat-out rock drama of the Who classic "My Generation" with room to spare for Jim and Andy's ever-developing original songs like "Adam's Hill," an instrumental named after a nearby hill where they went tobogganing in the winter. Andy played vibes while Ed filled in on drums.

Andy remembers seeing Ed and Steve playing songs together when they put on a show at camp. Some of those initial songs left an impression on him that lasts to this day, particularly a song called "Lilac Girl." "It was a great little song," Andy recalls. "Steven always felt that its teenage lyrics weren't that good, but we loved the song always. It's too bad it didn't get on any album." Sometimes when Ed and Steve played, Andy would impress the duo by picking up the third harmony and singing a little bit before going on his merry way. "I was becoming aware of them, and they began to realize that I could pick out a third harmony here and there. I always enjoyed that."

Jim had been a counselor at the music camp every year since grade six. Although he was aware of Steven Page, and had been impressed by some of his stunts, Jim didn't introduce himself right away. "He [Steven] was sort of part of the artsy crowd," says Jim. "I was kind of watching his group from afar. When there was a lip-synch contest they did really cool stuff, you know, like "These Boots Are Made for Walkin'." They'd have, like, fifty pairs of rubber boots onstage and chuck them into the audience."

Just to confuse things further, Jim didn't actually meet Ed at the camp. The one year that Ed was at music camp was the one year that Jim missed. So it fell to Andy to make that acquaintance. Even meeting Steven wasn't a foregone conclusion at camp. "I didn't really talk to Steve until I met him through Barenaked Ladies, but I knew about him," says Jim. "I actually remember he had an interesting kind of peer group. They were 'the Group.' I remember when he was a judge for some kind of contest or something and he had this sort of shtick going. I remember laughing; hey, there's something there. That's funny. He was really meek. He went on these little ramblings. It was pretty good. It was something that I just liked, this self-deprecating guy who was a judge. He got you into it. You get a little bit of a window into it and you're interested; he draws you in."

A few weeks before they got together with Steven and Ed to play at the Last Temptation, the Creeggan boys saw them play there. "I went to see them, and I just loved what they did," remembers Jim. "Then, they invited me and Andy to play with them. I was playing double bass, again; this was my first year at university.

"They began calling us up to play every show with them," says Jim. "We learned more songs and it just started rolling." Andy believes that, in a sense, the Last Temptation gig was a sort of audition for Barenaked Ladies. "They'd noticed that Jim and I had a strong thing going on and we had a good band. There was good music happening, and Jim and I had a laser beam between us, too. We were a unit, and we were interested in doing neat stuff. They knew their friends were going to come out. So they thought they should boost the show a little bit, so maybe they'd get us to come. So they invited us to come in. I think Ed said, 'Well, maybe don't bring electric bass and drums. I think we need something else.' I can't remember exactly who made that decision."

Steven says of Jim's contributions to the band's overall sound, "When people ask me to define the sound of the band, I think a lot of it is dictated by Jim's playing. That's one of the most distinctive parts of the group. Like in 'New Kid (on the Block.)' He just added depth and jazziness and bluegrass textures, some of which we had always imagined but also some things that we hadn't even thought of. He made it sound very full and more original."

"At the time," says Andy, "I was really getting into hand drums, so I thought maybe my conga would work, and Jim wanted to get more serious with bass. He wanted to get into U of T bass performance. So that's the way it was. There was acoustic guitar, acoustic bass, conga, and singing. That's the way we did that first show at the Last Temptation."

Here's the set list for that night:

> "The King of Bedside Manor"
> "Great Provider"
> "Lilac Girl"
> "Be My Yoko Ono"
> "Blame It on Me"
> "If I Had $1,000,000"
> "Crazy"
> "Really Don't Know"

Corky and the Juice Pigs, Part Two

The West of the Tour

"The western swing [of the Juice Pig tour] kind of fell apart," states Steven, flatly. "We flew out to Regina where we played at a place called the Venue, which later became Channel One."

From Regina, it was back in the Corky-mobile and off to Alberta and the Juice Pigs' shows in Calgary and Edmonton. Could Vancouver be far off? Okay, so I peeked at the itinerary. "We drove out to Vancouver and played on Valentine's Day at the Town Pump," Steven continues. "But nobody showed up; there were maybe fourteen people there." As it turns out, a huge, attendance-defying snowstorm had kissed Vancouver just in time for Valentine's Day. Still, it's better than a poke in the eye. Or a punch in the chest, for that matter. No, that would happen at the next show, up in Whistler, a resort town north of Vancouver where ski enthusiasts go to drink. "Buffalo Bill's, in Whistler, was so terrible," says Steven, hardly concealing his true opinion of one particular experience on the wild, wild west coast. "I actually almost beat a guy up there. The guy came up onstage and just punched me in the chest while I was singing."

Sean Cullen remembers that Steven was quite upset about the incident. "It was a strange night to begin with," Cullen reflects. "It was weird, because at the end of our show, we had done this thing that we used to do, where we would come out as 'the Solid Gold Dancers,' wearing these little G-strings, and it had gone over really well. The weirdest part was that at the end of the night, the owner of the pub came up to us and said, 'Uh, I'll give you a hundred bucks if you go out and do that again.'"

But in the mayhem of the moment, Cullen had failed to notice that Steven was not the picture of happiness, sitting by himself and brooding. "After the encore, I went out to where Steve was sitting and found him looking quite annoyed. I asked him what was the matter. He said, 'Well, a man just punched me in the chest.' I said, 'What are you talking about?' He said, 'A man just punched me in the chest, and I nearly got into a fight with the guy!' [Steven] just couldn't believe how terrible he felt that night."

Cullen says that while the band had great nights on the tour, it was probably the bad nights that really helped Ed and Steve to grow from the "little boys" they were at the beginning of the tour into the fully grown "Ladies" they were becoming. "I think that generally they were both incredibly mature in the way they dealt with what they had to deal with night after night," Cullen confesses. "I don't think I would have handled it as well as they did."

Among the things that Ed and Steve were learning to deal with was the indifference, bordering on hostility, levied at them by promoters as they refused to let Barenaked Ladies come back a second time, at least not as the opening act for Corky and the Juice Pigs. "The Juice Pigs had a bunch of shows booked on the way back," Steven says, "but some of the promoters didn't want us on the bill, and that was starting to happen a lot. They didn't know who we were or they had their own opening bands, so we ended up flying home from Vancouver."

This same indifference plagued them in 1991 after they'd played three nights with the B-52's at the University of Manitoba. "On the way back," Steven remembers, "we were supposed to play the Spectrum in Winnipeg, but they just canceled our show. They said, 'We don't want you.'"

It's been said that living well is the best revenge, so the boys didn't hold a grudge after Barenaked Ladies became an act that the Spectrum really did want. "The only time we ever played the Spectrum," Steven adds, "was in jams that we would go and do after shows when we were actually famous."

Cullen also remembers Ed and Steve's songwriting improving immeasurably on the tour, as the two began to define what it was that they really wanted to say with the music.

"I think they went through a sea change," Cullen states. "And they realized that they didn't want to be a comedy band so much." Flying home from Vancouver, Ed and Steven were far from daunted about their prospects. They already knew that, upon touching down back home in Toronto, the duo called Barenaked Ladies was history. But the quartet called Barenaked Ladies—now that was a different story altogether. Those guys were far from being history; in fact, with the help of Jim and Andy, they were gonna *make* history. But first, they had to get some sleep. In the comfort of their very own beds at home. At last.

9

Backstage in Beautiful Downtown Burbank, 1998

Of the many kinds of backstage passes issued at this show, a large percentage of them seem to bear the phrase *After Show Only*. And as this show is in Hollywood, the entertainment capital of the world, the list of after-show guests is large and high in celebrity content. And since "One Week" has lately dominated video and radio, there are many new friends and radio promo people here to shake the hands of the next big thing. But there are also those who've been there for the long haul, having been key to the success of the band from the early days. I ask drummer Tyler Stewart if he ever feels an enormous debt of gratitude to this vast and vocal support network.

"The great thing about Barenaked Ladies' career," he observes, surveying the packed reception area, "is that there's a half million people that think that they made this band's career. There's a hundred and fifty people at Warner Brothers who feel directly connected and are really proud that this band's gotten to where they've gotten and half a million fans who really believe that they personally made this band."

Backstage meet 'n' greets in big media towns like Los Angeles or New York can be potentially hazardous situations; one has to watch one's step lest one trip over the big names being liberally dropped around the room. And by the looks of this room, Barenaked Ladies seem to have attracted more than their share of folks who work in this business called show, which is only logical—this is, after all, a company town. Barenaked Ladies have been through town many times, whether to do *The Tonight Show* or to appear as the house band at the Peach Pit, the fictional hot spot on *Beverly Hills 90210*. Not surprisingly then, I'm introduced to a bearded Jason Priestley, friend of the band and Celebrity Fan No.1 who has just completed his rockumentary *Barenaked in America*. Then Fran Drescher arrives, best known to television viewers as the Nanny. But for me, and especially in this potentially schmoozy environment, she will forever be Bobbi Fleckman, the gutsy publicist from Polymer Records in *This Is Spinal Tap*.

And who's that beside her? Why, it's none other than Weird Al Yankovic, the song-parody magnate. Al ("Call me Weird," he says. "All my friends do") has shaven off his trademark pencil-thin moustache and is looking much less geeky in person than I would've imagined. At this point, I have no idea that Yankovic will go on to welcome Barenaked Ladies into his alumni of pop-culture icons, or targets, with the song "Jerry Springer," which borrows the hit du jour "One Week" as the backdrop to his lampooning of the *Jerry Springer* phenomenon. That makes it official: Barenaked Ladies have joined a club that includes Madonna, Michael Jackson, Nirvana, Red Hot Chili Peppers, and even Snoop Doggy Dogg. Weird indeed.

Oh, my, is that Janeane Garofolo I spy over there chatting with Steven? Why, yes, it is. Every man I know harbors a secret crush on Garofolo. There's something about her slacker cool, her improvised wardrobe, and her keen eye for spotting incongruities in modern life that makes her the poster girl for geeky guys. Ms. Garofolo has brought a friend to the show, and it's none other than Kathy Griffin, the flame-haired firebrand from the Brooke Shields hit-com *Suddenly Susan*.

Everyone's a comedian. At least at Barenaked Ladies' shows. In showbiz, there are several truths of association: Rock stars date models. Comedians are frustrated musicians, and musicians are generally frustrated comedians. Barenaked Ladies, of course, are far from frustrated, but their heightened sense of humor attracts a higher number of comedy professionals.

Somewhere in this crowd, I'm told, is Jay Kogen. Kogen is the co–executive producer of NBC's *Frasier* and one of the original writers/producers of *The Simpsons*. Kogen's presence here, and his support for the band, is as good an example of just how seriously the band's comedy is taken by professional laughsmiths as you're likely to get. For Kogen, who brings a message from actor David Foley who is unable to attend tonight, actually hired BNL to be funny in a film called *The Wrong Guy*, directed by veteran comedian David Steinberg and starring (former *Kids in the Hall* member) Foley. In the film, Foley plays Nelson Hibbert, a man who threatens his boss, only to find him dead hours later. All his coworkers had heard his earlier tirade, so Hibbert logically assumes that he's the prime suspect. He panics and flees, hoping to somehow prove his innocence. However, unbeknownst to Hibbert, the real murderer was caught on security cameras. He is, in fact, running away from no one. Cue the band. Barenaked Ladies play five Cleveland cops—five singing Cleveland cops, of course. Kogen goes on to explain their part in the film. "Nelson (Foley) sees a policeman and hides in a Dumpster until the cop goes away. Nelson waits for the cop to leave, but instead more policemen show up. Later we see the cops just hanging out, pitching pennies. Then, hours later, Nelson is still stuck in the Dumpster and hears doo-wop singing. He looks out to see five cops singing around a trash-can fire. Eventually, the cops leave."

The rest is movie history. So just how did BNL end up "copping out" in *The Wrong Guy*? Kogen says it was Foley, who's from Toronto and has been a fan since *Gordon*, who originally thought of them for the cameo part. "[David Foley] had even spoken to Steven Page about composing the music for the entire film," remembers Kogen. "Ultimately, the movie company insisted on someone who had more experience." A fine (and presumably more experienced) composer named Lawrence Shragg was hired to write the soundtrack score, but BNL did manage to compose and sing a little song called "Gangster Girl."

Although the idea for the cops to hang around way too long, goofing off and eventually singing a doo-wop song was part of the script, the band brought a lot more to it than what was on paper. "The guys," raves Kogen, "went over and above the call by writing a song especially for the movie. It was recorded the day they shot their scene at a nearby recording studio. The guys had worked out some lyrics and started putting music to them at the studio. Harmonies were worked out, and performance levels were set. It was amazing to see the guys work so fast and so well together. Very impressive."

Kogen says that the guys were a little nervous but excited to be in a real movie. They also required a bit of a police makeover to look the part. "We shaved off beards and moustaches and tried to hide the wilder hairstyles under policeman caps," remembers Kogen. "Tyler, to me, seemed like the best actor, but Ed also had a relaxed acting style I enjoyed. In the pitching-pennies scene, Tyler did an improvised running-man victory dance, which I think made it into the film." And unlike miming for their own rock videos, where they've generally lived with a recording for months, Kogen says they found it a little trickier to lip-synch to a track they'd only just recorded that morning. "Some of the doo-wop harmony parts go all over the place, and it's hard to mimic them exactly," says Kogen, adding, "I think the guys did great."

10

Toronto and Beyond, 1994

Around grade eleven, Andy Creeggan became
seriously committed to playing the drums. But in hindsight, he felt
he was too serious about it. His competitiveness and relentless
ambition began to eat away at his enjoyment of the music. "If I
noticed someone was better than me," Andy admits, "I had sort of
negative, jealous feelings about them. I would get in this weird
head space that I wasn't used to. I almost started treating music
like sports or something."

Then one day he had a moment of clarity: He was destroying
something he loved by taking it too seriously. And so he decided
to save what love was left by walking away from a music career
altogether. This simple shift in perspective had a profound effect
on his attitude toward music. "I started to lighten up," he
remembers. "If I noticed that someone was a better player than
me, I would be happy for them. I would try and learn from
them. I was cool about music, and I wasn't forcing it. I was just
really in a good way about it."

By magic coincidence (and let's be frank, the Barenaked
Ladies story is full of them) it was now grade twelve, exactly

when the new, improved Andy met Ed, who played music, too. So they played together now and again. And they played for the love of the game. It wasn't forced. It was fun. "I was enjoying this thing with the band . . . and I thought Ed was like God at that point. I just thought he was the greatest guy. Jim and I were playing. It was a good time." But at the same time, Andy became interested in the Canada World Youth program and its promise of travel.

"I didn't want to go to university right away," he admits, "just because that's what you did after grade thirteen. I wasn't even taking this Barenaked Ladies thing seriously. It was just something we did occasionally, maybe two or three times a month. I wanted to experience something other than Canada. I had this need to step out of my little bubble. So I decided to check out Canada World Youth."

But as Andy packed his bags and prepared to burst his little bubble, Barenaked Ladies had started to develop a small but loyal local following. Andy went to Steven with a question right out of the Clash songbook: "Should I stay or should I go?" "I remember Steve saying I shouldn't give Canada World Youth up, that it was a big opportunity."

So in spite of the band's burgeoning success, or perhaps in reaction to it, Andy made the decision to expand his horizons. It was a choice that would not only have a profound effect on his life, but a profound effect on his wife as well. But that's for later. First, Andy explains the Canada World Youth concept: "Canada World Youth is a program designed to give young Canadians a chance to discover their own country by spending time in a community other than their own. Participants try to discover their own culture by presenting it to people from other communities. They can also discover their culture vis-à-vis trying to fit into another one, then returning home with a new vision. The exchange works so that you do four to six months someplace in Canada before you go abroad."

A lot of Andy's learning took place in Canada—in a different community. Once he returned to his own life, he felt as if he'd come face-to-face with his own upbringing and culture, as if he were an outsider. "That was a pretty intense thing," he remarks. "I was driving home from the airport with my parents and I was just hyperaware of the fact that they were just in a certain culture and that I'd been removed from it."

Andy's foreign destination was to be Rwanda, but just three weeks before departure, the country suffered one of the most traumatic events in world history. "As history [shows]," says Andy, "this thing [the civil war in Rwanda] that became the travesty we all know about, in 1994, was just the beginning. Some of the rebels were starting to enter in, so it looked like there was some serious trouble, and that program got canceled." Some of the Rwandans, the ones who weren't in danger, went back home, and some of them are now refugees in Canada. Andy, however, had made up his mind to travel and asked to be placed in another group. Anywhere was fine.

As luck would have it, a last-minute cancellation opened up a spot in a group going to Uruguay. It was here that Andy met someone who would become a significant person in his life, future wife Natacha Hebert, an Acadian from Moncton, New Brunswick. The couple would eventually marry in July 1999, but the two didn't actually get serious about dating when they first met. "I never went out with her on the program," Andy admits. "I liked her from afar. Then, through touring with the band, I was able to visit all my friends from CWY, and our relationship was finally able to take some form."

After spending time in rural Quebec, Andy took a brief hiatus from the exchange to record what would become *The Yellow Tape* at Toronto's Wellesley Studios. "I got special permission from the head office to come back to Toronto," he explains. Then he was off to Uruguay.

Meanwhile, 1991 was shaping up to be a memorable year for the newly formed Barenaked Ladies. In late 1990, they'd been awarded Best Band of the Year by the young viewers of the YTV network. The Youth Achievement Awards had been televised across Canada, and the exposure helped the band gain momentum in the local clubs and colleges. While Andy was away, the rest of the Barenaked Ladies started doing a lot of busking, mostly to get people to come out to their gigs. Steven remembers that the band was getting pretty good at it, too.

Around this time, Tyler Stewart was becoming a fixture in the lives of Barenaked Ladies. I asked Steven to recount the events leading up to Tyler's arrival in the band.

"John King," Steven says, "who was then managing Corky and the Juice Pigs, was also booking the Waterloo Busker's Festival, which had all sorts of street performers, like clowns and magicians." King had booked the Ladies for the festival. "Tyler was there, performing with another band," says Steven, "and he saw us as we were setting up one day, and said, 'Hey, Barenaked Ladies, right on!' We were like, 'That guy knows who we are? Cool!' We just started getting along with him really well."

Tyler remembers his first impressions of the band: "First of all," he says, "their music was so incredibly catchy. Early stuff like 'Be My Yoko Ono.' They could sing so well, and then they'd do the rap, and it was so funny. Here were these intelligent goofballs playing amazing music. That's why I think I get what the audience gets from us; because when I first saw it I just thought, 'Wow, I have to be part of that.'"

"That's Ty for you," jokes Ed, "such an opportunist [laughs]. He was playing with this band called the Would-be Goods, and he saw us drawing all the crowds and thought, 'Hey, I've gotta be a part of that.'" It's safe to say, then, that Tyler had to be a part of that. But there was one problem: He was initially the only one who thought so.

"He said he'd love to sit in with us sometime in Toronto," Ed recalls, "and we were like, 'Whatever. We've already got a percussionist and he's coming back.' We didn't really want a drummer, per se. But he kept coming back and asking if he could sit in. Eventually we let him sit in for, like, one set, but just kick,

70

snare, and hi-hat. Every week he'd be back, but he'd ask, 'Can I just bring one extra tom?' Then two toms, and eventually he started building up this kit, and so he asked, 'Can I be in the band now?' And we said, 'No.'" But Tyler was nothing if not persistent. "Literally, I just knew I had to do this," he says. "So I just kept sitting in, and Ed said it wasn't out of the question for me to be in the band, and I said, 'Yes.'"

"Tyler played with us at the festival a couple of times," Ed continues. "In retrospect, he was really pushy trying to get into the band. Saying things like, 'So you guys play in Toronto? I'd love to sit in sometime. Just give me a call. Here's my number.'"

"Eventually we let him in," admits Steven, "mainly because we got along with him so well. We'd never really wanted a drummer. I always thought Spirit of the West [a popular Canadian group] did pretty well without a drummer, so we didn't need one. But he ended up joining, and things started to really happen after that."

11

Let's Begin: Canada Gets Caught Up in Yellow Tape
Toronto, 1991

Working as a quartet, Ed, Steven, Tyler, and Jim held down the tree fort while Andy was trekking through Uruguay with his Canada World Youth group. The band's sound was beginning to be described as part folk, part rock, part funk, part rap, and part spare parts left lying around, a sort of acoustic hip-hop. And with seemingly boundless energy, the band demonstrated this new sound for anyone who would listen and anywhere they could get a crowd: store grand openings, civic-award ceremonies, and on the street. "We'd busk on the street, right outside our own shows, to drum up customers," Steven remembers.

"We made ourselves really accessible to radio stations and other media outlets," Ed recalls. "We'd just play acoustically. And we concentrated on our live shows. Things like getting just the right set list and all the stuff we learned from Corky and the Juice Pigs. Word got out that we were fun to watch and that we had a good time doing it. People just latched on to it." It was always part of their agenda to try to give audiences something fresh and something different, but Ed doesn't discount the role serendipity played in their local success.

In an interview with *14850*, an Internet magazine, Ed and Tyler told journalist Dan Amrich that there was no secret formula and the knowledge of one probably wouldn't have made their odds of success any more likely. "I think whatever it was," Ed told Amrich, "if someone tried to do it again, it wouldn't work. We went out on a lot of limbs, and we did a lot of stuff that nobody thought that a band should do." "And besides," adds Tyler, "there's a certain danger, in the music business, of following trends. Because those trends tend to be, well, trendy. The music business attaches onto a certain way of doing things. For a while, it was 'You have to play every bad club in northern Ontario before you get any recognition.' Then it was 'You have to shop your demo around.' Now, it's 'Put out an indie tape, and see if it has any success. Finance everything yourself.' Well, everything keeps changing, and we just didn't follow any rules."

Barenaked Ladies were becoming something of a phenomenon waiting to happen on the Toronto-area club scene. Buoyed by word of mouth and their unpredictably frenetic live shows, the Ladies were regularly packing houses and making new friends everywhere they played. And everywhere the Ladies went, their tape was sure to go.

Essentially a live-in-the-studio recording, *The Yellow Tape* featured nascent versions of "Brian Wilson," "If I Had $1,000,000," "Be My Yoko Ono" and "Blame It on Me" plus an acoustic hip-hop makeover of, "Fight the Power" by Public Enemy. More than just a demo, *The Yellow Tape* gave audiences a formidable souvenir to take home and college radio stations something fresh to play. And quite a lot of fans seemed to be taking home the souvenir cassette, buying it from the band and through local record stores.

Before the rise of independent record labels like Seattle's Sub Pop, the term *successful indie* was still something of an oxymoron. While bands were custom-pressing vinyl albums and seven-inch singles as early as the late '70s, these were mainly to sell at gigs or to send, in vain, to radio stations. There were very few marketing or distribution options available. To most mainstream listeners, *indie* meant either a car race or a fedora-wearing, Nazi-beating character played by Harrison Ford. Any kind of alternative-music scene was, by definition, alternative to the mainstream and, as such, off the radar of the majors. Self-produced recordings were seen by the big record companies as demos to be rere-corded, remixed, or rejected.

And remember, there was no such thing as an MP3 in 1991. In fact, unless you were in the military or had a university hookup, there really wasn't much of an Internet to speak of. But with *The Yellow Tape*, Barenaked Ladies would forever change the way Canadian indies marketed themselves.

Barenaked Ladies began to garner local airplay on the mod-ern-rock station CFNY. The band, with Andy now back in the ranks, began to pop up with increasing regularity on *Speaker's Corner*, an interactive television program consisting of highlights culled from a street-corner video booth in front of Toronto's Citytv station. The guys were busking their asses off, and the mainstream was beginning to take note. Soon the tape was being stocked at the flagship store of one of Canada's largest record retailers, Sam the Record Man, on Toronto's Yonge St.

It was rather poetic that the downtown record shop carried the tape, because on one of its five songs, "Brian Wilson," Steven describes one of his many pilgrimages to that very store "just to check out the late-night record shop." Written in the summer of 1990, just after Steven's twentieth birthday, "Brian Wilson" employed a melancholy melody and self-effacing lyrics that con-veyed his adolescent depression and creative doubt juxtaposed against the myth that surrounds the Beach Boys' legendary leader, Brian Douglas Wilson.

"I was living at my parents' place at the time," Steven recounts in the BNL newsletter. "Sometimes I'd take their car down to Sam the Record Man and wander around all of the record stores. It was on those days that you just didn't feel like getting out of bed, and listening to music was there to help take you out of that. I used to really enjoy buying records; I was a record-buying addict."

Garwood Wallace, who also happens to be a funny guy and something of a pop musicologist, worked at the downtown Sam the Record Man store during the rise of Barenaked-mania. When *The Yellow Tape* broke all the rules, and sales records, Garwood was right there. Sort of. "Unfortunately," he says, "when the *Yellow* cassette was redefining the landscape for indie stuff in Canada, I was in charge of back orders for the whole chain, so I didn't experience it directly on the sales floor." From this unique position, however, Garwood bore witness to Barenaked Ladies' ascent from local to national phenomenon. He was inundated with requests from all the regional outlets across the country. It was his job to fill those *Yellow Tape* orders. "Massive amounts of *The Yellow Tape* began to go through my department to all the other Sam's stores," he reports. "The idea that anyone was writing songs about Brian Wilson or Yoko Ono did seem significant to me at the time. And the amount of airplay for "If I Had $1,000,000" was truly remarkable. I remember thinking this was a song that everybody seemed to know."

As stores across the country began stocking *The Yellow Tape* and its demand increased on a daily basis, Victor Page, Steven's dad, felt it was time to leave his job and oversee the production and distribution of Barenaked Ladies' hot little cassette. He founded Page Publications, later renamed Page Music. Soon, the little tape that could achieved gold-record status in Canada, selling more than fifty thousand units. Eventually, sales of *The Yellow Tape* would soar to platinum heights and in the process become a testament to working outside the system to reach the people. It was a feat previously unheard of, especially for an independently manufactured, cassette-only release.

Now, at this time, lurking on the Toronto music scene, there was a gaggle of musicians who'd formed a funky and politicized groove collective known as the Bourbon Tabernacle Choir. The

Bourbons featured the organic organ work of Chris Brown and the vocal stylings of Kate Fenner, along with Dave Wall, Jason Mercer, Chris Miller, and Gene Hardy. Chris Brown, fans will know, would later collaborate with Tyler Stewart on his album project, *Don't Talk Dance.* Many years later, on the *Stunt* tour, Brown would be called upon to fill in as keyboardist. "Their ascent was pretty quick," Brown recalls of the BNL. "I remember when I first started hearing about them. I first remember all the soundmen who worked in the local clubs, guys like Bo Cairo from Clinton's, talking about them."

House sound technicians often have to set up and mix as many as three different acts a night, often for seven nights a week. This volume of turnover affords the soundman the inside scoop about which bands are any good, which bands are really good, and which bands are good-for-nothing. The house sound guy is to the local music scene what the friendly old barber is to a small town. They're the spreaders of gossip, the tellers of truth, and the feelers of the local pulse.

The soundman usually begins conversing with bands about technical details, such as microphone requirements. Eventually, as sound check nears, the subject matter progresses, or digresses, into stories about which bands are hot and which ones are all hype. And, of course, who's hell to work with. Among the many excellent sound engineers on the Toronto music scene, some of the best and most friendly later moved on to important positions with high-profile touring acts. Gary Stokes currently works with Sarah McLachlan, and Robin Billinton is now the "Godfather of Sound" for Barenaked Ladies. And then there's Bo Cairo.

Bo is a character. In addition to being an ace sound engineer and a friendly soul, Bo has something of a reputation with local bands as a raconteur. A storyteller. The guy can talk. He knows all sorts of obscure facts about so many things that it's fun just to get him talking, so that you can listen. And Bo knows bands. So when Chris Brown got the news from Bo about Barenaked Ladies, he knew it was on the up-and-up. "'So," says Brown, remembering Bo's words, "'these guys asked me to set up four vocal mics, and you know what? It turns out they can all actually sing!' That was the first I heard."

The Barenaked buzz had started. "It was pretty extraordinary what they did," says Brown. "They were opening for various bands at that time and doing stuff around town, and then everybody was just kind of getting a vibe for them, and then suddenly it just went whoof."

"Whoof?" I ask.

"Whoof," repeats Brown.

As BNL approached new levels of fame, it became obvious that they required a manager to navigate the next phase of their career. At the time, they seemed to have found the best man for the job. His name was Nigel.

Nigel Best (whose name, I just realized, is an anagram of Let's Begin) was in publicity and promotions at Warner Music Canada when he was swept off his feet by Barenaked Ladies' charismatic stage presence and youthful exuberance. Vancouver-based music journalist Chris Dafoe, a columnist for Canada's national newspaper the *Globe and Mail* who's written a considerable amount on BNL throughout their career, became familiar with Best when they both worked at CITR, the University of British Columbia's radio station. Dafoe was the program director, and Best was a DJ. Dafoe's and Best's paths would cross intermittently for the next decade.

"I'd bumped into him in Toronto in the late 1980s," Dafoe recalls, "and he said he'd been earning his living as a sort of wandering journalist, filing freelance pieces from the Bahamas to the English tabs, doing stories about George Michael dancing with boys. Next thing I knew he was pitching me stories on behalf of Warner Music Canada." Dafoe figures that Best's innate charm, not to mention his gift for telling tall tales, had probably landed him the job with Warner Music. But, Dafoe told me, there was one tiny problem: He wasn't actually very good at it.

"He did, however, know how to make a splash, and he was conversant enough with the recent history of punk-rock outrage to know how to turn the Ladies into a household name, at least on a local level." Best, to this author, seems to be the kind of cheerleading soul who could really pitch you on an act if he believed in them. Which is why he was really useful in the early days of Barenaked Ladies' career. He really believed that Barenaked Ladies were the greatest band on the planet, and his enthusiasm was authentic and contagious. Think of his role in the band's career as somewhat akin to that of the legendary manager of the Beatles, Brian Epstein. Best may have been, as Dafoe says, "the right man to take them to the top," but like Epstein, he didn't really seem to know what to do next.

Barenaked Ladies were becoming really well known. As news of their sold-out concerts began to travel beyond a local level, so did the band. They were becoming citizens of the highway. Constant touring not only provided the band with valuable insights to the outside world, but the experiment also afforded scientists valuable and much-needed research into the effects of sleep deprivation. But who needs sleep?

The stuffy music business was getting tired, and Barenaked Ladies were, literally, its wake-up call. They sounded the alarm at high-profile music festivals such as the South by Southwest Music Expo (SXSW), in Austin, Texas, and the celebrated New Music Seminar (NMS), in New York City. One A&R guy, a recent attendee of the NMS, regaled some of his fellow A&R types on his return home with some of Barenaked Ladies' exploits in NYC. The guy was the textbook example of a jaded, cynical, but otherwise eagerly opportunistic, music-biz professional whom we used to call, back in the day, a *weasel*.

He was going on about how Barenaked Ladies went around to the festival hotels and performed wake-up calls for the delegates. Live, in person, singing wake-up calls delivered to your door by five guys with an acoustic guitar. At first he seemed to be mocking their innocent charm and tireless, yet childlike, sense of humor. But his tone went from mocking to one of sincere respect for the band's inventiveness. He couldn't find a cynical angle to the stunt, beyond the obvious self-promotional value. He and his friends stopped laughing and became curious about these new kids in town. Barenaked Ladies had awakened something in him, and he was touched, just a little, by their naive idealism. They were delivering an honest message, right to your door. Argue with *that*.

One fan in attendance at Barenaked Ladies' New Music Seminar gig enjoyed the show so much that he went home and told his mom all about it. Which seemed fair enough, since the band had sung a song named after her. The fan, of course, was none other than Sean Ono Lennon, and his mother, Yoko, was the subject of "Be My Yoko Ono." Backstage at the New Music Seminar, Sean told the relieved Ladies that his mother, the widow of John Lennon, was actually a good sport about the tune and found it all rather amusing.

12

Andy's Back
Toronto, 1991–1992

Andy wasn't bothered that, upon his return, there was this Tyler guy suddenly at the rhythmic helm, although he admits that he was forced to get to know him while in the course of playing in the band. And anyway, he still hadn't decided if he was going to jump in or jump ship. "I was considering planting trees that next summer. I wasn't really sure about what I was going to do. Then I thought, 'This band looks like an interesting thing—it might never happen again, and besides, university will always be there.'"

When Andy arrived home, the band was playing at Toronto's Harbour-front, so he checked them out and liked what he heard from the stage—and from the now very vocal fans whose legions loomed larger every day. "It was cool that the invitation was always there for me, so there I was, back. But I was used to playing congas, right?" In his absence, Barenaked Ladies had indeed become a local cause célèbre. Andy wasn't entirely sure if he still fit in, and neither was the band's new audience. As a result, he tried to blend in as much as possible.

"Everybody was a little bit suspicious," says Andy of the chilly reaction. "There was a crowd there that I had to fit into. They weren't ready to accept me quite yet."

Undaunted, Andy set up his congas and proceeded to get back to business as usual. But it soon became clear to everyone that business was not, in fact, as usual.

Before Tyler brought in his entire drum kit, Andy remembers that Ed was a big part of the band's rhythm. There had been an almost telepathic connection between Ed, Jim, and Andy. This had all changed, which tripped up the Creeggans. Not that they didn't like Tyler personally, it just felt weird musically. "There's no question about it," says Andy. "There really was an awesome rhythmical connection between Jim and Ed. Tyler didn't quite fit into that super–laser beam between them.

"When I was the drummer," Andy continues, "I was letting Ed's rhythm blossom a lot more. I would just sort of put in more spiky stuff and would try and enhance it." Andy began to feel that Tyler's more boisterous, rock-drumming approach was in conflict with this philosophy. "The sound of Ed's guitar and Tyler's drumming was very busy and continuous. There wasn't a lot of breathing space between them rhythmically, so that was something I found quite hard to fit into."

Tyler does admit to consciously influencing the band's rhythmic agenda a little away from a folk or jazz sensibility and headlong toward a heavy backbeat. And he admits to upsetting the applecart that existed before his arrival. "Jim is a very laid-back player, but I keyed off the energy of Steve and Ed so much that I was playing on top of the beat like you wouldn't believe. Which is another way of saying that I was concerned with pro-pelling the group more than Andy had."

If this had caused some tension with Jim's playing, that ten-sion was amplified upon Andy's return. "They're brothers," says Tyler, "and they have the same kind of nursery-rhymes-from-outer-space musical sensibility. They have that fluid groove thing that's not sort of straight ahead. It changed a lot when I joined."

And Tyler was determined to stay. Soon, the congas' loss was the ivories', and the band's, gain.

"So it just became natural that I go over and start playing more keyboards, which I was interested in doing anyway," Andy recalls. "I was always jealous when everybody was talking about chords, and I was just sort of sitting and twiddling my drumstick. So I was happy to switch to keyboards; it became quite natural, so that was cool." Andy stayed on, for the time being at least.

"I belong with these guys," states Tyler emphatically. "That's how we all hit it off in the first place, our common sense of humor." Perhaps Ed's following statement best sums up Tyler's contribution to Barenaked Ladies: "I guess we weren't really looking for a drummer; we were just looking for a Tyler."

The Tyler

TORONTO, AGAIN

Enter Tyler. Born in Scarborough in the summer of love, September 21, 1967 (okay more like the Indian summer of love), Tyler Joseph Stewart was raised by his mother, Sandra, and her husband, Bob. In the beginning, the family lived with Tyler's grandmother near Birchmount and St. Clair before moving to an inappropriately named neighborhood called Tuxedo Court. Tyler remembers the region, near the corner of Markham Road and Ellesmere Avenue, as anything but top hats and tails. In fact, he has a few sordid tales to tell. "Tuxedo Court," he begins, "is an apartment complex right behind Woburn Secondary School. It's pretty hellish nowadays, like absolutely crack-ridden. It's right by Woburn Collegiate, where Ed and Steve went to school. My dad went to Woburn, too. I guess he finished Woburn in '67 and Ed and Steve graduated in '87, I think. So, there you go, twenty years' difference."

Of course when Tyler says "dad," he's referring to Bob

Stewart, the man who raised him. He never actually met his biological father until around 1989. "I grew up with Bob Stewart, he's pretty much the only dad I ever knew. Bob played in a band called the Wizards of Id. They played Hendrix and Dylan and some original stuff. He was like a longhaired, motorcycle-riding kind of guy."

Tyler actually grew up in Newmarket, Ontario, a small suburban town just north of metropolitan Toronto. Although he attended school at Huron Heights in Newmarket, young Tyler spent a lot of time visiting family deep in the heart of "Scarberia." And as it turns out, he'd continue to visit as an adult because the band rehearsed new material quite frequently at Scarborough's Westbury Sound.

Before the buildings were demolished, Westbury Sound used to be surrounded by General Motors, where Tyler's grandmother, his mom's mom, worked for more than twenty years, and Phillips, where his grandfather worked for more than twenty years. "You know, it's so funny," he reflects. "I know it so well from those early years and from just going to visit my grandmother. My dad's parents were at McCowan [Road] and Ellesmere. The stomping grounds of the band and the whole sort of Scarberian beginnings are quite similar."

Although Tyler's grandfather passed away when he was only eight years old, Norman Sullivan nonetheless made a huge contribution to Tyler's early upbringing. "He was the one who kind of sent me on my way," Tyler remembers proudly. "He would do things like take me downtown to Commissioner Street and show me big ships in the harbor. He also helped me with reading by getting me to say all the road signs out loud. He was a very generous man."

Young Tyler, barraged by suburban culture and a glut of infotainment from television, movies, and radio, became curious about where all this stuff was coming from. This curiosity led him to initially pursue a career in the broadcast industry. One dial twist of fate, and the drummer man might have been a weatherman. Yet, when you look closely, the two fields are not that distant from each other.

Canadian communications guru Marshall McLuhan observed that drumming and radio and television broadcasting are joined at the hip, so to speak. You see, back when people had no mass media (or cars, for that matter) to communicate with far-off tribes and villages, it was the role of drummers to sound the news of the day, beating out, as it were, the headlines. Drumming was, in a way, the original village radio, globally speaking. So Tyler's ambitions to get into broadcasting are not that surprising. As an extension of his desire to communicate, not to mention his latent extrovert tendencies, Tyler enrolled in the prestigious Radio and Television Arts (RTA) program at Ryerson Polytechnic University (RPU) in downtown Toronto.

Tyler learned a lot about both drumming and broadcasting at Ryerson. Perhaps most importantly, he learned that his heart wasn't really into a career in broadcasting. Drumming, however, was another matter. "People respond to drumming," Tyler comments. "They have no choice. It's so loud. You can make people dance. It's great. Make them laugh or make them dance. I always wanted to do that, and RTA kind of took me off that track."

Leaving Ryerson, Tyler suffered through a variety of decidedly unglamorous production-assistant jobs in the television field. He was a self-described techie for the *Super Dave Show*, which was taped in Scarborough but syndicated around the world. Super Dave was a fictional, low-grade daredevil who attempted to emulate real-life stunt jumper Evel Kneivel. But like Toonces, the cat on *Saturday Night Live* who could drive a car, he just wasn't very good.

(Hey kids! Here's some useless, unnecessary, and totally uncalled-for trivia: Super Dave Osborne was played by former Smothers Brothers *writer Bob Einstein who is also the brother of comedian Albert Brooks. Brooks, you see, changed his stage name when he realized that the name* Albert Einstein *had already been used. Super Dave and Albert Brooks, now that's relativity!)*

After his stint with the stuntman, Tyler went through a few more crew jobs, including holding umbrellas over other people's heads, photocopying scripts, and being a crew driver. And while working on a kids' show called *Eric's World* (hosted by Canadian children's performer Eric Nagler) Tyler found himself relegated to cutting up carrot sticks as the craft-service guy. His job entailed feeding the entire cast and crew, and while Tyler made the best of it, he also made a wicked baba ghanouj.

"Everyone hung out in my craft-service room," Tyler recalls. "They'd come in to get carrots or I'd have baba ghanouj, but it was also sort of the place to hang out because I'd have tunes going and I was an amusing guy."

Exclusive! Tyler's Job-Saving Baba Ghanouj

Makes 2 cups

1 large eggplant

2 tablespoons extra-virgin olive oil

2 garlic cloves, minced

3 tablespoons lemon juice

2 ¼ tablespoons tahini (sesame paste) available at health-food or Middle Eastern shops

½ teaspoon salt

¼ cup chopped fresh, flat-leaf parsley

Preheat oven to 450° F

Prick eggplant several times with a fork, then place it on a baking sheet. Bake for 35 minutes, until the flesh collapses and is soft. When the eggplant is cool enough to handle, scrape the pulp into a food processor or blender. Compost the skin.

In a small skillet or pan, heat the oil over low heat. Add the garlic and cook for 2 minutes, until soft.

Add the oil, garlic, lemon juice, tahini, and salt to the eggplant. Process until smooth. Add the parsley and process for another 20 seconds or so. Serve at room temperature, garnished with a bit more parsley and a drizzle of extra-virgin olive oil. Serve this with pita bread, veggie sticks, or crackers to your coworkers or friends. They'll love you, and you won't get fired.

The year was 1990, and Tyler was moonlighting as a drummer here and there with bands like Three Day Bender and Cow Tools. During this time, Tyler plastered the walls of his craft-service area with posters of these and other bands. That year, one of the bands, the Would-be Goods, attended the Waterloo Busker's Festival, held in Waterloo, Ontario. It was here that yet another of the many cosmic coincidences in the story of Barenaked Ladies took place. For, as longtime fans (or people who just read the last chapters) know, this is where it all came together. Barenaked Ladies, ready or not, had found their Tyler. And Tyler had found his kindred spirits.

Tyler claims that it was their shared sense of humor that initially sparked his enthusiasm. Here was an ensemble of wired extroverts born in the electronic age, who could be wickedly satirical one minute and drop-dead serious the next. As they got to know one another, they unearthed still more common ground. Steven wrote lyrics about stuff that Tyler knew all about, because Steve was describing his life, too.

> *Drove downtown in the rain*
> *Nine-thirty on a Tuesday night*
> *Just to check out the late-night record shop.*
> —from "Brian Wilson"

"We all grew up in the suburbs, which we maligned," Tyler points out. "Where do you learn stuff? Mainly from the TV or the newspaper. As soon as you get bored with shopping culture, you pick up a book or go to a movie or go downtown to the record store. I was impressed with that angle because I was thinking I was media-savvy as well."

Tyler knew that the time had come to leave the Would-be Goods and join in with the could-be greats. "I started sitting in with them at Ultrasound [Showbar] in Toronto, and other clubs in town," Tyler says.

Ed recalls the first time Tyler played with them in Toronto, at Clinton's Tavern. "I remember we didn't rehearse back then," Ed confesses. "Tyler just showed up. I had said to only bring his kick drum, his snare, his hi-hats, and one cymbal, so that's what he did." By way of example, Ed recounts an incident from the show that, to this day, still makes him smile. The band had, of late, been playing a cover of "Still Ill" by the Smiths, but they were in the habit of doing it a little differently. "At the point where the chord changes to E minor," recalls Ed, "we'd always throw in this little Led Zeppelin guitar riff, as a little joke."

Tyler had never rehearsed with the band, and yet he played along with this little change as though he knew it was coming. "We were playing it in this sort of ballad style," Ed recalls, "but I turned to him as soon as we hit the E minor and yelled out, 'Led Zeppelin!' and he got it right away. It was cool."

It wasn't long before Tyler's parallel world began to merge with his other life at *Eric's World*. "The first time I ever rehearsed with the Ladies was on the *Eric's World* set." Tyler says. "We went after hours, and it was a big open space and we rehearsed in the living room of the set." Gradually cast and crew people from *Eric's World* began to come out to see Tyler at his other job, drumming with Barenaked Ladies.

"It was a nice production," Tyler recalls of his old work buddies. "People were cool and stuff—they started to come out to my shows, and eventually I just went, 'Okay, I'm going to do this.'" By all accounts, Tyler's media connections played a small but crucial role in the promotion of the band in its nascent stages. Not to mention the fact that many of his former classmates at Ryerson were now working at scattered media outlets all over the country. As the band began to get interviews, Tyler was often amused to discover that the interviewers were old friends.

"On our first-ever cross-Canada jaunt," Tyler reveals, "I'd run into people who were in my class at Ryerson who operated the camera or were doing the interview or who edited the piece. It was really cool that way, in that respect. I'd be in the newsroom, and there'd be somebody there who's a reporter."

Did Tyler have any regrets about straying from the broadcasting path, especially when he started seeing his fellow alumni out in the real world with real jobs? Nope. In fact, these encounters only confirmed to Tyler that he was doing the right thing. "I was playing in a band," Tyler explains. "I got to do all the things that I went to RTA for. I got to be on TV and be a nob with Barenaked Ladies and play music."

And playing music, Tyler soon learned, was just one part of what the band was striving to achieve. Ed and Steve had learned a lot about showmanship watching the frenetic antics of Corky and the Juice Pigs night after night. They knew they didn't just want to be musicians; they wanted to be performers. Tyler recalls getting this message loud and clear. "The show always must go on," he says, as if checking off an imaginary list. "You must be on top of it. You can't slack. And a good way to be on top of it is to challenge yourself every night. So I learned."

13

If I Had $100,000 (Canadian)
The Road to *Gordon*

Disc one,

It's where we've begun,

It's all my greatest hits,

And if you are a fan then you know

That you've already got 'em.

—from "Box Set" by Steven Page

In 1991, Barenaked Ladies entered the Discovery to Disc contest, staged by Toronto modern-rock radio station CFNY. First prize was $100,000, for the making of a master recording. They won, and the cash was now theirs for the taking.

John Jones, CFNY's music director at the time, described the phenomenon of Barenaked-mania to Toni Ruberto of Ontario's *Niagara Gazette.* "It was almost like they were riding a very large wave at that point in time," Jones told the paper. "They captured a large audience through the success of their independent cassette, and all of it was entirely deserved because they are great songwriters, great lyricists, and phenomenal entertainers."

Through funding from CFNY's Discovery to Disc program, the band was able to independently bankroll their first full-length CD. The bed was sufficiently warmed for a full album of Barenaked Ladies music. So with their $100,000 prize tucked under their collective arm, the band set out to choose a producer.

Tyler remembers the process being both exciting and, at times, humbling. "Mitchell Froom [American producer of Suzanne Vega, Crowded House, and Elvis Costello] turned us down," laughs Stewart. "He said he didn't do 'joke bands.'"

Undaunted, the band continued the search for a producer who'd not only see their whimsical side but who'd also understand and nurture their more heartfelt musical ambitions. One promising name on their list was that of a talented young Toronto producer who'd impressed them on recordings by some of their favorite local bands like Change of Heart and the Rheostatics. That producer, Michael Phillip Wojewoda, remembers well the day he received a tape from the band's early manager, Nigel Best. "I knew about them as this local phenomenon," admits Wojewoda. "There had been quite a buzz in the city."

Having only heard BNL's "collegiate schtick" on local radio, the producer was pleasantly surprised by the diversity of the material on their eclectic demo. One song particularly piqued his interest. "Many of the songs [on the tape]," recalls Wojewoda, "I had already heard on the radio. But it was "The Flag" that made me realize that they had this great potential. There was definitely some wisdom in their young years. Like the best Shakespeare, they liked to surf that line between comedy and tragedy. I realized that we could maybe make a really great record."

Wojewoda telephoned Best to declare his interest in producing the album. He'd need to meet with the band to get an idea of who they were and what they hoped to achieve. As fate would have it, the producer was recording a new album with the Rheostatics, *Whale Music*, and wanted to add a layered vocal section, à la the Beach Boys, to a song called "California Dreamline." Remembering the impressive vocal arrangements on BNL's tape, and sensing the perfect excuse for them all to get better acquainted, Wojewoda invited Barenaked Ladies over to the studio. "Everyone in the [Toronto music] community knew each other," confides Wojewoda, "so the Rheos were really into having them in to sing. Plus, as singers go, they were just really, really good. They went out and sang their parts, with all their jazzy voicings, and everyone was very happy."

Wojewoda witnessed what he describes as an unbelievable confidence about the young band. As it transpired, Rush drummer, Neil Peart, a certified rock star to be sure, happened to be making a guest appearance on the Rheostatics' album on the very same day as the Ladies. Yet, Wojewoda says, the band appeared unfazed by Peart's celebrity status, opting instead for a tone of respectful admiration toward an accomplished peer. In addition, he also got a firsthand look at the band's winning sense of spontaneity and improvisation. "After the vocal part was done," he remembers, "I had to set up a production effect in the control room before I could play it back to them. This was a fairly time-consuming process, so members of Barenaked Ladies and [the] Rheostatics all went out into the studio and began jamming together." Two hours later, Wojewoda called everyone back into the control room to hear the fully mixed vocal tracks. On playback, Barenaked Ladies liked what they heard.

As December 1991 arrived, Barenaked Ladies had selected Wojewoda as the midwife for their unborn baby, the as yet unnamed *Gordon*. While the fun and professionalism of the *Whale Music* session had cemented the band's choice of Wojewoda, Tyler says, "We loved his work and were leaning toward him anyway." "I think they just sort of dug the vibe and extrapolated it into what it would be like on a full album," guesses Wojewoda. "Of course, if you ask them," he adds, "they may have just liked my hair."

The road to *Gordon* began in earnest with rehearsals at a cramped studio in Toronto's west end. The band had no shortage of songs from which to choose. Together, Steven and Ed had amassed a truckload of material. They'd also collaborated with the Creeggans on "I Love You," and the whole band had written "Grade 9," a boisterous dissertation on high-school life.

Out of about twenty songs, fourteen were selected to take into the studio. Wojewoda remembers this process flowing organically, with everyone more or less in agreement about which songs made the cut. Wojewoda's expressed desire to include what he viewed as their more mature material, songs like "The Flag," "Wrap Your Arms Around Me," and "What a Good Boy," turned out to be perfectly in sync with the band's shared vision. "They knew what they were already," Wojewoda maintains. "We had basically the same ideas about what the shape of it should be. In preproduction, they didn't need a lot of shaping. It was really just a matter of sifting through a lot of great moments and finding the ones which fit best on the record."

Many of the songs chosen for *Gordon* reflected an acute awareness of the pitfalls of the music business and its star-making machinery, which was seemingly at odds with a band at such an early stage in its career. "New Kid on the Block," written by Steven and Ed with Toronto songwriter Scott Dibble, may have taken its cue from the flash-in-the-pan career of Donnie Wahlberg's teen-beat crew, but the song's precocious lyrics also poked an irreverent finger at fame and conveyed a sense that the band didn't take its own newfound fame too seriously.

Likewise, Page's "Box Set" was a scathing commentary on the music business's predilection toward the endless repackaging of a recording artist's greatest, and not-so-greatest, hits. While sardonic in tone, the band's cheerful exuberance and honest love for the music part of the term *music business* dispelled any notion of hypocrisy. Today, Steven says of "Box Set": "I love the irony of being five albums in. Like, I told you so. 'Box Set' was always intended to be a warning to myself. I had always said, 'That's just so if we ever hit it big, I can say I called my own bluff, when we do the boxed set.' I don't know who I was writing about. The first line, when I was first writing it, I was thinking about someone like Sting, and his fabulous ego. But then I started thinking about somebody who has this body of work, yet people only want to hear one thing. Lindsey Buckingham of Fleetwood Mac, for instance."

In addition, their constant name-checking of a wide range of recording artists from Yoko Ono and Duran Duran to Tom Jones and Milli Vanilli—and, of course, Brian Wilson—indicate that they probably spent as much time in record stores as some people do in church. Ironically, Steven wasn't all that enamored with the Beach Boys when he was growing up, but later became curious after hearing stories about Wilson, the mad genius who was said to have a sandbox in his living room. Tales of Wilson's legendary stage fright, his partial deafness and descriptions of mythical recording sessions for his long-lost album, *Smile*, finally coaxed the inquiring record addict into the Beach Boys section at Sam's.

"I started listening to their stuff from the later sixties that I'd never heard before," says Steven of Beach Boys albums like *Pet Sounds* and *Smiley Smile*. "I got quite turned on to it. I then became really interested in the band and Brian Wilson himself." In January 1992, Barenaked Ladies were, at last, ready to breed some pet sounds of their own. To capture the basic instrumental performances, commonly referred to as "bed tracks," both band and producer packed into a small van and ventured east to the legendary Le Studio in Morin Heights, Quebec. Nestled among the scenic Laurentian Mountains, in the middle of a private forest on its own private lake, Le Studio is a cozy, live-in facility some fifty miles north of Montreal. Renowned for its state-of-the-art recording equipment, but especially beloved for its secluded location, Le Studio's client list reads like a Who's Who of international recording artists. Artists as diverse as Rush, the Police, Rod Stewart, Bryan Adams, Celine Dion, Shania Twain, Chicago, David Bowie, the Fugees, Ramones, Keith Richards, and the Bee Gees have all made major recordings at Le Studio. And now Scarborough's Barenaked Ladies, *les nouveaux enfants dans le bloq,*" as it were, added their own, mildly controversial name to that illustrious list.

Wojewoda remembers loading up the van for the long drive to Morin Heights. "We picked up the Creeggans at their parents' house in Scarborough," relates Wojewoda, "and Andy and Jim were packing in their cross-country skis. I remember thinking, 'These guys look like they're planning a ski trip.' Watching them load all this extracurricular stuff into the truck, I wondered if they realized just how much work was actually lying ahead of them." Once in the studio, though, the producer's fears were instantly allayed by the band's disciplined work ethic and exceedingly high standards.

"The sessions were really focused," Wojewoda reveals, "very long ten- to twelve-hour days with very little band conflict. No fights at all. I've worked on other albums where emotions have run high, but they had really worked out their musical ideas. They had a real clarity about what they wanted it to be, so they seemed to feel very inspired."

Bringing the skis actually turned out to be a somewhat practical, albeit recreational, way to get around the frozen landscape of Morin Heights, especially since the studio was directly across the lake from the band house. Tyler recalls how Jim, always the athlete, got right into the ski-commute. "He skied across the frozen lake to the studio every day," says Tyler. "It was definitely a good time for him."

Wojewoda, an avid astronomer, notes that the sessions corresponded exactly with the waxing and waning of the moon—a fact that not only guided them home on their evening ski-commute, but also left them profoundly moved. "Most of the nights," he recalls, "when we were finished doing the sessions, we would ski back home in a full [or nearly full] moon. It was really beautiful."

Tyler remembers his surprise and delight upon returning from a downhill ski trip with Ed in nearby St. Saveur to hear the sonic mayhem that the others had been up to back at Le Studio that day. "Ed and I went out skiing with a visiting friend from Toronto," reports Tyler, "and when we got back, Steven, Michael, and Andy had added all sorts of crazy noises to the song 'Crazy.'"

Crazier still was the time that all the Barenaked Ladies paid a visit to a local sauna. "We had a chef named Sylvain catering our stay," recalls Tyler. "Sylvain worked at Maestro, a restaurant in St. Saveur, and he was sort of like 'da mayor' of the little tourist village. He was so connected, in a francophone-mafia kind of way, to everything that happened in that town, and he took it upon himself to show us around. Like any European alpine sauna, the idea was to bake yourself in a steamy, way-hot room and then plunge yourself into the icy river. [We] culture-less suburban kids had never tried this decadence, and we were in heaven. We would sit in the sauna with the local gangsters and Sylvain, who was shaving without shaving cream in the hundred-and-forty-degree jungle, and talk about the differences between Toronto and St. Saveur. Sylvain would translate for the francophones. Also, he would introduce us to each new *French Connection* extra as 'le rappeurs from Toronto' because the first song we recorded at Morin Heights was 'Fight the Power' by Public Enemy. So the first time Sylvain heard the band, it was Chuck D's rhymes coming out of Ed's mouth over me, Jim, and Andy trying to sound as urban as possible. Classic."[1]

But by far, the craziest thing is the hitherto untold story of a rather unique dress code that was strictly enforced during the recording of "The King of Bedside Manor." The song was among

---

[1]Although "Fight the Power" doesn't appear on *Gordon*, the song was re-recorded at Le Studio for inclusion on the *Coneheads* movie soundtrack.

the last bed tracks to be recorded, and the band just couldn't find the right groove for it. After a couple of unsuccessful attempts, the frustration became too much to, well, "bare." Indeed, when the going gets tough, it seems the tough go naked.

Here, for the first time anywhere, producer Michael Phillip Wojewoda exposes the Barenaked truth about what may have been the world's first all-nude recording session. "It was either Jim or Tyler," Wojewoda reveals, "who said, 'You know what we have to do? We have to get naked!' They all just had this unspoken understanding and started hooting and howling as they took off their clothes."

The nudist policy even extended to the men behind the recording console. "I was in the control room with the assistant engineer, Jean Diamont," discloses the producer, "and at this point, you felt more awkward if you had your clothes on. So I ditched my clothes, too. Of course, I went out and took some photos of all of them buck naked."

To maintain continuity on "The King of Bedside Manor," nakedness was strictly enforced during every single step of the recording process. Thus, when the project moved to Reaction Studios in Toronto to do the final overdubs, the whole team went full monty once more. "We set up all the microphones and adjusted the levels," continues Wojewoda, then, when we were ready to do an actual take, they had to get naked again. That's when it was decided that anything to do with the song had to also be done naked. Steven did a little guitar punch-in, for instance, but we all had to get naked, even for that. Even during the final mix, we were naked. I think the recording has this totally over-the-top nervous energy as a result of being naked."

Although band and crew had sworn at the time never to reveal their literal nakedness, Tyler feels that it's time that it was all out in the open, so to speak. "I have the pictures of us naked," confesses the extrovert rather coyly. "We should publish them! Especially since we edited out my screams of 'I'm naked!' at the end of the track!"

Musically, however, the band dressed up the naked bed tracks with a whole new wardrobe of musical accessories. From sensible basics like fiddles and pedal steel guitars to the full-blown, designer horn arrangements that adorn "Box Set," "Wrap Your Arms Around Me," and "Enid," little *Gordon* was dressed for success. In a bold fashion move, the band cinched the album's closing track, "Crazy," with a brave-hearted swatch of tartan in the form of some amazingly graceful bagpipes, courtesy of the song's cowriter, Tim Wilson.

Wojewoda humbly admits that most of the album's "endless production ideas" came from the enterprising young band themselves. "I think I may have had a hand in offering enough enthusiasm to really go all the way with things like 'Grade 9,'" the producer readily admits, "but they had hinted at it, live, already. My influence may have been introducing them to the dynamics of a studio; I think I just captured what it is they do."

He also speculates that recording in a proper studio with better microphones went a long way toward capturing stronger vocal performances. "While I never consciously referenced *The Yellow Tape* while I was doing *Gordon*," declares Wojewoda, "if I listen to the two today, I notice that the cassette sounds like a band that's still singing over bad monitors while the album sounds like it's sung with a really nice headphone mix."

According to Wojewoda, it was the Creeggan brothers who first came up with horn ideas for what would be the first single from *Gordon*, "Enid." It was, he notes, a pretty standard rock-and-roll animal until the day, back home in Toronto, when it grew horns. "I remember the Creeggans going off and working at the piano then coming back and showing us their ideas," the man they call "MPW" recalls. "Then Steven, Ed, or I would modify what we heard."

Yet as Andy remembers it, he and Jim, along with Steven, had always envisioned "Enid" as a many-horned beast. "Steve, Jim, and I worked out the horn chart for 'Enid,' and then Jim and I went back and wrote out the charts." When it was all done, the vibrant horn chart for "Enid" was further fortified by the sweeping pedal steel guitar of kindhearted Lewis Melville, a favorite sideperson of the Rheostatics and the pride of Guelph, Ontario. "Lewis played a great part," says the producer, "which you can hear very clearly on the verses. But when the horns come in, especially on the choruses, he gets kind of buried by all this brassy debris. The end result is just this wash of tonal colors supporting a very strong band track."

Indeed, the Ladies had no shortage of supporting players for their debut album. In their short time on the Toronto club scene, they had begun to make a lot of musical friends. Consequently, many of the best players in the city made cameo appearances on *Gordon*. With characteristic whimsy, the band made up joke names for some of the various guest groupings on the album credits. So while it may say that the Jimmy Crack Horns appear on "Enid," the Horn Cuskers featured on "Box Set" are in fact one-half of the Jimmy Crack Horns. Or something like that. Rounding out the chorus of "If I Had $1,000,000" was a chorus of friends and associates that the band gathered around a microphone. They're billed on *Gordon* as the Suburban Tabernacle Choir in honor of their suburban Scarborough heritage and because the choir contained many members of the Bourbon Tabernacle Choir. The Suburban congregation was augmented by local heroes Bob Wiseman (ex of Blue Rodeo), Meryn Cadell, Arlene Bishop, Blair Packham and various members of Moxy Fruvous, the Waltons, the Skydiggers, and the Rheostatics, including Rheo guitarist Dave Bidini, who was credited as "Veteran Warhorse."

"I don't think there're many musicians from Toronto who aren't on *Gordon*," says Chris Brown. "They were very intent on having everybody in there, so to speak, I think because they were genuinely moved by and wanted to be part of the community, and secondly, because things got so big so fast for them, they probably felt a little sheepish and decided to involve a few more people."

Just getting the crowd into the studio was a bit of a party in itself remembers Wojewoda. "It was a real love-in," says the producer. "Everybody was just having fun. It took about an hour, then we booted everyone out so we could keep doing overdubs."

Gordon was finally mixed in March 1992. As a result, the band was now in demand by the major record labels. Inevitably, if not unexpectedly, the album that had been recorded and financed entirely independently would eventually see its wide release on Sire Records, the prestigious New York–based label that was home to seminal artists such as Talking Heads, the Ramones, k.d. lang, and Madonna. Coincidentally, an A&R man at Sire, Andy Paley, had even produced a 1988 solo album by none other than Brian Wilson himself.[2]

As fans will attest, among the most unpredictable and exciting things about a Barenaked Ladies show are their frequent, off-the-cuff renditions of other people's songs. This practice, which the band is fond of referring to as live sampling, continued unabated on the sessions for their debut album. While he reveals that the Depeche Mode–like sample that presages "Enid" is in fact a Barenaked Ladies parody of the U.K. synthesizer band, with Wojewoda himself on lead vocals, the producer says the band didn't shy from their old live habits. From singing a line of Styx's "Mr. Roboto" in "The King of Bedside Manor" or a whole chorus from the Housemartins' "Happy Hour" over "Hello City" to the unlikely merging of Vince Guaraldi's "Charlie Brown Theme" and Rush's "Tom Sawyer" in "Grade 9," their irreverent referencing style was still very much in evidence. But now, with the involvement of Sire's corporate lawyers, a poten-

---

[2]According to Steven, Paley once played "Brian Wilson" for the ex–Beach Boy. Frustratingly, the band never heard whether or not the reclusive icon approved. But in 1998, Wilson agreed to sing "Surf City" with the Ladies live on a Chicago radio show—before backing out, with no explanation, at the last minute. Of course, Wilson would eventually make up for this by recording "Brian Wilson" on his *Live at the Roxy* CD.

tial legal complication threatened to quash distinctive parts of *Gordon*'s major-label release.

"Of course, when Sire got on board," relates Wojewoda warily, "they had to go out and get clearances for all of these songs. In some cases, we literally didn't know which songs were going to make it to the record until the last minute. The 'Charlie Brown Theme' was the hardest to clear with the publisher. In fact, it was almost pulled from the album." *Gordon* was, however, finally released intact in July 1992 and immediately sold a record-breaking eighty thousand copies in Canada alone during the first twenty-four hours of its release. A week later, it became the number-one record in Canada—a distinction it held for another eight weeks.

Jon Pareles, the celebrated *New York Times* music critic, was among the first U.S. journalists to "get" Barenaked Ladies. "It's not easy to be hyperactive, brooding, and whimsical all at once," Pareles wrote in the *Times*, "but the Barenaked Ladies do just that, balancing breezy melodies with unsentimental lyrics and delivering them with plenty of amiable schtick." Pareles later went on to describe the band as "Fishbone recast as a skiffle band."

Gordon continues to be a favorite with BNL fans, new and old. According to their Canadian distributor, Warner Music Canada, Barenaked Ladies' auspicious debut album has gone on to sell more than a million units in their native land—diamond status by Canadian Recording Industry Association standards. America, on the other hand, has been a slow but steady climb for the band. While border towns like Detroit, Chicago, and Buffalo, and a handful of more central U.S. cities such as Phoenix, Denver, and Santa Fe, were early strongholds, it really wasn't until later, with the *Rock Spectacle* album that the debut began to pick up sales momentum. Based on U.S. fans' curiosity and familiarity with the remake of "Brian Wilson," and what is sometimes called the "back-catalog effect," key industry insiders speculated that the U.S. multiplatinum status of *Stunt* significantly boosted sales of *Gordon*.

Today, Barenaked Ladies' live shows, constant touring, and general affability have made them a welcome concert act in the United States. And although *Gordon* didn't actually sell big numbers there upon its initial release, Steven has witnessed the ironic sight of legions of American fans, all of whom seem to know all the songs from an album that supposedly none of them bought.

Steven speculates that, according to his own informal calculations, "*Gordon* must be the most bootlegged album in U.S. history." He reckons that the ratio of fans who know every word of every song to the amount of actual units sold there is close to four to one. "We find that our older fans heard us in college, and the younger ones heard a tape while camping in Indonesia or Colorado. People seem to bring our music along on long journeys and make it a captive experience for others around them."

The road to *Gordon* had itself been quite a memorable journey, not to mention the beginning of a dangerous time.

14

Tension Builds
Back at It, Toronto

Tyler is certain that adding his own energy to the sound helped take it to the next level. But, not everyone was so sure about this new level. "When Andy came back," says Tyler, "I think we were headed toward a different musical place, one that he wasn't particularly interested in. I think that Barenaked Ladies was a folk band when he left for Uruguay, even though the energy level of the shows bordered on punk rock. I think my louder drums and straighter feel gave the group a certain kick in the pants or whatever."

But as Tyler became more interested in showmanship and "kicking the band's pants or whatever," Andy became increasingly concerned about a very big musical issue.

"It changed a lot when I joined," Tyler admits. "I keyed so much off the energy of Steve and Ed. There was musical tension and even more when Andy came back. I mean, Andy is an incredible musician, way more than me, and I think, unfortunately, that Barenaked Ladies wasn't his thing. I could be bold enough to say there wasn't room for both myself and Andy, and there was no way I was going to quit."

And although Andy switched to piano, for a while he still kept the congas going, even if he found that his old rhythm patterns didn't quite sit with the new kid on the drums. "I still played my old parts, even though a lot of the time it didn't really work with the new setup," remembers Andy of that tense period. "I still did it anyway. I tried to play a different style, tried to play just sort of ornamental things and not do the main rhythm. I was pretty stubborn, or whatever, about that."

But Tyler saw Andy's stubbornness as a passive-aggressive attitude toward him personally, and wasted no time in confronting him. "He [had] an ego that needed to be served," observes Tyler, "but I don't think he thought that he did. That's one of the things I said to him after we made *Maybe You Should Drive*. I said, 'Man, if you're going to fight for something, fight for it. Don't wear the guise of humility when it's not in your heart.'"

Nonetheless, Andy stayed on, playing keyboards and the aforementioned "ornamental things" on percussion. In addition to playing things like maracas, shaker eggs, and tambourines, did he ever feel compelled to use Tyler's head as an ornamental-percussion thing? I asked him. "We were very polite," Andy says. "We had some things in common that were fun to realize. Pat Metheny was one. No one else was really into him, and Tyler had a huge musical knowledge about different stuff. He was pretty amazing about that, so we were able to connect on different things. We also were drummers, and we'd done rudimental training and stuff. I knew more about rudiments and stuff, and Ty was heavy into march drumming and stuff like that. So we were able to connect on that level, although, once again, the last thing he needed was another drummer breathing down his neck. That didn't help our relationship. I think I intimidated him. The fact that I knew a little more theory than he did was another source of unease."

Up to then, Andy and Jim's natural familial connectedness and mutual musical sensibilities had made for one happy stand-up bass player. Fans may not have noticed, but an unspoken tug-of-war had begun in Barenaked Ladies' rhythm section that wouldn't be resolved for many years. So while Jim lamented the passing of the groove, Tyler was reveling in his newfound status as a celebrity. A single, unattached celebrity who'd basically run off and joined the circus. "I was definitely into the circus," confesses Tyler. "Absolutely. I had lived out of my house already for six years in Toronto. I'd gone to Ryerson and was working and playing in bands and hanging out on the scene in Toronto. I think how I got through that period without totally losing touch with who I am was the fact that I'd already been dealing with some of that stuff."

Even though there may have been trouble under the big top, the band continued to become even more popular. But this circus, like most good circuses, was often intense.

"It's interesting," Tyler reflects. "In that whole period we were so carried by the audience, it was screaming approval no matter what. The music took a backseat in a live performance, and I think I kind of rode that a little. I was more interested in keeping up the energy live, so the music and the grooving at times, I think, did suffer. But I had a vision of what was happening and served the entertainment side of it."

Around this time, Jim, for whom music had always been front seat, was not at all entertained by this lack of concern for groove coming from the backseat driver on drums. "Jim's correct," Tyler admits today. "We had some groove problems. You can hear it in the early stuff, so much so that what ends up happening is that on the records I would sound very restrained because we were forced to use a click track."

A "click track" is a kind of audio metronome often used by record producers to keep drummers from speeding up or slowing down on a given song. An electronically generated click, repeating in short, even intervals is fed into the headphones of the drummer while he tries to play the drum parts as though there were no click there at all. The click track is usually not heard on the final recording, the idea being that a perfect drum part is all that's left for the listener. But perfect is not what makes rock and roll. Charlie Watts, of the Rolling Stones, while having a very steady sense of tempo, tends to go a little faster on some sections of a song and a little slower on others. This is often referred to as swinging the beat. It's much harder than it seems to swing with any kind of excitement when you're intimidated by a click track. What often happens is that the drummer becomes so fixated on staying in the mechanical rhythm that the beat sounds timid or lifeless. It's kind of like trying to ride a BMX stunt bike with training wheels on. Needless to say, Tyler didn't feel too secure in those early recording sessions. "I was kind of scared," he remembers of his first taste of click-tracking. "It's like, 'Okay, now we've got Tyler in his place.'"

Maybe You Should Drive was a particularly humiliating experience for Tyler. Producer Ben Mink, a fine producer most known for his work with k.d. lang, put the drummer under microscopic scrutiny. "I felt like a retard," Tyler admits. "Making the second record, I was treated like a retard by Ben Mink. It was like, 'Oh, that was good. Do it again.'"

Sometimes they would record one bar at a time, an insane yet often expedient way of ensuring metronomic regularity. The idea is to build a kind of Frankenstein's monster out of little separate drum bits and then have the band play over the assembled drum track. Tyler says that the producer wasn't entirely up front about this process, and didn't tell him that he was cutting and pasting whole drum tracks. But a drummer can tell when his performance has been altered, and that's just what went down when Tyler heard some early bed tracks on playback. "What would happen was, Ben would say to take a break to fix something or do some business, saying, 'Oh, we have to do some stuff.' We'd go out for a while, then I'd come back in to hear the track we'd just recorded, and I'd hear the same fill in the bar, and I'd hear it again. It didn't end up on the record like that in the end."

So it wasn't too easy in the beginning. Like a kid brother you look out for by kicking his ass, Tyler had, from time to time, been dealt tough love—or intimidation—at the hands of every member of the band. "Steve was a difficult guy to get to know," Tyler confesses. "He intimidates a lot of people, except when he's onstage and then everyone just goes, 'Wow, look at him. He's amazing. Look at him dance. Look at him sing.' But offstage it's like—he doesn't talk. I definitely got deep with him the earliest, but he also freaked me out the most. He was very moody. There were a couple of times there I definitely wanted to kill him.

"He's a very shrewd guy," Tyler continues. "Every angle is covered, always. The thing is, when he fucks up, he can't admit it. It's really hard for him to admit it. I think it comes from him being a genius child and sort of being under observation more than he was allowed to just be. I mean, his parents are both educational psychologists as well. If you break something it's not 'Oh, well, that was too bad.' It was like, 'Why did it fall, and how did it fall, and why, why?' And he always had to have the answer to the questions because his parents are bright, and he was bright, so he never got to be a child. He never got to goof off. So what does he do onstage? He goofs off like a sexually deviant, chubby-guy clown. It's amazing, combined with the fact that he's an incredible singer and he writes very bracing lyrics. He's a weird guy."

Tyler remembers rebelling against both Ed and Steve for entirely different reasons. Although time, too, has softened his rebel stand. "With Steve, I was like, 'I can't like what he likes because it's too fuckin' esoteric.' Whether it be wine or cigars or cooking or whatever. But now what do I like? I like cooking. I like wine. I like some of the esoteric songwriters that he likes." In those early days, though, Tyler worked very hard to break Steven down and get into his head. He admits that more than once he resorted to drawing out Steven's dark side, pushing his buttons to trip him up. The result was part bonding ritual, part hazing.

"I think the only way that we really got to know each other was by me indulging in the ambiguity of things. Hey, you're in a relationship, and you don't have the answer to this beautiful girl who's tempting you. You don't have the answer to the way you feel right now. Or else, what happens when you smoke this joint and you have ten gin and tonics? You don't know what's going to happen, do you?"

Steven is well aware of his ability to appear moody or intimidating offstage. But he blames much of his perceived complexity on people's expectations of him. You can't always be on. Even Robin Williams has to chill out now and again. "When the fans meet us," Steven admits, "I always have the reputation as being the cold and aloof one. I come offstage and they're so used to seeing somebody who's extroverted onstage with no inhibitions, then I get offstage and I'm quiet and I don't know what to say to people; I don't have a lot to say."

Steven and Ed's natural humor and constant one-upmanship created a kind of wall around them at times. Tyler often felt excluded by this impenetrable force. So while Ed assumed the role of father figure in the band, Tyler became the enfant terrible, the naughty child, just to bug him. "It was like, 'If Ed likes it, I don't like it,' Tyler confesses. "Just because. And yet, Ed's actually easier to deal with on a day-to-day basis. He's pretty straight. He's so straight that he's not, so he's really easy to like."

Considering the flip side of this equation, Tyler offers that given the right scenario, Ed could be just as easy to dislike or maybe just ignore. "But," Tyler reflects, "he has such a force of will that he gets his own way." When I point out that, like Reg in an old *Kids in the Hall* sketch, he'd probably be hard to kill, Tyler finds this notion amusing. "Yeah. Absolutely hard to kill. He's Bruce Willis. He's in a fucking burning building, and he's saving everyone just because he believes he can. He believes he can fly."

Ironically, while Ed may have been a kind of father figure and Tyler may have represented the wild child, Tyler was actually the eldest in the band, and the only one who struck out on his own. "It's funny, because I think I was the one who'd gone through the most in life in terms of confronting stuff," Tyler notes. "Meeting

BARENAKED LADIES

110

my father *x* number of years later. I was living with my girlfriend when I met the band, and they were living at home. I'm the oldest, and slightly less calculated and controlled."

According to Tyler, this unspoken worldliness balanced his initially shaky musical status within the band. Over time, he would have one-on-one discussions with each band member, applying his personal life lessons to the lives of his band mates. "They're nice boys from Scarborough," says Tyler of his fellow Ladies. "Straight up, incredibly talented. I'm speaking now from a purely social point of view. There were times on the road where they'd end up talking to me on some level, be it a girlfriend or a death in the family, whatever. Each guy in the band has had moments with me where I felt I had something to offer."

15

Reborn on a Pirate Ship
April 1995

. . . and in walks the Fantastic Four

> —from "Same Thing" by Ed Robertson

And if I always seem distracted

Like my mind is somewhere else

That's because it's true,

Yes, it's true.

> —from "Break Your Heart" by Steven Page

Discussing the fraught sessions for *Maybe You Should Drive*, Steven says, "we had considered calling the second album *Car Rear-ender* or *Career Ender*." But *Born out of Hardship* could have been a more appropriate title for Barenaked

113

Ladies' third studio album. Ultimately, though, the process marked the end of their first blue period. They would be reborn on this pirate ship, but it was going to cost them.

"When I think back to *Born on a Pirate Ship*," says Ed today, "I just think about what a distracted band we were then. We really wanted to make a good record, and I think we did. But we were all over the place, personally and as a unit."

Finally delivered in the autumn of 1996, *Born on a Pirate Ship* had been a difficult labor. Deciding to stay with the group after his brother Andy's departure, Jim now found himself doubting why he should stay. Once buoyed by mutual respect and camaraderie, the group was taking on water in their lower decks. And if there was ever a time to abandon ship, Jim thought, maybe it was then. But if he was going to stay, things were going to be different. "I was asserting myself in a way that was like, 'If I'm here I'm going to commit to this thing in a big way,'" Jim says. "'I'm going to work at it and I'm going to write and bring songs to the band.'"

Jim's two songs on *Born on a Pirate Ship*, "In the Drink" and "Spider in My Room," were significantly more fleshed-out than Andy's "Tiny Little Song" on *Maybe You Should Drive*. Jim's increased output was a direct reflection of the bass player's increased input during the making of the third album.

By 1993, Steven had married his music-camp girlfriend, Carolyn Ricketts, but the strain of Steven's celebrity lifestyle, and the fact that he was never home, was causing problems in their domestic life. Prescription antidepressants helped him to a degree but hindered him in other ways—the medicated Steven could be unpredictable. Jim says he never knew which Steven would walk through the door, that is, when he was there at all.

"I remember how Steven's moods had definitely simmered," Jim says. "It took a while for me to trust where he was coming from. Maybe I just needed to know that it was really him talking and not the drug. Also, I had to realize and respect that he was on medication because he really needed to [be] and that it wasn't just an escape."

To add to Barenaked Ladies' increasingly complex world, Ed and his wife, Natalie Herbert, were blessed with the birth of their new daughter, Hannah, which meant that Ed had the demands of new fatherhood to add to the mix. If the band was to make it to the next album, maybe Jim should drive. At least that's how Jim saw it anyway. Jim says that while he'd realized that he'd have to be the designated driver on the road to *Born on a Pirate Ship*, he even surprised himself with the amount of drive he actually had.

"Once I made the decision to go for it on this record," Jim says, "I couldn't believe the amount of energy I had for the project. I was going bananas writing horn and string charts and participating in any way I could. I think there was a definite effort on my part to take on Andy's old role as well as mine."

Michael Phillip Wojewoda, the producer of *Gordon*, was brought in to oversee the band's resurrection, only this time he shared the producer credit with the band. If everything was going to change, they thought, then maybe it was a good idea to bring back at least one of the elements that had helped them back in the good old days, only two years earlier. "He's just so good at facilitating the vibe and letting the band have ownership of the record," says Jim. "I think also it was definitely a let-it-rip experiment, and I was totally into that approach to the record, maybe to take us to the next step. It was really experimental."

That's not to say the album could be described as experimental music. "Whenever I've heard music described as experimental," says Jim, "it always seems to give the impression that the music was too self-conscious and overly thought out. We were pretty brave about trying new ideas during this album, but we still managed to follow our gut instincts and serve the songs well. This seemed to give the album a soulful quality throughout all the experiments. Maybe a better way to describe the overall tone of the record would be 'adventurous'—yeah, that's it."

While Ed has some unpleasant memories of that time in general, the album produced two of his favorite Barenaked Ladies songs. "It was a very difficult process," Ed remembers.

"Everybody was redefining their roles after Andy left; we were struggling with Nigel and generally discontent. But that album produced two gems. 'When I Fall' and 'This Is Where It Ends' are two of my favorites. So I'm glad we stuck it out. That's the understatement of the year!"

Ed describes this point in time as being "very weird." "Nat was pregnant," Ed recalls. "It was a hot summer and we'd just done *The Anne Murray Christmas Special*. We'd also just done a big photo shoot with Nigel for the cover of a *Canadian Musician* feature on band managers in Canada, only we were right on the verge of firing him." In the end, Best was dismissed just one day before the issue bearing a smiling photo of him and his former associates hit the newsstands.

"It was just bizarre," Ed recalls. "We were definitely all in different places at that time. I remember finishing off the background vocals for the record—it was just me and Jim staying up all night with Michael Phillip Wojewoda. Steven was there in the control room, but he was so exhausted that we couldn't physically wake him up. I was just working for the spaces in between. Working for my time off, and I think everybody was kind of working for the weekend. In some disconnected way, we all still believed in what we were doing, but the communication was really bad; we weren't a good solid unit. We weren't a good band, in terms of unity. There's a period of years there where communication was bad. Honestly, it's hard for me to remember how we operated then."

Jim, on the other hand, feels that in hindsight he may have overcompensated and worked too hard to force everything. It's not something he'd do so willingly in the future. "I remember after we completed the bed tracks," he says, "Mike just swiveled around in his chair and said, 'All right, this song needs a little something special. What do you think it is?' In the past, this would be the exact moment where Andy would find that special little something. I immediately felt the loss and tried every trick I knew but still didn't know how to make up for it."

Still, he soldiered on. "I was overly present," he admits. "I think in a way I kind of saw the gap and tried to fill it all. And I went bananas. I was all about, in retrospect, making my statement, stating my presence. I had this huge hair, and I was all about 'Here I am in the room, I'm doing it, here I am.' It was all about being this strong spiritual guy. It became limiting. I was starting to lose my freedom. I never want to do that again. That's when I wanted to take out the hair and take with me what I learned from that time, but not to exert that all the time, to just exert one side of myself."

Wojewoda says that, at the time, the idea was to make the antidote to *Maybe You Should Drive*. And it was also the first time that the band began to realize that the spontaneous combustion of their live shows had never been truly captured on record. It was about time. It was also about trying to have a good time again. Even if it killed them. So in April 1995, Wojewoda and the Ladies hauled a ton of auxiliary recording gear into Don Kerr's little warehouse studio, the Gas Station. The room was noisy in all the right ways. Jim remembers how the ambience made a big difference to the sessions.

"The studio was on the sixth floor of an old industrial building," Jim recalls. "There was a fire escape connected to the studio that had a clear view of downtown Toronto. One occasion, when we were all listening back to a take of 'The Old Apartment,' Tyler, who was thoroughly enjoying his performance, stepped out onto the fire escape." Jim wondered why Tyler had left so suddenly during the triumphant playback, so he looked outside to see what was up. "The music was permeating out to the platform where he stood," Jim remembers, "and he seemed to be doing a curious dance. Arms outstretched and bobbing up and down to the beat, it was as though he was gesturing to the entire city of Toronto, giving them the rock-and-roll goods that they'd desired for so long. Here he was, appeasing the masses. I had a laugh and wrote it off as some ridiculous impulsive move on Tyler's part."

Imagine Jim's surprise during a gig in upstate New York a

few months later when Barenaked Ladies performed the same song: "While playing 'The Old Apartment' at a show in Rochester that summer," Jim says, "I saw something that proved to me that Tyler's reaction to the song was no passing dance move. I gazed into the crowd only to see two gals doing that same curious gesture that Tyler had done on the fire escape. But instead of facing the city of Toronto, they were facing the band. In a state of disbelief, I looked over at Tyler to see if he was witnessing this strange coincidence. He just flashed me this all-knowing glance and nodded his head assuredly."

"'The Old Apartment,'" says Jim, "was the first sort of rock thing we'd recorded since 'Alternative Girlfriend.' It's really very melodic but grooving stuff. The bass line is really slippery all over and pretty awesome. I was just going for it." Jim went for it big time, using an electric bass, by choice, and playing it with a wah-wah pedal. "I was just in there," Jim reckons, "staking my claim to the band, I guess."

"The neatest thing about the song," Ed later told the late, great rock writer Timothy White in *Billboard*, "is that it tricks people into thinking someone's breaking into his old girlfriend's apartment. But actually, this guy and his girl are revisiting the building from which they've recently moved, and it's painful to them. Things have changed there, and they're thrown by it, thinking, 'Hey, don't people understand how important the physical evidence of memory is?' Because even the addition of a handrail on the steps where you once played as a kid can ruin your ability to ever have a game of tag there again. It's a song about how you identify with places and structures that you had almost created for yourself by living and growing in them. This is the sort of stuff Steve and I write about, and like our live shows, it's funny and sad to us at the same time."

"As a result," Steven adds, "some people in our audiences may resist the roller coaster of our concerts, but when the crowds are willing, they see the larger picture, which is that red, for instance, is not just the color of blood but also of clowns' noses."

By the way, there is no truth to the claim, made by some fans, that the freckle-faced, red-haired kid whose grinning face adorns the album's cover is one of Jim's baby photographs. But he concedes that the flame-haired kid may have symbolically represented his power role on the album, however unconsciously. "I don't know how much of that played into it," Jim reasons. "The name was already chosen way before and who was the most evil-looking—you know, a red-haired, freckled kid—was kind of the main idea."

In case you don't know the gag, try stretching out the corners of your mouth with your fingers then try to say the words "born on a pirate ship." In most mouths we surveyed, it ends up sounding remarkably like you're saying "born in a pile of shit." "It's just a stupid grade-six joke," Ed says. "It's just a title that we'd wanted to use for a while." Their love of goofy sounds and words punctuates the proceedings as well. "We got in some good words on this record," Ed laughs. "Words like 'stomach,' 'gastrointestinal,' and 'squeegee' in 'When I Fall.'"

"Craig from the Odds," Steven recalls with pride, "actually pointed out 'squeegee' the first time he heard 'When I Fall.' He was listening really intently, then he turned and said 'squeegee' while nodding approvingly." But isn't "When I Fall" one of Ed's more earnest songs? "We've always thought that wackiness and earnestness coexisted," Ed points out. "Even on the first record there were a lot of novelty tags. We never felt like we were a comedy band—we never had a big focus on humor; we just liked funny things and said funny things."

"The Beatles," Steven jumps in, "could get away with putting 'Yellow Submarine' on *Revolver*. It's a classic pop record that has 'Tomorrow Never Knows' as well as 'Yellow Submarine,' but that doesn't make them a novelty band; it just makes it a great record with lots of breadth to it. Our second record came around, and I don't think any of us were feeling all that 'funny' when it came time to write the songs. We were so exhausted by the success and the work that we had to do on the first record and touring that it was time for introspection."

Steven compares this approach to the novels of one his favorite American authors, Kurt Vonnegut Jr. "He doesn't get the respect he deserves, because he's not only a brilliant thinker but a really absolutely entertaining writer. It's not easy to write something that's easy to read. It's so easy to read that he makes it look easy, so you see his books in the sci-fi section and go 'Aw, that's for high-school kids.'"

The real main idea, for the sound of the record at least, was to get back to their live roots. As such, much of the perform-ances are what is called "live off the floor." They even brought in stage-tech-to-the-stars John Farnsworth and enlisted their per-sonal live-sound engineer, Robin Billinton, to act as Wojewoda's assistant for the sessions. "Almost all of my vocals are live," Steven says. "It's taken me up until recently to realize that I sing best when I'm onstage, so that's what I wanted to do on this, just sing."

Wojewoda set Steven up in the same room with everyone else, eschewing the traditional isolation-booth approach to vocal recording. He also had Steven sing into the kind of microphone he would normally use onstage (a Shure SM58) in lieu of more exacting or sensitive studio mics. "I had a '58 on a stand," Steven remembers. "Most of the live stuff was done that way. We tried others, but I like the sound of a '58. I like the way it feels. I'm just figuring that out."

If there was a problem with other, louder sounds, like the drums being too audible on the vocal tracks, Wojewoda would cave in and do some of the vocals in a separate area, but he'd move the singer back immediately to keep the flow going. "If Michael wanted to try some neat sonic things," Steven recalls, "he'd say, 'I definitely want you to do the vocals separately.' For instance, if he wanted a great acoustic guitar sound or whatever, we'd do vocals separately, but it would be right there. He'd say, 'Okay, there's the mic. Let's do it right away.'"

Ed credits Steven with helping him find his way in recording his vocals for the album. "Steve's helped me to be a lot more comfortable with my singing," Ed said at the time. "Steve's a more trained singer who can turn to you and say, 'Just do that,' where in the past, I've had trouble with being comfortable singing in front of a microphone in the studio, as opposed to live, where I'm fine with it."

"For Ed," Steven explains, "it was much more of a problem for him to just sit in front of a microphone and get a good, honest performance. But he's great when it comes to just sitting with a guitar and singing; he hits you like that, so it's a matter of us learning how to achieve that in front of a microphone."

In Vancouver, Ed tried to record the lead vocal for the song "Great Provider" every night for a week. "I was flat or sharp, or just terrible," he confesses. "By the time we got it in tune, I felt so distanced from the song. It was a really strange process, recording in a studio. I was even uncomfortable with some of the stuff that went down on *Gordon.* I just felt uncomfortable in front of a mic. But with this album we did everything live, and we were so relaxed that everything worked."

Besides being the first Barenaked Ladies album to feature additional multimedia, *Born on a Pirate Ship* was also their longest album to date, featuring fourteen brand-new songs. Usually, for reasons of economy, track listings are limited to ten or twelve. "We just didn't want to let anything get left behind," Ed says. "For us, there's always a sense of change and growth. It's like a journal, documenting where we are at a time. That's what we consciously did with this record. We said 'instead of making the bible for Barenaked Ladies at this time, let's take snapshots . . .'"

"It just happens to be this year's photo album," Steven adds, "rather than this year's *Farmer's Almanac* or anything." Of course, there is one very striking farmer's song on *Born on a Pirate Ship.* "Straw Hat and Old Dirty Hank" concerns itself with an obsessive and fanatical agricultural worker, or "corn stalker," who becomes fixated on singer Anne Murray. Based loosely on a very real story that made the news in the 1980s, the song was not only one of the high points on the album, it has since become a staple of the band's live shows, as the live album, *Rock Spectacle*, would later attest.

> *I'm the farmer*
> *I work in the fields all day*
> *Don't mean to alarm her*
> *But I know it was meant to be this way*
> —from "Straw Hat and Old Dirty Hank"
> by Steven Page and Ed Robertson

The recording features a guest appearance by another Canadian singer named Murray McLauchlan. It was McLauchlan who lent the song a certain threatening tone by putting the *harm* back into the harmonica. McLauchlan's inclusion on the recording is something of an in-joke, actually. Steven and Ed unearth the subtext: "The song was originally called 'The Farmer Who Likes Anne Murray,'" Steven explains. "Then," continues Ed, "we started calling it 'Farmer's Song.'"

Of course you can't copyright a song title, but it's not good for business to call your song "Farmer's Song" in Canada, where there had already been a very well-known hit with that title several years earlier. And the guy who wrote and sang that song was none other than Murray McLauchlan, who at that time hosted a weekly radio series *Swinging on a Star* for the Canadian Broadcasting Corporation. Canadian folk and pop songwriters would come on and play and talk a little and so on. Barenaked Ladies had been guests. "One of the first people I'd ever talked to about the song when I was writing it was Murray McLauchlan, when we did *Swinging on a Star*," Steven confides. "And every time I saw him, he'd ask me, 'Have you finished that song yet?'" Personally, this author thinks the whole thing is like one big, brilliant word-association game. A line from McLauchlan's "Farmer's Song" inspired the title of a song about a farmer who stalks Anne Murray—it don't get much prettier than that.

Then there's "Shoe Box," which had been recorded before the other songs and had been released on the soundtrack album for the then-new NBC television series *Friends*. Fan reaction on the Barenaked Ladies Internet mailing list was mixed but always entertaining. Steven was an infrequent lurker on the mailing list, where he didn't want to be seen lest he intimidate the fans from sharing their valued real opinions.

"I think a good portion of our fan base are compugeeks," Steven said at the time. "The mailing list is great, but I try to stay out of it as much as I can. If I was in there all the time, people would be more inhibited about saying what they actually think. When "Shoe Box" came out, fans were trying to figure out what the lyrics were. I had them on my computer anyway, because I'd done them on my computer, so I just sent them to the mailing list and they could all have it."

But when someone on the list made a disparaging remark about the band's motives for writing "Shoe Box," Steven was moved to cross the line and respond vocally. "This one guy on the mailing list said that we'd been commandeered by studio execs to be more friendly by singing 'la dee ah dee ah . . .' on 'Shoe Box.' The logic was supposedly that the song should be more friendly because the song was on *Friends,* and I just mailed back, 'Are you retarded? I wrote that song. I don't remember any pressure from above, and if you listen it says, "Shoe box of lies," which isn't the most friendly thing to say,' and I told them that there was a backward message that says, 'Drink more Pepsi; corporate America is cool!'"

Speaking of subliminal messages, Ed once got some snail mail from a man he describes as "this transient, Deadhead kind of guy." "He wrote us a letter saying, 'You guys are right on. I've only seen you once, but my girlfriend really likes you guys.'" Ed recalls, "Then he said, 'You guys are excellent, and you make people happy,' then he ended, saying, 'This girl at my work was really upset, and I put on your tape and she was really happy.' But then he put in a 'P.S.' that asked, 'How do you do it? Subliminal messages?'" Ed wrote the man a reply: "It said thanks for listening, but I added in brackets all the way through the letter 'You Love This Band' . . ."

There's a good chance that both these fans were American. Because in Canada, after *Maybe You Should Drive*, Barenaked Ladies' glory days were over. For the time being anyway. There was an active backlash. They were grossly overexposed. They had succumbed to the "sophomore jinx" with their second release and Canadians had been there, done that, and in fact, bought the T-shirt. Ex–Juice Pig Sean Cullen had watched Barenaked Ladies' rise from boys to men (but not Boyz II Men) when they opened for his comedy troupe four years earlier. He remembers the Canadian media backlash against the Ladies. "In Canada," says Cullen on the phone from his new digs in L.A., "Barenaked Ladies suffered from the tall-poppy syndrome, where people kind of abandon you when you make your second album. But in many ways, I just think a lot of it is sour grapes. In Canada, there's this pressure to always be the struggling soulful performer but never to make it to the big time. If you mess up, you become a legend. People who actually make it are considered traitors because they've gone away and they've done it. It's amazing."

But even as BNL's Canadian career was experiencing a lull, they were beginning to see a shift in their fan base. They were becoming bigger in America than they were at home. To paraphrase Neil Diamond, "We're comin' to America!" "We just toured the States," Steven said around the time of the *Born on a Pirate Ship* release, "and things are going well. We played to five thousand people in Detroit and six thousand fans in L.A."

Craig Northey, whose then-band the Odds had opened a slew of northeastern U.S. dates for Barenaked Ladies, says that the warm reception afforded the Ladies by the American fans during the *Born on a Pirate Ship* tour was nothing short of vindication. "Canada had quietly dismissed what they were doing," Northey recalls, "and yet all these college venues were jammed! They had quietly built up something on their own, and we could all feel it getting ready to break through. Canadians so quickly doubt their own, until they prove themselves elsewhere. That's like telling your six-year-old that you'll only love him if he can beat up the neighbor's nine-year-old."

Every night, the Barenaked Ladies' show features a moment where Jim steps forward and takes control of his bass in the form of a big solo. In these moments, Jim can open up and fully demonstrate his abilities and inventions on the big double bass. During the last few years, a common melody has popped into his solo, that of the children's song "Itsy Bitsy Spider." "Maybe," Jim quips, "the bass player in me appreciates this creature's low-grounded stance, it's keen finger on the pulse of its web that might catch and support any free-flying lead-guitarist flies in the vicinity."

"In the Drink" is one of the two tunes that Jim brought to *Born on a Pirate Ship*, but being a confessed arachnophile, he was most excited about his other contribution, "Spider in My Room." When asked if he's, well, obsessed with the little creepy crawlers, Jim answers, "It's true, spiders keep showing up in my music, and I do cry whenever I read *Charlotte's Web*, but there really is no master plan at work here. 'Itsy Bitsy Spider' appeared in my solo mainly because it's a melody that's sympathetic to the simplicity of the bass."

> *If a spider gets killed how does that make it rain*
> *How could I be the one to blame . . .*
> *But the Hoover was quick, termination complete . . .*
> *I hear the thunder from outside*
> *And the water's gettin' high*
> > —from "Spider in My Room" by Jim Creeggan.

"Spider in My Room," Jim continues, "stemmed from a memory of gazing at a spider in my sandbox[1] and pondering the

------

[1]Legal Notice: A sandbox from his childhood. This story took place when Mr. Creegan was just a kid, and as such, it must be made clear that Mr. Creegan is not currently in the possession of such a sandbox in any room of his current dwelling. Nor is this the sandbox referred to in Steven Page's "Brian Wilson." We regret any misunderstanding this inference may have caused. Thank you.

125

consequences of killing it, with the old wives' tale resounding in my head that seven days of rain follows the killing of any spider. This contrasted with the spider hunts my older brother, John, went on in his room with the vacuum cleaner. But there is something about spiders. Something that draws me to them."

Ed remembers the highly independent and highly secretive circumstances surrounding what he calls a "crazy Jim Creeggan vision." "Jim didn't really let us in on it until it was done," Ed says. "He just said, 'Ed, you play bass because I want to play guitar.' And Tyler didn't play his regular drum set, either." Oh, yes, the drum set. Ruefully, Jim remembers how his perfectionist drive to get the drum parts to swing the way he wanted resulted in what he refers to as "one of the biggest fights" he ever had with Tyler.

"The drum groove wasn't happening for me," Jim says frankly. "I think Ty and I both wanted this song to work. For me, it was my first time writing a full song for the band, and Tyler wanted to support my effort. But the combined weight of my ambition and Tyler's loyalty nearly kept the song from flying. I didn't like the way the drums swung, but he thought the feel and the tone of the drums had a Tom Waits appeal. We couldn't agree. He finally said, "Someone's going to have to drag me in there to play that again," and that's when I hit the door. After the shouting match subsided, we managed to find a unified vision and pull it off. We almost smothered the song by loading too much significance on it, no matter how well-intended."

Then Jim got the idea to get the Stoney Park Pow-Wow Singers to sing on it. "The Pow-Wow group in the song," Jim explains, "represents the all-knowing conscience." And without much more explanation than that, Jim was on a plane, ADAT recorder in hand, headed for Saskatoon's Right Tracks Studios where he would have the Stoney Park Pow-Wow Singers sing over the band's bed tracks. Ed recalls that Jim's urgent need to give his spider song total priority was a little confusing to the others.

"It was this thing," Ed recalls, "where we were doing this whole record, but Jim got intent on 'Spider' and flew to Saskatoon.

It was like, 'Where's Jim? Oh, he's in Saskatoon, he's working on 'Spider.'" Back home, Tyler, Steven, and Ed wondered why Jim had gone "to the wall" to record a simple song that might not even make it onto the completed album. "We had no idea what was going on until he came back and played this tape and we all just went, 'Oh, this is what he was doing.' It was an amazing transition, we just trusted him on that one."

Making Plans Without Nigel

BNL's original manager, Nigel Best, who'd been full of great ideas at the beginning when the band had nowhere to go but up, was now becoming unresponsive and hard to reach as the band had nowhere to go but down. His days as Barenaked Ladies' manager were numbered, as were the band's own days if something wasn't done to reverse the negative trend. "It was a long demise, and we were in a bad state ourselves, in a lot of ways," Jim told me in a frank discussion of the topic that I had referred to as "the Nigel Problem." "We weren't in good shape," says Jim. "Andy had just left the band, and Nigel was handling our finances very loosely. We kept asking him for financial statements, and nothing would be done."

Then, according to Jim, Best started firing key staff members, people that the band didn't want to let go. People who, Jim says, didn't deserve to be fired. "After a while it was just him and his secretary," recalls Jim. "The initial united spirit of the office had left. We just stopped trusting Nigel's decisions. But the incident that really made us question our manager's integrity was the AGO crisis."

The Art Gallery of Ontario (AGO) was the Toronto host gallery for the Barnes Exhibit, a touring show of classic paintings. Since many of the works on display were of nude female forms, the promotion people for the AGO commissioned bus-shelter posters, took out print ads, and sold T-shirts, all bearing two simple words: "Rarenaked Ladies."

"The AGO had been trying to get in touch with Best for some time to get permission for the Rarenaked Ladies shirts," Jim remembers, "but they hadn't heard back from him and went ahead and did it anyway. Our lawyer got word that these shirts were being sold and asked us if we would like him to write a cease-and-desist document to the AGO. Not knowing the seriousness of a document like that and how it would make us look bad in the media, we said okay."

While BNL was out on the east coast, they happened to hear a CBC radio interview with a high-level representative of the art gallery. "He was saying that the Ladies had lost their sense of humor," Jim recalls, "and that we were suing the AGO over a simple joke. It seemed as though the media was all too ready to lump us into the 'once-they-were-innocent-but-now-they've-been-corrupted-by-money-and-fame' category. We were all just in a total state of shock, just sitting around the bus and staring blankly at the floor."

They pulled into a gas station and tried in vain to contact Best. "The more time passed," Jim says, "the more we could feel people's impression of us quickly slip into the toilet. It was panic time." Jim remembers that in the absence of any direction from Best, Ed took matters into his own hands. "Ed came up with the idea to counter the AGO's Rarenaked Ladies shirts," says Jim. "He called our T-shirt manufacture guy and got him to make a T-shirt saying 'the Barnes Exhibit' and displaying three different pictures of barns. The farm kind."

Phase two of the plan was to sell the Barnes-busting T-Shirts at their next show in Fredericton, New Brunswick. "Then," Jim recalls, "I think we sent out a press release advertising the availability of our new shirts. The media had a laugh, and the word went around that the Ladies hadn't lost their sense of humor and were still good guys." The incident, while saving their reputation, only underscored their increasingly estranged relationship with their soon-to-be-former manager. "The absence of Nigel at this critical point," says Jim, "contributed to our growing lack of confidence."

Basically, although no one in the group would stoop to bad-mouthing their former associate, it seemed that the honeymoon was over between Best and the band. It was time to go their separate ways. So upon completing *Born on a Pirate Ship,* Barenaked Ladies said bon voyage to their former manager and began making plans without Nigel. In the interim, Ed took up the slack.

Ed, however, offhandedly dismisses any notion of his being a serious rock manager. "Well, I certainly wasn't managing the band in any real sense. I was just bridging the distance, as it were. I was liaising with the record company re artwork and label copy for *Born on a Pirate Ship* and going over release dates. Hmmm, maybe I was managing the band for a while," Ed says. Jim confides that "Ed was starting to be more or less like the military police of a third-world country, you know, like ruling?"

Do the math:

> Lead Guitarist
> + Military rule
> _____
> = Marshall Law

"It seems a bit of a blur to me now. It was pretty fuckin' hectic," Ed says. "I was on the phone all the time." Ed is very thankful to a lot of people for guiding the band through that time. "Howie Klein, from the label, was incredibly helpful, as was everybody at Reprise Records, Steve Martin our former agent, and our lawyer Len Glickman.

"My main focus was just keeping the release of *Born on a Pirate Ship* on track and getting a new manager in place."

On the *Born on a Pirate Ship* CD-ROM, Jim describes a kind of tribal rap party he'd attended with his new friends in the Stoney Park Pow-Wow Singers. That night, Coleman Beaver and his associates had presented Jim with three items of spiritual significance: a braid of grass, a bit of tobacco, and the feather of an eagle. All three of these items are involved in a spiritual-cleansing ritual, but the eagle feather was given as a symbol of brotherhood.

Then, Jim says something that makes a lot of sense: "Barenaked Ladies had been going through their own spiritual house-cleaning, as it were. They had lost their way, but now they were coming out of the fog. They had seen the void, and yelled back, 'Hey, void, what are you lookin' at?' And while they still live with it every day, as we all do, defining the darkness had helped them to define the light. There was no turning back now. They had some music to make, dammit, and somehow they just knew it was meant to be this way. Some shows you might see the feather in the top of my bass. That's when I feel Barenaked Ladies and I need a little help from Stoney Park."

16

Kevin Hearn Gets on the Bus. Stays.

Enter Kevin.

Kevin Hearn still remembers the day he came to the studio to meet up with Barenaked Ladies. The meeting had been arranged at the band's request, and they wanted to see if Kevin was at all interested in joining their ranks. At that time in the band's history, boarding the good ship *Barenaked* may not have been such an easy choice to make. Andy had left, and the band was now rife with tensions, both among themselves and with their soon-to-be ex-manager.

Kevin sensed that in terms of career peaks and valleys, Barenaked Ladies' career was in a valley. "They were experiencing a backlash in Canada," recalls Kevin. "This was reflected in lower record sales and bad press. Yet they were grinding forward with determination and making a record, which I felt had healthy creative growth."

In an effort to find their way musically, they had returned to Reaction Studios to mix *Born on a Pirate Ship*. The familiar surroundings brought them some much-needed comfort. And for Kevin, who had worked at Reaction on other projects, it turned out to be a great place to meet up with the band. "I suppose it was a situation where I usually would have felt a little nervous. But it was a beautiful summer day, and I felt genuinely excited."

"Eventually," Kevin says, "the four of us met in a small side room, which seemed to be used as a storage room for odds and ends, outboard gear, equipment racks, and a couple of analog synthesizers."

Tyler, Ed, Jim, and Steven were anxious to find a keyboard player within their own circle. They didn't want to hold auditions. They'd known Kevin from the Toronto music scene where he was the keyboard player in a band called the Look People. The Look People had a sound that could best be described as a busload of virtuoso musicians driving headlong through a circus tent pitched right in the middle of Las Vegas. Their singer was a flamboyant lounge lizard, an A-list Toronto socialite, named Jaymz Bee. The drummer went by the name of Great Bob Scott and managed to live up to the hyperbole when he played. If they were "the Munsters" of music, then choirboy Kevin was like Herman Munster's "normal" teenage niece, Marilyn. Except that it was clear in his playing that Kevin was no "normal" keyboard player. He peppered his playing with digital samples of cartoon sound effects and, hey, wazzup with that little bald-headed statue and rotating hand atop his keyboards? The guy shared the Ladies' offbeat sense of humor and he possessed what musicians like to call "chops," which means that he could really play.

"Apparently," explains Kevin, "my name was mentioned in a conversation between Tyler and Dave Bookman, a music-loving fellow who promotes many new live bands from in and outside of Toronto. Tyler first told me of my invitation during a chance meeting at the Horseshoe Tavern. Then, sometime later, I bumped into Tyler on the street. He said, 'It's so funny to bump into you; we were just talking about you.'" But four months went by, and Kevin was sure that they'd changed their minds about him or that they'd found someone else. Then out of the blue, he received the call to come out and meet the guys on the eve of the *Born on a Pirate Ship* tour, which was proposed as a two-month stint. (A two-month tour. Yeah, right, I seem to recall that the SS *Minnow,* from *Gilligan's Island,* was supposed to be on a three-hour tour. And just look how that turned out.)

Kevin was excited and flattered that the band had approached him specifically, and didn't audition anyone else. "Being asked, and then joining the band, was completely an out-of-the-blue, curveball turning point in my life," he says. "So much has happened since. It feels like twenty years ago. Ultimately, I was given about two weeks' notice to learn most of the band's repertoire and get on the bus. Oh, and Steven added that part of my job would be entertaining the guests in the hotel lobby lounges after the show."

During their meeting at Reaction Studios, the band made it perfectly clear that they were in no way looking for some hot-shot session guy to come in and replicate all of Andy's old riffs. "They wanted me to come on board and be myself. With this in mind, I approached learning the material, which I happily found out was more diverse than I had thought. I particularly enjoyed 'This Is Where It Ends,' 'Just a Toy,' 'I Live with It Every Day,' and Jim's 'Spider in My Room.' 'King of Bedside Manor' and 'A' reminded me of Look People songs. I wrote parts, wanting to include homemade sounds as well as the organic piano and organ features. Based on the other groups I'd played with, I've never been sure as to why they figured I might be the right guy."

It was true. Other than knowing the song "Brian Wilson," which he quite liked, Kevin had heard very little of Barenaked Ladies' music and was unfamiliar with their recorded work. He'd seen them live once, though, at the Ultrasound Club and had really enjoyed them. Now he was being asked to join the show and take it on the road. But given the band's declining fortunes, he wondered if this was the road to success or the last mile of the highway to hell. But when he finally got to talking with them, he realized that the band was anything but resigned to the delete bins of life. To quote Frank Stallone out of context, Barenaked Ladies were "far from over."[1]

"As a group," notes Kevin, "I've found that they're good at making tough decisions and they're strong when dealing with hard situations. And they're not afraid of trying something different." Neither, it transpired, was Kevin. He took the chance and hit the road. "I felt that I was joining the underdog team, which has always appealed to me. My energy was 'Let's go fellas!'"

The road, for Kevin, began just outside of the Essex Park Hotel in Toronto where he was told to meet the band and get on the bus. "When I boarded the bus for the first time, I realized that I was going on a trip with a close-knit group, which also included some dedicated crew members, Robin Billinton, John Sulek, and Craig Finley. I also had years of inside jokes and stories to catch up on."

Two months came and went, but Kevin stayed on the bus and now knows pretty much all of the inside jokes and stories all too well. He's lived many of them. "The stories are still funny," he says, "even when hearing them for the three-hundredth time." Before we get our motor runnin' and head out on the highway looking for adventure, perhaps you would like to know some historical facts, stories, and trivia about Kevin Hearn's life up to this point. If facts about Canada are called Canadiana, and facts about America are called Americana, then I suppose facts about Kevin Hearn could be called "Hearnia." (Yes, I know I'm on thin ice with the bad puns and wordplay.)

Kevin learned from day one that change could be good. In fact, he owed his early life to a timely change at birth. "I was born with jaundice," Kevin recalls, "so I had to be rushed from Grimsby, Ontario, to a hospital in Hamilton for a complete blood transfusion at birth. I guess I got off to a weird start."

---

[1]"Far from Over" was the theme song from the Sylvester Stallone film *Staying Alive*, which was billed as the sequel to *Saturday Night Fever*. The song was performed by Sly's brother Frank Stallone.

The Hearn family made many changes in location, moving to Montreal before settling back in North York, then a suburb of Toronto (now part of the "megacity" of Toronto), when Kevin was six. There was a piano in the house, and at age five young Kevin began learning a few changes of his own. Such was his prodigious talent that in 1975 he was shipped downtown to Toronto's prestigious St. Michael's Choir School. It was there, in one of the city's most esteemed learning places, that Kevin had an early lesson in contradictions. It was a lesson that would be learned again and again in the years to come. "My first piano teacher," he recalls with astonishment, "told me that the white keys and the black keys were separate, they were different, which I've always questioned. Why would you do that? She was trying to teach me sharps and flats by distinguishing black and white, but it didn't make sense."

In addition to challenging the wisdom of keyboard apartheid, Kevin was being exposed to popular music. The ever-curious keyboardist started innocently but had soon gotten hooked on the harder stuff. "The first record I ever got was by Andy Williams," he confesses, seemingly without shame. "Then the Beach Boys' *15 Big Ones* and the Beatles' *Magical Mystery Tour*." His seven-inch-vinyl memories include singles like "The Boxer" by Simon and Garfunkel, "Theme from Mahogany (Do You Know Where You're Going To?)" by Diana Ross, and "Daniel" by Elton John.

Pop would have to wait, though, because in grade-four piano, Kevin fell in love with classical music, and more significantly, piano improvisation. "I practiced every day on this upright piano," he remembers. "But before I'd practice, I'd improvise for about an hour or until my mom made me stop."

Kevin credits two key teachers for nurturing his latent song-writing talents with their enthusiasm. "Mr. Eleskovich once came into the room where we were playing and asked if we were writing songs, and if he could hear them," Kevin remembers, adding that a teacher named Mr. Pengelly was just as encouraging. As a result, Kevin still has some of those early songs lying around somewhere.

In grade six, Kevin got his first taste of life on the road as a member of the fifty-voice St. Michael's Choir. The choir would often perform at senior citizens' homes, and it was here that Kevin had his first experience with the after-show meet-'n'-greet.

"After you played you had to go out and say hello to all the people," Kevin explains. "I always loved playing; it didn't seem like extra work to me." The choir also sang on a television skating show called *Stars on Ice,* featuring Canadian figure-skating star Toller Cranston. Although he was chosen to sing a solo, Kevin still has bittersweet memories of the occasion. "I sang 'Ave Maria' solo with the choir behind me," he recalls. "In the studio there were these pillars right behind the choir. Right in the middle of the shoot, this guy thought he'd lean back on the pillar but it wasn't rooted down, so this huge pillar fell right over. Toller Cranston was upset, and we had to shoot the whole thing over. It was very Spinal Tap."

The choir also made a few records. At one session, he even got to meet Dan Hill, the Canadian superstar whose biggest hit was "Sometimes When We Touch." "I remember hanging out with Dan Hill one night by the pinball machine at Manta Sound," Kevin explains. "He was telling me stories of hanging out with Elton John and I thought 'wow that's cool.'"

Among the better gigs that the choirboy remembers was the debut performance of Mahler's Eighth Symphony with the Toronto Symphony Orchestra, under the renowned baton of conductor Andrew Davis. This performance happened to be before His Holiness the Pope during the pontiff's visit to St. Michael's Cathedral.

Outside of the choir, Kevin took to walking on the wilder side. The altar boy developed a bit of an alter ego, one that wanted to rock and rebel. Just as Ed—who Kevin would not meet for several years to come—had formed a band called the Rage up in Scarberia, the bad boy Kevin began joining or forming bands with names like Renegade and the Slide. The Slide managed to learn both the chords in Lou Reed's "Walk on the Wild Side" in addition to writing some original rock songs. "We had this one song called 'Extinction' that featured a fast, distorted guitar," Kevin recalls. "Because of my choir training, though, I was singing very sweetly on songs that shouldn't have been sung very sweetly at all.

"Our drummer, Basil, was also in the Look People, and he invited me to play with them. Here was a band that wanted to rehearse five days a week. For me, that was amazing!" A wildly eclectic rock group, the Look People was one more thing that would change Kevin's life forever. With them, he recorded four full albums, went on three European tours, and even got asked back to play Lollapalooza two years in a row. "I liked it for the mix of theater and humor plus actual serious music. There wasn't a lot of melody in the singing, but it was a real musical thing. Before the Look People, I would disregard things that I did while improvising. But jamming with them, I'd just go nuts and they'd say, 'Hey, that was neat, grab that.' I started realizing that I could actually use things from jams. That opened up whole new worlds to go off and explore."

"His playing was very good," remembers the Look People's former front man, Jaymz Bee. "But we didn't know just how talented he was until we began composing with him." Bee maintains that Kevin's seasonal fave, "It's Christmas Time, Oh Yeah," which was eventually recorded by Barenaked Ladies, had its origins as part of a holiday-themed concept album that Bee put together. He even recorded it yet again, after Barenaked Ladies did their version. "Look People was also a close-knit group, with years of inside jokes and stories. We were constantly going against the grain, striving to put on a surprising, tight show that often verged on being some sort of politically incorrect musical-performance art circus." This included years of crappy temp jobs, living on Kraft dinners (yes, it's true), and the occasional jar of peanut butter. "This experience" says Kevin, "helped me realize that I would not be able to understand what made Barenaked Ladies tick overnight and to just take things one day at a time, go with their flow."

Bee recalls in vivid detail how he first met Kevin in the summer of 1989. "He was wearing navy blue Levi's cords and a Scooby-Doo T-shirt and he looked like 'the boy next door,'" Bee says. "Great Bob Scott and I knew that getting the vibe right was crucial because we toured so frequently. Everything about him seemed to mesh with Look People. He was a great collaborator, and became a solid friend." According to Bee, touring with the Look People's traveling circus toughened Kevin up to the rigors of the road. "Great Bob Scott and I loved to pull pranks on him, which I'm sure prepared him for life on the road with Tyler Stewart."

The Look People were briefly hired to be the house band on CBC's Friday-night variety show starring Ralph Benmurgui. A late-night show in the David Letterman style, Look People and Jaymz Bee were brought in to be the "Paul Schaffer" to Benmurgui's Letterman. Kevin says that the experience of doing a weekly television show was good preparation for future shows like *Saturday Night Live* and *Beverly Hills 90210*. "When it came to performing on shows like [*Late Show with David*] *Letterman* and [*Late Night with*] *Conan O'Brien*, relaxing and playing comfortably with cameras moving close by is not something I could just do so easily. On *Beverly Hills 90210*, they only showed my hands, so I found simply having hands useful in this case. The Ralph [Benmurgui] show was definitely a good exercise because Ralph's a good person, as well, so I felt fortunate to have worked with him."

After his Look People years, Kevin was asked to accompany his cousin, Harland Williams, in a comedy-theater project. Williams has since appeared on *Late Show with David Letterman* on numerous occasions. His film work includes a starring role in Disney's comedy *Rocket Man* and a memorable cameo as an unhitched hitchhiker in the Farrelly Brothers' hit comedy *There's Something About Mary*. Kevin still remembers with fondness the time they played the renowned Just For Laughs Comedy Festival in Montreal. "It was just me and him," he recalls. "I love comedy. I don't consider myself a comedian, but most of the bands that I've worked with have had a good sense of humor."

Okay, here's another weird crossing of paths in a book that's packed with them: In 1994, Kevin was enlisted as musical director for Corky and the Juice Pigs.

"I'd always been a big fan," Kevin says of the Juice Pigs, "so I did a run of shows in Toronto before touring with them all the way to the Edinburgh Festival." Yes, it was those very same practitioners of musical comedy and manic mayhem who had taken Ed and Steve across Canada early in their partnership.

Juice Pig Sean Cullen says of their highland fling with Kevin, "I knew him from the Look People. We just wanted to add more music to the show and allow Phil Nichol, who'd been trapped on guitar, to get more into the sketches. We were looking to free ourselves up to do more complicated scene work. Kevin had just left the Look People, which at that time had just sort of self-destructed, so he was available. We were glad he could come to Edinburgh with us, and it was a great time."

In addition to playing piano and organ sounds on his keyboard synthesizer, Kevin began to use digital samples for their sound-effect cues. "He's such a talented guy," Cullen says, "and he's just the nicest guy in the world." Having worked with Barenaked Ladies in their nascent stages, Cullen remembers how thrilled he was that the band had hooked up with Kevin after Andy's departure. "When he went over to Barenaked Ladies," Cullen recalls, "I thought it was just a perfect fit for them."

"Ed and Steve had learned and been influenced so much by their show," Kevin says of the Juice Pigs' ability to hit the ground funning. He points out that Ed and Steven's freestyling and irreverent stage banter owes a little, if not a little more, to that of Corky and the Juice Pigs. "Although," he interjects, "the Barenaked Ladies' stage improvs tended to be somewhat tamer in subject matter."

But for Kevin, it's the spontaneity that makes it all so exciting, night after night. It's about living in the moment, a fleeting and often memorable moment in time, and the feeling that everything could change at any second. "The feeling of going out on a limb with someone onstage and the energy that this can generate—little gems in my memory, like 'Father Beard' or 'MC Mouthful of Toast' are like shooting stars to me. They happen once, out of the blue, and may never happen again."

So did Kevin experience any weirdness from Jim upon boarding the Barenaked bus? He was, after all, taking the seat of Jim's brother Andy. "I was afraid Jim would be giving me the 'evil googly eye' all the time," says Kevin, "as if to say, 'You're not my brother Andy. Where is my brother Andy? Andy's my brother, but you, you are not my brother, and your name is not Andy!'" But his fears were unfounded and such an eye, googly in nature, was never cast upon Kevin Hearn.

"Jimmy is a good guy," Kevin says, "and I figured, to the best of my ability, I'd just bring what I had to offer as a musician and performer and hopefully work as a positive force in the band's sound. I also needed to be open-minded to new ways of approaching this music. The role of the keyboardist was more pop and commercial than anything I'd taken part in previously." The transition was no doubt made smoother due to the fact that Kevin felt immense respect for Andy, both as a musician and as a person. "I think he's incredible," says Kevin. "When I was first learning the songs, there were parts that I just loved and didn't want to change. Like the riff in 'Intermittently' or in 'Jane,'" Kevin says, pausing to hum the riffs out loud. "Andy's voice often sends shivers up my spine. I don't know if he wrote those, or what, but I recognize the technique from my piano training, and they're very keyboardy parts and I play them. I also admire his dedication to music and his harmonic taste. Plus, he has a knack for simple, catchy melodic statements, which to me often add an essential charm to a song."

Musically, however, Kevin was more concerned about filling another gap in the band, and didn't wish to unravel any complicated, delicate yet unseen balance of personalities. Interpersonal dynamics, in any band, often consist of unspoken politics and established systems for working out musical ideas or making decisions. And let's not even get into the possibility that Jim, who'd collaborated with Andy for many years, might have been experiencing what psychologists call separation anxiety. But none of that happened. And as Sean Cullen stated awhile back, it was a perfect fit. "He had," Cullen adds, "the same kind of childlike innocent quality and love of foolishness and silly performing."

Finally, when asked rather bluntly just what he really thinks he's brought to Barenaked Ladies, Kevin, ever humble, won't take himself seriously enough to give a straight answer, instead hamming it up with "Rock-'n'-roll dreams baby! Make 'em come true! That's what I do. With my electric guitars, keyboards 'n' shit. I got sounds. They go pop, zoom, and ping. It's like a cutout of a lightning bolt getting pointed right into your ear!" Then his tone becomes decidedly more reflective, and he says, "Seriously, though, that's a tough one. I just try to add what I feel or hear the song needs."

17

Nettwerk and Terry McBride

For the record, the band really meant it when they wrote, "Take care, Nige" in the *Born on a Pirate Ship* credits. And when the Ladies began shopping for a new manager, among the first people they called for advice was Pierre Tremblay, who at the time worked for Universal Concerts Canada. Tremblay had been involved with the Ladies during their "salad days," when he organized and promoted Mr. Rockin's All-You-Can-Eat-Salad-Bar, a marathon tour after the release of *Gordon*. Tremblay accompanied the band for the whole thing—he even had his own bunk on their tour bus.

"When you're out with a band for three and a half months, sleeping on the same bus and you're with them every day, you become good friends," Tremblay says. "We did well over seventy shows in close to fifty different markets. We went everywhere from Yellowknife in the Northwest Territories to Cornerbrook, Newfoundland, in the Maritimes."

Steven described one of their more memorable, and isolated, tour stops, a tiny Inuit town in the Canadian Arctic, now part of a new province called Nunavit, to journalist Michael D. Clark of the *San Jose Mercury News*. "We played a high-school gym in a village called Iqualit," Steven told Clark. "All the local elders were in the front row. They didn't know English, but they were extremely gracious and took us dogsledding."

> *Get out of the slush*
> *Tell your dog pack to mush*
> *Go home*
>
> —from "Go Home" by
> Steven Page and Ed Robertson

In fact, the scope and scale of Mr. Rockin's movable feast had broken new ground—some of it tundra—within the Canadian rock-touring industry, so much so that BNL was honored with a commemorative plaque by Tremblay's bosses. While it's true that the Ladies bonded with Tremblay during that extensive and exhaustive tour, they'd actually known each other since the early days, well before *Gordon* or even *The Yellow Tape*. It all began when Tremblay booked them into Ottawa's Café Deluxe, where he worked prior to becoming a national promoter. "I'd brought the Rheostatics in from Toronto and booked the Barenaked Ladies in the support slot for fifty dollars," Tremblay recalls. "I thought they were great and instantly offered them a regular night at the club, every Tuesday for the next two months. The first Tuesday that they played, there were like fifty people there. Then the next Tuesday, it was a hundred. Then two hundred, and so on, until they were completely selling out the club every time. Word of mouth was huge, and they just put on such a great show."

And that's why, in 1995, Barenaked Ladies called upon their old friend Pierre with the musical question "Who is better than Best?" "I said, 'If you're looking for a manager in Canada, you've only got one choice, and that's Nettwerk and Terry McBride in Vancouver,'" Tremblay recalls. "Bands like Barenaked Ladies are rare in this industry, and Nettwerk were the only people who I

144

felt were appropriate for the guys, who could take the band beyond Canada."

Shortly after dispensing that critical wisdom, Tremblay took his own advice and dispensed himself from the concert-promotion business to join Nettwerk. Today, he and McBride share all the front-office managerial duties for Barenaked Ladies. McBride mainly runs the American networking, while Tremblay deals with things like video production and, most important, helming the band's next frontiers: Europe and beyond. "One of my main reasons for coming over here was to work with Barenaked Ladies," Tremblay says. "From very early in my relationship with these guys, I felt that there was something very special and unique about them, and I felt that no matter what, they would be successful."

Enter Terry McBride. I'd spoken on the phone with McBride only once before I finally got to meet the renowned impresario in person. Having never really seen a picture of the highly respected entrepreneur, I was a little surprised that the crop-topped kid in a simple grayish-green T-shirt and running shoes was actually one of the main architects of Lilith Fair and the careers of Barenaked Ladies and Sarah McLachlan. And I really had trouble believing that this "kid" was actually a forty-year-old music-business veteran.

And seated beside him on a couch at Cello Studios, was Tremblay, a hipster in a green short-sleeved shirt and San Francisco Giants baseball cap. Tremblay, sporting a moustache that could only be called a "Fu Manchu," once joked to me that Nettwerk's management approach was strictly "new skool." But listening in as the pair went over a contact sheet from a Barenaked Ladies publicity-photo shoot, it soon becomes clear that he and McBride are still quite grounded in "da old skool," championing such old-fashioned ethics like honest hard work and really giving real people real entertainment for their very real, hard-earned money.

McBride, however, feels that it's not entirely about the

money. "We're in the entertainment business," McBride says. "I have a whole philosophy. The first couple of years with an artist, I'm not going to make any money on them. The BNL had a booking agent who was interested in getting the biggest guarantee moneywise, and that usually means going into clubs or bars of some nature—not necessarily the venues that they should be playing if the band is to grow. So getting a ten-thousand-dollar fee versus a one-thousand-dollar fee is of no value to me. It's sort of a weird thing. I'd rather take the lesser money, play the right building, and promote the show in a certain way. It's basically micromarketing."

If BNL was going to go to the next level, they needed a manager who would level with them. Terry McBride was just that manager. As far as he can tell, he was the first person who was actually honest with them about the state of their career. "They had a lot of 'yes' people around them," he says, "and I was like, 'No, no, that's stupid.' I don't think anyone had sat them down and said, 'You know, your imaging sucks on this record. You have this and this, but you don't have the following things. . . .'"

Among the first things to change were their album covers, which McBride felt were "god-awful." He had a lot to do with reissuing the *Gordon* CD, replacing the original in-your-face cover with a more subtle one depicting the red-white-and-blue ball that was something of an icon for the band at that time. "You know," McBride begins once more, "I really, truly believe the music should do the speaking. When you do an album cover that in no way represents the music that's on the actual CD, you confuse people. For the better part of about fifty to sixty percent of all album covers, you can look at them and know pretty well what the music is about.

"The original cover of *Gordon*," McBride continues, "on the first issue, was horrible, like a kid's record. It was for nine- or ten-year-olds. I mean, their songwriting and wit was far beyond nine- to ten-year-olds, far beyond. There were little tiny things like that, and it was all due to the fact that no one would say no."

INTERMISSION: Photo Album

Steven, already a ham

Kevin—bare naked (almost)

Steven, testing the waters

... and Tyler was kung fu fighting

Jim and Andy, inseparable
from the beginning

Ed makes wish, grows up to be rock star

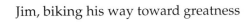

Jim, biking his way toward greatness

Hmm . . . wonder what Tyler wants to do with his life?

Jim loses teeth, finds fish

Jim's fifth birthday

Jim, starring in
Blair Witch, Canada

Jim with double bass

Tyler doing the big brother thing

Kevin modeling very
early BNL costumes

Steven in his school band days

Tyler in the drum corps

Ed as basement rock god

Steven busts a move

Steven
and family
at his
bar mitzvah

Early Brothers Creeggan
jam session

Jim is used to running
away with the prize

Jim and Andy in
a cappella group

Jim and Andy,
still inseparable

Tyler and mom
at his graduation
from Ryerson

The Ladies as
lawn ornaments

Rockin' out
at the house

Steven and Kevin are family men

Barenaked Ladies onstage at Scarborough City Hall

The Ladies
with Michael Phillip
Wojewoda
(second from right)

Ed signing
autographs

Taking notes at the press conference

A packed house in Washington, D.C., 1998

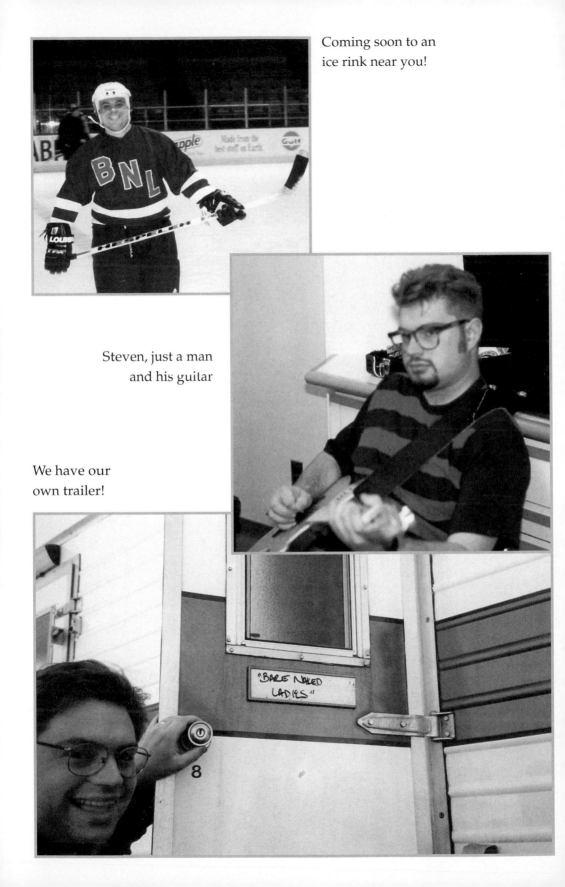

Coming soon to an
ice rink near you!

Steven, just a man
and his guitar

We have our
own trailer!

8

Tyler and Jill get married

Tyler + Jill – Milli

Ed and Nat
are the king and
queen of their
shower

Ed and Nat
get married

Barenaked Ladies, San Francisco, 1998

The Ladies themselves, as McBride is quick to point out, also knew that they could do better, and he's proud of them for pushing themselves that little bit further.

"It was all them," the manager demurs. "It wasn't me that came up with the album-cover design. It was them. It wasn't me that came up with the music. It was them. But it was someone telling them they could do better."

So if the Ladies' previous manager had seemed to be all over the place and nowhere—all at the same time—their new management, all high-tech and fully wired, seemed to be everywhere at once—all the time. "When I first met the band," McBride recollects over the phone from Nettwerk's Vancouver offices, "they wanted to put this record out in two months, work it for two months, and then they all wanted to go away for six months." But McBride would have none of it. He told them to go away for six months now, because when they came back, he'd own the next eighteen months of their lives. "You basically go where I say," he informed them.

And yes, McBride acknowledges his "I own you" management approach has earned him a reputation as a dictator now and again, but he swears by the need for total commitment in the face of war. "Go away for the next six months," he told them. "I'm going to learn your record label. I'm going to build bridges. I'm going to talk your record label into marketing an artist versus marketing a mere album. I don't want them focused on *Born on a Pirate Ship;* I want them focused upon *Gordon, Maybe You Should Drive,* and *Born on a Pirate Ship.*"

McBride's plan was to get the band to prioritize their life agendas. Wisely, he realized that the band members' personal lives had a great effect on how well they conducted their career. As the demands of a runaway career eroded the stability of their home lives, the reciprocal effect became damaging to the band. The answer was to put everything on hold and take a much-needed walk away from it. I think it was English poet laureate Ted Hughes (or was it Sheryl Crow?) who said, "A change will do you good."[1] After all, every day is a winding road, and all they wanted to do was have some fun. If being in one of the most successful bands in Canadian history made them happy, then why the hell were they so sad?

McBride was also underwhelmed by the band's imaging, which he thought bordered on infantile. "Imaging," McBride explains, "is really your own self-confidence. It wasn't about reinventing the Barenaked Ladies. It was about giving them the confidence to do it in a more professional manner. What they needed to do was to represent what they were, which was witty, cutting edge—because they weren't writing, 'Ooh, baby, I love you'—and have that sort of imaging. So that what they wore and how they looked and how they were marketed reflected the music they were actually making. Again, it all came from them."

McBride had seen how multimedia and the Internet helped Sarah McLachlan to not only reach her existing fan base, but also to broaden her reach into the world marketplace. Aware that Barenaked Ladies had a similar groundswell of dedicated fans, McBride set about projecting the band's inherent "coolness." "I said, 'Let's start building a coolness around you. Let's use your humor, but let's treat it like Chris Rock instead of like some bimbo. Let's get some edge there. Get your personality out.' We started getting them onto the Internet and adding multimedia content on their CDs."

McBride realized that these changes needed to be made right away, while the band was still relatively young and while they still had the stamina and desire to take on the biggest challenge they would ever be faced with. "They, of course, had a meteoric rise here in Canada," McBride notes, "and then they had a meteoric crash. I think the first album did about nine hundred thousand and the next one did about two hundred thou-

---

[1]Definitely Sheryl Crow.

sand, so obviously that's going in the wrong direction. They had horrible imaging and were definitely burnt out."

McBride had his work cut out for him. The odds were that even if they could get back on the Canadian charts, it would be next to impossible to duplicate the Barenaked-mania of *Gordon*. "That just doesn't happen very often," McBride observes of BNL's first record. "They were very overexposed in Canada, and I guess nothing had really gotten going in America, where they were seen as a minor novelty act." Doesn't exactly sound like a band poised on the brink of success. And many of McBride's music-industry peers didn't think so, either. "My focus was to break America," he admits, "then, and only then, bring it back to Canada. I actually got ridiculed a lot for it, which right now makes you sort of smile."

So why, oh why, Terry McBride, did you take them on? "Well, the bottom line was they write great songs, and they're great live. Plus, I had time, which I hadn't had in quite a while, and I was willing to try something new. I was looking for something that already had some of the road work done, already had some awareness of what needed to be done—and everything starts with the actual songs."

According to McBride, the songs come first, followed by the singers themselves. Entering Nettwerk's world, it would seem, requires checking one's ego at the door. "I met with them," McBride says. "They're really nice people; I refuse to work with artists who have egos. I'd rather not work with them." Barenaked Ladies, humbled but not hobbled by recent events, had no problem finding the ego-check booth and emerged with their claim tickets, ready to work. "They're just really nice people," says McBride, echoing the sentiments of pretty much everyone I've talked to about the band, "and they were willing to listen."

They could do worse than to listen to McBride. Back in 1984, McBride started Nettwerk Records out of his "old apartment" in Vancouver. "I went to university and took civil engineering.

149

Never graduated," McBride is quick to admit. But then he "fell totally in love with music" and started his own record label.

But his first time around as a label boss, he says, didn't work out. "The second time around I was lucky enough to have a few hits. I've been lucky enough to have partners that I've worked with for sixteen, seventeen years now." He doesn't really regret not graduating; in fact, these days he doesn't seem to have regrets about anything. "Definitely the engineering background helped, because it teaches you a certain way of looking at things. But there is no education for this business. There just isn't. Probably the best education one can do is either go into radio or into retail and at least get some sort of base, but it's just using your head."

McBride was definitely using his head in 1987, when Nettwerk signed a singer, from all the way on the other side of Canada, to a recording contract. That singer, Sarah McLachlan, moved out west to Vancouver, and the rest is history. McBride focused her career south, to the much larger U.S. music industry. After impressive showings for her initial stateside releases, McLachlan and McBride, along with everyone at Nettwerk, broke new ground when they launched a touring festival called Lilith Fair. The rest, as they now say, is herstory.

Plugged into the world of music and data-management tools like SoundScan, which tallies sales directly from the bar codes on CDs as they're sold, McBride is fanatical when it comes to high-tech data tracking. He's also a firm believer in building things. Building a marketing campaign for an album or building a career for an artist. Building up the public's awareness of that artist. And when artists are overexposed, McBride says, building a mystery around them may be the best plan of action. "Whoever was at the helm didn't realize when it's sort of smart to pull back and leave a little bit of mystery there, to create a sort of coolness or novelty around it."

While McBride admits that Best didn't "bury" the band, as managers so often do, the fact remains that Best's efforts didn't help put the band over the top in America. In fairness to the former manager, McBride wonders if the band themselves might not have been ready, at that time at least, for the big time. "I don't know," says McBride, mulling over such possibilities in his mind. "If they'd had the same breakthrough in America based on the same perception and novelty image that they had in Canada, I don't think anyone could have saved their careers, personally. You know, Nigel obviously did a lot of right things, but I don't think he understood the business well enough to step out of what was happening and look down the road. It all just happened. From what I can see, he did the best he possibly could."

> What does it mean to wake out of a dream
> And be wearing someone else's shorts?
> —from "Same Thing" by Ed Robertson

"You can have shorts," McBride offers by way of interpretation, "but don't look like you came from the farm. Your look is all people will think of you initially, if they just see photos or a video without really hearing the music. If you look like a bunch of clowns then, as such, how are you to be treated seriously? How is your song craft going to be looked at? It won't be looked at seriously, even if you're great writers."

Although BNL was now holding back the release date on *Born on a Pirate Ship*, there was one new recording going out. The song was "Shoe Box" and its inclusion on the soundtrack to the hit television series *Friends* was considered by many to be the first shot fired in the revolutionary war to get Barenaked Ladies out of their doldrums and into American consciousness. McBride says that he was against that idea, but it was already out of his hands by the time he got into position.

"That was already rolling," says McBride. "The 'Shoe Box' thing was something that Howie Klein [at Reprise Records] wanted to do, and the guys had already said yes to it. So be it. It wasn't where I wanted to go, but there were certain things that were already in motion that one couldn't stop. It didn't hurt us any, and it obviously brought enough royalties in for Howie to allow the rest of the process to happen, but Howie and Richie and especially Eric [Fritchie]—the product manager—were very instrumental in changing a key philosophy at Warner Brothers. That was when we went out to play live."

Just after the *Shoe Box E.P.* was released, I had the occasion to ask Ed and Steve about it.

> **Me:** You just had "Shoe Box" on the *Friends* sound-
>   track. This leads me to ask, "Which *Friends* cast
>   members would you want to have play you in a
>   Barenaked Ladies made-for-TV movie?"
> **Ed:** Matt LeBlanc is not in the movie.
> **Steven:** Lisa Kudrow would be Jim.
> **Ed:** Jennifer Aniston would be me, because of my
>   perky hands.
> **Me:** And, of course, your famous haircut.
> **Steven:** I would be the monkey.
> **Me:** Marcel?
> **Steven:** I've only watched it once. The week before
>   the soundtrack came out, I thought I better
>   watch this because people are gonna ask me
>   about it.

McBride tells me point-blank that he'd only heard one single on *Born on a Pirate Ship:* "The Old Apartment." As a result, McBride says, the band's relaunch plan included releasing the *Shoe Box E.P.*, a five-song CD, a sort of setup for *Born on a Pirate Ship.*

"No matter how much they fought me on it, it had only one single," McBride asserts. "I can remember having a big debate with them. They thought there were four or five singles on it, and I'm going, 'No, there isn't.' And they're saying, 'What about "When I Fall?"' I said, 'Beautiful melody, great chorus, but the bottom line is the verse is talking about some guy falling off a building. Radio's not going to play that.' They'd ask, 'What do you mean?' I said that the radio guy is not going to play a depressing song about someone jumping to their death. That's not what radio is about. 'But it's such a great song,' they pleaded." Then McBride retorted, "Well, you know what? It is a great song, but it's not a great single."

"I don't remember fighting about that at all!" says Ed. "I've always really liked 'When I Fall,' and I'm really proud of that song, but I don't remember it ever being talked about as a single." McBride then dispensed some priceless advice on the difference between good singles and merely good songs. "My whole thing with any artist," McBride states, "is 'Go write yourself an album. When you're finished writing it, be happy with every song on it and then give it to me, because I'm going to be picking the singles.' The bottom line is don't put on a song that you don't like because the chances are it'll be the single that I pick. So be happy with your album."

"But while you're writing," he adds, "think about this: What you've got to start doing is, if you're going to take the lyrics to the left, take the music to the left; if you take the lyrics to the right, take the music to the right. It doesn't mean that you have to change the way you write songs. You've just got to be aware of how you do it. Thinking about what you're actually writing, the crafting of your music. There's no sense writing an incredible melody with an incredible lyrical hook if you're going to put such a different twist on it that no one's going to play it. Then all you're really going to do is sell to the converted."

"We were making the switch to Nettwerk," says Ed, "and they'd made a decision to stall on the release to try and get more setup happening. That provided a nice little break, almost a three-month break. The record was in the can, ready to go, artwork was done—just waiting for the right time to come out. Consequently, when Hannah was born, I was able to be home for the first three months of her life, which seems like years compared to what subsequent 'band births' have been like. I think Steve was on the road days after Ben was born; I think he was actually on the road the next day, because we were on tour at the time.

"There was so much flux in what the band was at the time, you know," Ed continues. "We'd just started playing with Kev; we'd just started off with Nettwerk, so there was a real process of trying to get to know them. Trying to get a sense of Terry McBride. I really felt like Terry was all business, in the beginning, you know? Now I think he's just mostly business. It was a long process of trying to get a read on somebody, on the phone, because they were in Vancouver and we were in Toronto. I did get a sense, though, that they really believed in us, [that] they thought we had something great but that we needed to learn how to present it better or something. His big initial push was he just wanted us to lose the goofiness. Like, we would go out of our way to be goofy just because that would make us laugh."

For instance, the shorts . . . "We were like that," says Ed. "We wore shorts offstage; we thought, 'Well, this is how we are,' and we thought that everyone would just accept that. But the truth was that people were going, 'It's those fucking guys in shorts. What's the deal?' We didn't realize that we were being identified as 'guys in knee-length shorts.' We didn't want that; we wanted it to not be an issue. But the fact is, it was an issue. So then we got a stylist for a photo shoot, and we all felt a lot better. But not the styling on *Maybe You Should Drive*—that was the record company trying to style us out.

"I think we wanted to be successful," Ed continues, "but I think we wanted to be successful in a very nontraditional way. I don't think we wanted a little cult of secret fans that were really cool. I think we wanted the quarterbacks on the football team to go, 'Those guys are great!' you know? But there were things that we thought were kind of sublime and ridiculous, and the kind of low-rent aspect of them never bugged us. But the truth is, the whole world doesn't love independent films. We were just really being obtuse all the time, esoteric, not even in a highbrow way, just in a goofy way," Ed observes. "So Terry's big push in the beginning was 'I want you guys to be seen as a legit band. I want you to lose the kind of hamminess and goofiness and wackiness. I know you guys are funny, and I know there's humor in the music, but let's not be goofy.' And he was pretty relentless about that. He wanted good styling in the photographs and on and on."

Then, Barenaked Ladies toured. And toured. And toured. And toured. And then, when they'd finished touring, and they were almost home, they toured some more. Then, let's see, oh yeah, they toured again. As you can see, McBride's philosophy on artist development involves lots of roadwork. But there is a method to the madness, which I asked McBride to explain: "I think the guys, for the longest time, thought that I had a map of America and that I would just put on a blindfold and randomly determine where they'd go next, because they'd never worked like that before. They would do a tour, and then that was it."

But in the new Nettwerk regime, those days were deader than disco. McBride's new way meant more playing time, less playtime. "The bottom line," says McBride, "is that they're really nice people and that they got a tutorial on the business, because I don't think they understood the actual business. I'm a manager that will educate the artist so I can have a sensible conversation with them. I honestly believe in taking that method and putting them fully in control of their career, making them understand every single element of it."

To get the message to the band, McBride's first priority was to bring tour manager Craig Finley into the office for a crash course in Nettwerking. McBride wanted to make him a part of the management team versus just acting as the traditional road manager. With Fin plugged in, as it were, to the head office, he could easily disseminate the game plans from the bunker to the troops on the front lines. And when the band itself has an understanding of the big picture or game plan, that makes McBride's job, and everyone's job, that much easier.

"They can see where I'm going," McBride says, "and we can have much more logical conversations. A lot of managers want their artists to purely focus on the music. Yes, I want that, too, because that's their job, but I want them to understand every single thing that we in management are doing."

McBride's e-mail updates go out daily from his desktop to the laptops of everyone concerned. "They know where it's going and why it's going a certain way," he says. "They don't walk into a city and question why they're doing three different radio stations. They already know what to do, but now I have to point out to them why, when something comes naturally to them, they should do it just slightly differently. Then do it enough times, and they'll do it naturally. The band didn't understand the business before, and now they have a great grasp on the business as a whole, and they understand how all of the little micromarketing parts fit together."

McBride prefers to see himself as a coach who works with star players, rather than a dictator issuing orders to his lowly troops. "You know, if you know why you're doing something, then chances are you'll put more effort in, versus if you're just told to do something, which is almost a military point of view, where it's the general trying to tell the private what to do."

Among the things that Barenaked Ladies now know all too well are:

The Touring Truths of Terry McBride

BUILD, BUILD, BUILD

"Six weeks on, two weeks off, six on, two off, never ending," explains McBride. "The idea is that I'm going to visit a city five or six times over about an eighteen-month period, and I'm going to market this band. Every time I come through, they'll play a bigger venue and we'll just build it."

NEVER PREACH TO THE CONVERTED

"I always believe," McBride says, "that you should never

play only to those who already know you. So I'll always stick Barenaked Ladies in venues that are slightly bigger than what they need, and I don't care if I don't sell that venue out. I just want to make sure that people who decide to come that day can still buy tickets. If a venue sells out, so be it. But I want to make sure that everyone who wants to come to that show has a chance to come to that show because I'm so confident that my band is so good live that people will walk out and buy the records."

YOU CAN'T GO BACK

"You know," continues McBride, "sometimes a city has a three-thousand-seater [theater], and then the next biggest room is like an eighteen-thousand-seater. You've already sold out the three-thousand-seater. It makes no sense to go back to that again. You've got nothing to gain. So you know what? You've just got to go into the eighteen-thousand-seater, knowing that you're only going to get six thousand people. So be it."

WALK-UP TRAFFIC GIVES YOU "BUMPS"

According to McBride, when you play in front of three thousand people, your record sales are likely to go up three and four hundred units. "That tells me," McBride says, "that someone brought a friend or someone decided at the last minute to go with a bunch of friends, saw the show, was completely blown away, and went out the next week and bought the record. You know, another fan down. A convert. Like, ten percent of the people at a show went right out and bought the record on the way home. Pierre and I used to sit there, with Eric [Fritchie] the [Reprise Records] product manager, and watch the SoundScan bumps just to judge how good a job we were actually doing. We've seen it happen time and time again, where the SoundScan week-after ratio showed a huge bump. Funnily enough, the band started watching them, too. And that's what gave them a lot of the extra juice to keep going, because they actually saw it working."

The band was concerned about playing the same set of songs

in a town within such a short time, and worried that it would sound stale if they did. "Well, then," McBride told them, "you'd better think of another set to play. Because you know what? This is what you have to do. You know, any artist that I have has to be able to perform, to portray their character. People have to be able to get sucked in and walk out going, 'Wow, I really liked that.' So that when I come back four months later you're coming back to the show because you had such a good time the first time. They were forced to entertain, and the bottom line is, one of the two magical ingredients you need in order to have a long-term career is you've got to be able to entertain live." After a while the band was not only really good, but they were also getting really good at localizing their stage patter to each town they played.

McBride's faith in the band's musicianship and songwriting gave him the faith to put his saturation plan into action. His philosophy was, that if they were going to win any kind of audience in America, they were going to have to do it one fan at a time. So they'd better get to work, hadn't they? "Given time, and in enough cities," McBride continues, "there would be a natural momentum to it. They got a second chance because they hadn't been overhyped inside America. It's sort of like you have to win every fan one by one. You've got to win every radio programmer one by one."

Nettwerk's plan required the flexibility to respond in a timely fashion to sudden interest in far-off territories. The band couldn't be locked into long-term plans that would preclude them from capitalizing on even the smallest amount of airplay. As such, McBride says that he made sure that the band wasn't booked more than six weeks ahead at any given time. And it wasn't just the band and crew who were working these markets. Just as the band had busked outside the clubs back in the early days in Toronto, Nettwerk's plan was to rustle up all the promotion muscle they could muster to hustle the band in every place they played.

"When you go and play a show," McBride continues, "don't

just mention it over the radio and put an ad in the local newspaper. Do the posters. Do the Internet marketing. Do two or three retail visits with an in-store connected with a radio visit, even if the radio station isn't playing you a lot. Get the retailers, the radio, the media all down to the show. Do all the basic stuff, and do it over and over and over again."

In a 1998 interview for *Hits* Magazine, Tyler told Canadian music journalist Karen Bliss that Nettwerk had employed "a tour-your-fucking-ass-off strategy." Tyler noted that McBride had an amazing relationship with radio people and would get them on board. McBride was also good at forging relationships with the record company, Reprise, suggesting things and not taking no for an answer. "The only trick for Terry," Tyler mused, "was getting people out to see us. It's been a developing game plan."

Radio: We interrupt this program to explain a little bit about commercial radio and the mechanics of getting a single to be added to a station's playlist. You see, as it turns out, commercial radio is all about the money. And while you and I may see the radio as a kind of faucet that brings music flowing freely into our lives, they who own the faucet are not in this business for humanitarian reasons. The music is free in your house because advertisers, who sell products that they'd like you to know about, pay that radio station a whole batch of money to tap into the faucet—and your attention span—while you enjoy the music of your life. As the hits just keep on comin' on a given channel, that station attracts people like you to listen to it over another station. Surveys are published that tell advertisers just which stations you and others in your demographically attractive age bracket, midteens to early thirties, are listening to and when. Advertisers want you to buy their stuff, and conversely, radio wants to play music that attracts higher numbers of listeners. It's like an FCC license to print money.

So getting played on the radio, you see, isn't as easy as just being good or writing great songs. It's about showing the programmers that enough of the target audience will be attracted to the single. And that means, in the case of McBride and those try-ing to get Barenaked Ladies' music heard, showing the "suits" just how big and loyal Barenaked Ladies' audience is. And just how serious the band is about entertaining that audience.

McBride factored all of this into his master plan for blowing away the radios of America.

"If a radio station starts to spin a record, even lightly, then it's a spark. I'd make sure the band, six or seven weeks later, would have a show there. I'd go to that station. I'd work with them. I'd do creative promotions and market the hell out of it so that by the time the band came through town, the radio station was sort of getting into it. [Radio programmers and music direc-tors] would come down to the show, and there was [the radio station's] target audience.

"And then," says McBride, and these are his words exactly, "the radio station would be pounding the band.

"That's why you have to go back and back and back. They just went and toured and toured and toured with *Born on a Pirate Ship*. As it was, we only had the one single on the whole album. I was looking for a way to keep the momentum from 'The Old Apartment' going. I needed another song without putting them back in the studio. So I needed to go back into their earlier songs, which were all hits to me, but no one had done it right. And when I couldn't work it anymore I got them to do *Rock Spectacle*, a live album of older material, which I can't say they were really willing to do."

For once, that's an understatement.

"It was all Terry's idea, actually, to release a live album or a live EP, and we weren't really interested," says Jim, looking back. "We thought it sounded like a live greatest-hits album. Why would we want to do that after three records? We thought it would be just way too early for that kind of thing. We didn't really want to do it."

"The fight with the Barenaked Ladies to make it work," adds McBride, "lasted, like, three to four months. I felt like I'd been stomped all over. I would go out to see them play live. I'd take a weekend, fly out for one or two shows, get all my enthusiasm back, and then fly back to Vancouver and work eighty-hour days trying to keep it going or to fight the same battles, but a little bit harder."

But as McBride went to the shows, he couldn't help thinking it was a shame that some of the older songs, many of which had never been heard in the States other than at live shows, weren't hits the first time around. "You know," McBride told the band, "all of these early songs are hits." Why they weren't hits the first time around in America made no sense to him. "I mean, it did make sense when you knew how they were approached," he concedes. "So I decided I wanted a shot at that."

The initially reluctant band finally relented when they started to see a buzz building as their audience became bigger and more loyal. "They'd just spent fourteen months on the road," McBride says, "and they were seeing themselves being marketed, and they could see the success beginning."

It was just like when Tremblay had booked them into the Café Deluxe years before, only now it was theater shows with full lighting and sound crews. "They could feel it beginning to happen," remembers McBride, "so they were like, 'Okay, okay. We'll just do it, but we have to do it this way.'" McBride said fine, and let them know which songs he wanted.

The live album, *Rock Spectacle*, was culled from recordings of two Barenaked Ladies shows from the *Born on a Pirate Ship* tour in the spring of 1996; one in Chicago, where the band was rapidly becoming known, and the other in Montreal, a largely French-speaking part of Canada, home but not home, as it were. And it's an odd thing that, for all of McBride's push to get the album out for the American market, the album's title, *Rock Spectacle*, is actually pronounced "Rock-Spek-TAK," the way a French-Canadian person might pronounce it.

Besides the fact that both Montreal and Chicago were early adopters of Barenaked Ladies' music, there wasn't really much discussion or strategy about where the shows would be recorded. "It wasn't really that well thought out," Jim concedes. "It was just, like, 'We'll just record these dates.' But it ended up doing really well. People really liked it. We all kind of thought, 'Well, I guess we are a good live band.' It sort of reaffirmed our belief in our live show."

"Audiences in Chicago have always been fun," Kevin said recently, "so I'm glad we recorded there. Montreal was nice, too, as I had lived there for a few years; I always enjoy being there. I don't think that either of the shows were particularly outstanding performances. I think the new Barenaked Ladies lineup has become a better unit since that time. I've always felt it was a bit soon to make a live record, at least artistically."

"What turned us around," Jim says, "was when we heard the recordings. Then we agreed to go ahead with the greatest hits, and it turned out to be the best thing for us at that time. It totally set up *Stunt* perfectly."

"*Rock Spectacle* was a great tool for the American market," Tremblay says. "People weren't overly familiar with the material; it emphasized the live side, which they're so good at; and it gave us something to start the groundswell before we released *Stunt*. It went gold [five hundred thousand copies sold] before *Stunt* was even mixed."

"*Born on a Pirate Ship* was all about *Rock Spectacle*," says McBride, "and *Rock Spectacle* was all about *Stunt*. Once we got it going, we knew it would be pretty unstoppable. It was just 'Build it, build it, build it, build it.' It's definitely worked, no argument."

McBride says Ed's quote about the buildup puts it best: "A myriad of small steps add up to something way, way bigger than the sum of the parts."

Now that McBride had his live recordings, he had to pick one song to be the single. The answer was clear in his mind. "Once they'd done it all and done a great live album, I just looked at 'Brian Wilson' and said, 'That's the one we have to go for.'"

But the record label was reluctant to go radio with a live track as a single. "Everyone was like, 'But you can't make a live song work on radio; it's not gonna work, it's not gonna work. We have to give them a studio version.' I said, 'I'm sorry, but I think you can.'" Still, to appease the naysayers, McBride sent Barenaked Ladies into a Seattle studio, with producer Gavin MacKillop, to create a brand-new studio version of "Brian Wilson," with the live version as the B side. But it was always McBride's intention to push the live version as the A side. "I didn't like the studio version one little bit," he confesses. "So I put that second. Everyone played the live version. It totally captured the energy and the emotion. Michael [Wojewoda] mixed it beautifully."

In fact, says McBride, the whole *Rock Spectacle* album was as finely and attentively crafted as any of BNL's studio recordings. "You know, the guys paid a lot of attention to it. Once they focused on it, they made a great live album. In essence, it was a greatest hits without being a greatest hits, and it allowed me to go back to what I considered to be great songs that hadn't seen the light of day in six months."

The never-ending tour now had yet another album to support. "We were going to go out there for eighteen months," McBride says. "We wanted to sell three albums, not one. Then when we did *Rock Spectacle*, we wanted to sell four albums. So the record company did catalog programs."

Normally, record companies will market an album week by week, based on how it sells. If something is selling well, they'll spend a lot of money to keep it going. Reprise Records, however, broke from tradition and began to view the entire Barenaked Ladies back catalog as a whole. That way, the company could better gauge the impact of promotions and touring. "What they did was take the sales of *Gordon, Maybe You Should Drive, Born on a Pirate Ship*, and *Rock Spectacle* and looked at it as a band driving album sales, as a career artist selling all albums," McBride says. "As such, all of the catalog got dragged along with whatever we were currently working. They worked it as an artist, versus just a current record. Now that really helps at the end of the day. Reprise probably spent more marketing on that band than they would have traditionally spent."

McBride gives kudos to Reprise for this bold shift in approach. "They bought into it, and they worked. They must have worked the 'Brian Wilson' single for nine, ten months—just worked it and worked it and worked it till we were only about a month or a month and a half away from delivering the first single from *Stunt*, 'One Week.' They just worked it through different radio formats, and it never looked like it was a hit single, but if you combine all three of the formats together over the nine-month curve and put them all into the traditional three-month curve, you'd have a hit single."

The perception inside the industry was that it never was a hit, but McBride is quick to point out that it was. "It was actually a really big single," he emphasizes, "but because we took it from Triple-A Modern Rock to Modern AC to Hot AC to Top Forty—of course, by the time you're four months in, you're losing the people who were there first. 'Brian Wilson' broke radio for Barenaked Ladies and sold a lot of *Rock Spectacle*," McBride says. "I smashed that curve [and now] you're looking at two million copies in six weeks. People were sitting there going, 'A live album that hasn't fallen out of the top ten in its first week? It's still selling a hundred thousand units a week!'"

Tremblay first realized that "Brian Wilson" was happening when he was in Montreal around Christmas. "I got a call from Bob Divney, who is head of modern-rock promotion at Reprise Records," Tremblay remembers. "He called to say that we'd gotten over twenty adds that week at modern rock. That was due to the fact that two weeks prior we'd been fighting and fighting to get a couple of the key influential modern-rock stations to add it. I think we got Q 101 in Chicago, the big modern-rock station, to add it, just two weeks before Christmas. After that, it just avalanched, and we basically had a hit at Top Forty."

The band even redirected some of their own financial

resources into keeping the "Brian Wilson" dream alive. BNL didn't get the tour support they'd ordinarily receive from Reprise, and they did free radio shows at no charge to the label's promotional budget. Reprise was impressed at the self-sacrifice, which inspired the label to keep up the fight. "They just took a different view of it because we were willing to go out there and work and we weren't drawing tour support, and I didn't want to draw tour support," McBride says. "I'd do enough big shows to zap out the small shows. I didn't bill them for radio shows, because I wanted all of the money to go toward marketing."

So the guys weren't making anything at all for the shows? "They sort of broke even," McBride says. "But it built a career and got them out of the hole. They were a royalty-positive band even before *Stunt* came out in both publishing and the record-royalty side. I have to give the guys credit. They trusted. I knew intuitively where we were going. They couldn't come up with a good argument except that they didn't want to do it, so I was like, 'Give me one good reason, please,' and they couldn't give me a good reason. So there you go."

The band was put on a meager salary, a kind of living wage. It was more like an allowance. Terry McBride was Dad. And their weekly "chores" were to play countless promotional radio shows for free. "It wasn't all that much, and they knew they had to work," McBride comments. "They knew they couldn't stop until I was ready to have them stop. Now they've come to the rationalization it will never really stop, but at least now they'll have one out of every three months off."

McBride is quick to state that he doesn't hold the key to all the wisdom in the industry. "I don't know everything yet, either," he confesses. "I like learning every single day. There's always going to be someone who does a concept that I find very interesting, so I'm always looking at what everyone else is doing. When I see something work, I'm always trying to find out why."

18

Stunts
Scarborough, 1998

Stunt was the product of a concerted effort by Nettwerk management to revamp Barenaked Ladies' "men-in-short-pants" image. "The goal," says art director John Rummen, who designed the *Stunt* cover, "was to promote the Ladies as serious contenders in the world of pop music, USA."

When Rummen began to conceptualize various themes and images for the new album, the band hadn't even settled on a name for it yet, so they let the designer run wild with his imagination. McBride had wanted a multipurpose motif, one that could be used for more than just the front of *Stunt*. One that would establish a brand identity around Barenaked Ladies, and which would tie in to all of their merchandising and staging as well. "McBride not only wanted an album cover," says Rummen, "but something that they could leverage for marketing purposes."

When the band did eventually arrive at the album title, Rummen had to define, for himself, the meaning of the word *stunt*. "Bravely doing something stupid" was what he decided. "I wasn't too keen on doing something obvious like a motorcycle through flames or even resorting to a nostalgic image of children doing some kind of stunt, because it's too obvious and only promotes the comedic side of the band." So it wasn't just a matter of defining *Stunt*, it was a matter of defining who and what the Barenaked Ladies were.

"To me," Rummen offers, "the Ladies' music is like good comedy: Both have fun, shiny surfaces but are rooted in something tragic or dark. There's something about irony that keeps us laughing on the inside." Due to the complexity of where the band was in their career, Rummen opted for a more illustration-based concept, as opposed to one that employed basic typography or mere photography. The result was a collaged character, a little cutup he called "Stunty." "We're not sure if he's performing a stunt or if someone has pulled a stunt on him," Rummen notes, "but we do know that he's all tied up and will have to do some tricky maneuvering to use his scissors to cut himself out."

During their project meetings, the guys spoke constantly of the concept of rebirth, a notion that Rummen represented in the cocoon of string around the stunt guy. Because of his belief that Barenaked Ladies' records are less likely to be taken back to used-record stores, Rummen wanted to keep the design timeless: "I see the Ladies' records as classics in that they're in the pile everyone hangs on to," he says. "With this in mind, I chose to root the illustration in a sort of dadaist collage—a style that won't go out of fashion tomorrow."

In this case, it would seem, everyone was a winner. Management got their serious-funny image. Marketing got a tool to use for promotion. The live show–set decorators had a theme. Stunty found his way onto T-shirts, hats, and even starred in a short animation that was played before the live show. And Rummen got a Juno Award (Canadian Grammy) nomination for Best Album Design.

While the band had more or less managed to get their career back on course and headed down the road toward revamping their image, they weren't so sure they were ready for the stunt they were about to pull off. In the months leading up to the initial recording sessions for *Stunt,* Ed says that he has no idea how they even managed to function as a band at all. "I can't speak for everybody," he admits, "but I think I'd lost touch with the joy and the reason of it all. And I didn't really find that again until making *Stunt,* when I thought, 'This is good, and we're great at it and we need to realize that and celebrate that and work for that.'

"But," he points out, "it's honestly difficult for me to remember how that stuff felt because it seems like another life." In that disconnected other life, Ed had been trying to get a read on just what the hell was going on with Steve, who was trying to figure out what was going on with Ed, who was talking to Tyler, who had been talking to Jim. Everybody was talking, but no one was listening. In going after the tiny day-to-day issues in a kind of broken telephone circle, they weren't going to the heart of their bigger problems. As Ed put it, everybody was dancing around everybody else. Finally, Ed realized, the dancing had to stop. If not, the music would stop, and then no one would be dancing, in or outside the group.

A kind of intervention was arranged at Scarborough's Phase One Studios, so close to where it all began. The five band members all went off to a small, isolated studio room to let the dancing end and the honesty begin. The meeting began with Ed's assertion "This is just so fucked," so you can pretty much imagine what went down. In fact, *meeting* might just be the best way to put it. It appeared that, after a gazillion meet-'n'-greet sessions with countless fans, radio programmers, promoters and their dogs in Canada, Europe, and the USA, the only people left to meet were themselves.

While Ed was one of the first to voice his concerns, he doesn't see his call to action as being the product of intelligent reasoning or any deep psychological insight. He'd just reached his emotional breaking point. "I don't think I was thinking [puts on calm analytical voice], 'Now I see a sociological problem here.' I was just reacting through sheer frustration."

And as Ed admits, for him to *react at all* was a new thing for him at the time. "I'm not overly analytical," he confides. "And over the years, I've come to realize that it's a defense mechanism on my part. It's not like I realize it at the time; it just happens. If stuff is bugging me, it just goes away, and I never get back to it or deal with it consciously." But that would all change on that January morning in 1998. It was time to deal with something they'd all been rather good at avoiding: one another. It was now or never. "We kind of sat down in an empty studio, and I said that things were getting really exciting, you know," says Ed, setting the scene. "*Rock Spectacle* had just gone gold in the U.S., and everybody was really hyped about the new record. So finally I just said, 'Okay, this is just so fucked. This next record could be huge and we are in no way prepared for it to be huge.'"

Then there was the wanton opening of emotional wounds and a general letting of bad blood all around. Flowing freely in every direction. For Ed had not only stated his feelings, he'd invited the others to air their own grievances in return. "Look, you know, this is what I think," he'd begun. "This bugs me and I think this bugs you—I don't know. But we have a chance here, a chance that this album could be quite successful, and I think we gotta drop the crap. We've got five guys going through the same thing, who aren't using each other to get through it, you know?" Ed says of that time, "I think we just tried to clear the air and get some support from each other. And I think it put us in a really good place for *Stunt* to come out. We started actually hanging out together, when we were on the road again, having dinner together, going to movies and stuff. I think, to a large degree, we realized why we were doing it in the first place—all over again."

And while each band member continues to maintain his own distinct private life, the clearing of the air has been a constant process within the group ever since. In Ed's opinion, the alternative to this rigorous honesty would be the group's implosion from the weight of its own internalized anger. "So I'm really glad we do it," Ed maintains. "We just keep each other in check and just deal with shit as it comes up rather than letting it slide and fester. It's a lot of work—it's like Group Therapy 101." So began the road to number one, the road to *Stunt*.

Released on July 7, 1998, *Stunt*'s life began in rehearsals shortly after the air-clearing at Phase One. The album was produced by Susan Rogers and David Leonard, but not together as such. While they share coproducer status on the record, as do Barenaked Ladies, the two producers didn't actually work together side by side during the recording process. Like so many great inventions, their tag-team arrangement was born out of necessity. Rogers, approached by the band in December 1997, was eager to accept the job but had to pass, due to a prior commitment. She just didn't have time to squeeze in another full album production, certainly not on the timetable that they proposed. Politely declining, she explained the situation to the guys, adding that if they needed any help, she did in fact have a tiny three-week window of availability to provide any preproduction or consultation. The Ladies really wanted to work with her, so a plan was drawn up wherein Rogers would attempt to complete basic tracking, lead vocals, and whatever overdubs they could muster over the course of twenty-one action-packed days. At that point, Leonard would finish the job, including the final mix. So the *Stunt* tag team was set.

The process began in earnest when Rogers flew up to sunny Scarborough for four short days of preproduction, which is basically where the band and producer familiarize themselves with the songs and their various arrangements. This is often a time when a midtempo rock song becomes a full-blown funk rocker, or a ballad can suddenly adopt a reggae groove. Verses are cut out, choruses are altered, and keys are changed, all in the name of having some vague idea of where the album is going to go.

Having familiarized herself with an advance demo cassette of Steven and Ed's new songs, Rogers liberally suggested minor rhythm, tempo, arrangement, or instrumentation changes, and

171

the band quickly ran through those changes. Her suggestions ranged from trimming a chorus on Page's "Call and Answer" to recasting his "I'll Be That Girl" with a decidedly surf-rock rhythm. And Ed's "Leave" got a little bit more country, while "Light Up My Room" took a more soulful turn.

"Susan Rogers really encouraged me to try more fills and stuff," says Tyler. "She was the first [producer of Barenaked Ladies] ever to say to me, 'Just because it's an Ed song, you don't have to automatically use brushes [on the snare drum].' She said, 'Let's put some tom fills here and there, and play with it.' Like on 'Leave,' that was a song that had hung around since *Maybe You Should Drive* days; it changed a lot by the time it got on *Stunt*. And songs like 'Alcohol,' I tried adding more fills. Then, on 'She's on Time,' I was thinking of the Beach Boys, which was different."

Rogers asked the powerhouse drummer to simplify some of his parts, or just stay locked on one steady groove to provide a simpler frame for the singer and his words. And the words, as it turns out, are a very big deal for Rogers. "It's very important in communicating a song," Rogers explains, "that the music provide the subtext for what the singer is trying to say. What can you do, musically, that would support the emotion of what this singer is trying to get across? What is the gist of the song's message?"

For Tyler, Rogers's message of emotional support was very important. Her approach went a long way toward healing some of the wounds he'd encountered in Vancouver years earlier. "Susan was really ready to explore the pop-music songbook and just go for stuff," says Tyler, "whereas, I think Ben Mink and Marc Ramaer, on *Maybe You Should Drive*, saw the whole band as an obstacle; they had a way of working between them that was more suited to solo artists."

Preproduction under their belts, band and producer packed their suitcases, fastened their seat belts, and flew to Austin, Texas. In Texas, Barenaked Ladies began tracking the album, deep in the heart of Arlyn Studios. Arlyn is owned by legendary country star, Farm Aid founder, and celebrated former tax evader Willie Nelson. While the red-haired stranger does not appear on *Stunt*, Steven and Ed did, in fact, record many of their lead vocals with the very microphone favored by Willie himself. "If it's good enough for Willie," figures Rogers, "it was good enough for us."

Just to indulge in a little tangent: The Willie Nelson Connection is more prevalent than you might think. For instance, late in 2000, Barenaked Ladies were invited to play at Farm Aid. And of course, nerds like me will like to point out that both Willie and Barenaked Ladies have written songs called "Crazy." Willie's "Crazy" was a hit for Patsy Cline. Barenaked Ladies' second album was produced by Ben Mink, a member of k. d. lang's band the Re-clines, named in honor of k. d.'s obsession with Patsy Cline. Barenaked Ladies' security person, Joe Self, is an Austin native who's worked with Willie Nelson. Willie sang, "You were always on my mind," while Barenaked Ladies later sang, "You were the last thing on my mind" in a part of their song "Tonight Is the Night I Fell Asleep at the Wheel" from their September 2000 album release, *Maroon*. The comparisons are eerie, don't you think? Hey, wait a minute, Susan Rogers once worked with the artist once again known as Prince, whose full name was originally Prince Rogers Nelson. Man, this is getting crazy.

Things were looking good for Barenaked Ladies as they moved their traveling circus down to Austin. Yet, these sharp-dressed men-who-would-be-Ladies were well aware of the high expectations placed on their first studio album in four years. "I think my mood was terror as we went into the studio," Steven announced in the official Reprise Records bio for *Stunt*. "I was so scared writing these songs. The first couple that I wrote came out fairly easily and quickly, songs like 'In the Car,' and 'It's All Been Done.' Then Ed and I started to get together at my house, every day for a couple weeks. For the first couple of days, we'd just sit and stare at each other for hours. But once the songs started coming out, I was really happy with them."

When *Rock Spectacle* went gold in the United States (it later went platinum), Barenaked Ladies' American audience multiplied overnight. That, as record executives like to say, "warmed the bed" for *Stunt*.

According to Rogers, although that career bed may have been warming up, the band didn't sweat it while laying down the bed tracks. On the contrary, she credits the Ladies' abundant recording experience for the album's relaxed but focused confidence. "The thing about this record," Rogers says, "is that it was their fourth studio album. When a band first gets signed, they have to learn how to be recording musicians, how to play to tape. It can take several albums to really learn that. I can't emphasize enough how marvelous it was to work with guys who'd reached that level of feeling so comfortable in the studio that it became a playground to them. It was a lot of fun."

For the most part, Rogers captured the basic tracks live-off-the-floor with all the musicians out in the room together just as they'd done on the *Born on a Pirate Ship* sessions. The one change was that the band was now decidedly more electrified, and therefore, louder. "If it was kind of a loud song," Rogers recalls, "we'd go ahead and have the singer out in the room with the drums and just give him a talkback mic to sing into. Tyler's such a loud drummer that we didn't worry about the guide vocal bleeding into the drums."

Bleeding? Into the drums? Sounds messy, doesn't it? But unless you're Iggy Pop or Marilyn Manson, bleeding is not as messy as it sounds. In fact, it's nothing more than a messy sound mix, and it has no relation to precious, or potentially biohazardous, body fluids. It's an audio term used when one microphone, aimed at an acoustic guitar, for instance, picks up the sound of an instrument that it's not designated to pick up. Often, to control this bleeding, a player will be put into another room, known as an "iso booth," which is a specially built box not unlike the soundproof booths employed by various game shows.

According to Rogers, Barenaked Ladies are all incredibly good musicians. "Those guys are such excellent players," declares the proud producer. "There was never a problem with execution. When the players are that good, you can throw out idea after idea and it's almost like tossing a ball to a crowd. One guy will catch it and pass it to the next guy and so on."

The precious and fluidly bawdy bass work of Jim Creeggan is at the core of much of Barenaked Ladies' sound. This is pretty impressive, considering that the lanky redhead's weapon of choice is an electrified double bass, an instrument not usually associated with precision. *Stunt*'s other tag-team producer, David Leonard, who ultimately provided the final mix on the record, says that Jim's dedication to "good tone" made the mixing process a lot easier. "Jim's double bass sound is so full," Leonard says, "with none of the usual clacky characteristics that you find in a lot of double-bass players."

Rogers seconds that emotion. "Jim is something else," she adds. "He knows the bass so well, but perhaps more importantly, he also knows what the song needs [in terms of] bass. He's one of those guys who's great in a supporting role; he can hear the track and know right where he fits in. That's invaluable in the studio and in a band." And Rogers maintains that a good example of Jim's musicality was afforded by his string-bass contributions to the recordings of "When You Dream" and "Call and Answer." "Jim would take a cassette of the songs into the next room," Rogers remembers, "then come back with four or five parts written. We just set him up, and he'd lay down track after track after track of these things."

"Some Fantastic" also came together in the studio. Well actually, it came together just outside the studio, in the parking lot. "Ed had an idea for wanting to do it with a Brazilian rhythm," recalls Rogers. "We started by sending Ed and Tyler out into the parking lot with these snare drums around their necks to play them. It goes without saying that a snare drum is a really loud instrument, but you notice it even more when it's outdoors because the sound really travels. So we had to put a couple of towels over each snare, which actually made them sound better. They played the whole song, five minutes or something, until the neighbors complained. Then we brought them back into the studio and added the other instrumentation."

And speaking of waking up the neighbors, the boisterous choruses, crunchy guitars, and crashing drums of "One Week" not only woke up America when it blasted out of their clock radios in the morning, but it also gave a little jolt to longtime fans of Barenaked Ladies. Rogers says that the band's demo version of "One Week" was actually more of an acoustic affair. "It was played on acoustic guitar, with a small drum sound. It was really appealing that way," says the producer. "The most appealing thing about it, of course, was the rhyme. It's the kind of thing you want to memorize; they're just fun words to say."

Apparently, the band and Rogers had agreed to keep "One Week" as a simple, natural, acoustic guitar–based song, to accentuate the lyrics. So what happened? Evidently, a series of small steps, from tracking to mixing, inched the song toward its final, rocking outcome. "After we had cut the basic track and started treating it," says Rogers, "we wanted to have just a bit of electric guitar here and there. Kevin and Ed both came up with some great electric-guitar hooks, and we put on a few different tracks just to incorporate all of that. Then I had an idea that I wanted a very big sound coming from a very small sound source. Tim Blunt, one of their guitar techs, had one of those little tiny Marshall amps, about four or five inches high, so we set that on a chair, put an SM57 in front of it, and Ed plugged in his guitar and just played. The idea was to sound as if it was a guy in his room; it could be a guy who couldn't actually play, playing along with the record. We had a few of those little licks, very tiny but very, very distorted, on there. Mainly, they were just decorative."

Steven loves "One Week" because it's so radically different for Barenaked Ladies on record, but he points out that it's an approach common to their live shows. Ed agrees, although it was hard work to make it sound so easy. "I never thought I'd finish that song," Ed said at the time. "As soon as I started I was afraid to write it. Hip-hop and rapping and freestyling have been a part of what we do as a live band since the beginning, and we're big fans of that kind of music. But it's never really reared its head on any of our records, although it's a huge part of what we do live."

During an online chat on Yahoo, Steven was asked, by a user named Fiznarp, just what the heck was the meaning of "Chickity China the Chinese Chicken?" "That's a reference to Chickity Chaco the Chocolate Chicken, as said by Busta Rhymes in the [A] Tribe Called Quest song 'Scenario,'" Steven revealed to a presumably relieved Fiznarp. "But it's also, apparently, a reference to some chickens in Hong Kong [that] were contaminated and had to be killed."

Due to the compressed schedule and an overall lack of pre-production time, some songs could only be developed and realized during the recording sessions. One case in point is Steven's paean to his young son's slumber, "When You Dream." The soundscape that adorns the song began in the studio with a series of loops made from Kevin's collection of digital samples, which includes the sounds of air conditioners and various motor noises. Steven also added some of his own samples to the mix, culled from an assortment of vintage music boxes. Once this sonic tableau was complete, Steven took his acoustic guitar out and sang, folk style, against it.

But for the record, Kevin still has what he calls bittersweet memories concerning the version of "When You Dream" chosen for the record. No, he doesn't so much mind the *Stunt* version, which is lovely in its own right. He just remembers what might have been. "I was really into making that into a dreamscape," Kevin said a year later, "and maybe not even have any tonal reference other than the vocal.

"There's a version of it that I liked better," Kevin continues, "a board mix of it, kicking around somewhere, just Steve's vocals, and I had the air conditioner–sample loop and all the cycles of the music boxes and the reverse guitar and stuff. Susan Rogers was happy with it, Steven liked it, and I liked it."

Board mixes, often known as "scratch" or "pencil" mixes, are quickly performed mixes that give a brief idea of just how many different sounds are on the twenty-four-track (typically) tape. This mix can be taken home for a time so that everyone can strategize about which sounds they would like to hear on the final mix.

However, Kevin's favored dreamscape version was deemed a little too avant-garde by his producers and band mates, and was therefore voted off the island, er, record. "I was knocked down again by the others," adds Kevin wistfully, "so we put an acoustic guitar on it. There was a bit of split of opinion on that song. We had two producers, and one was willing to play that way, and the other one wasn't, you know. I had to go for a long walk that day, when that guitar was added. But when you look back, you know, hey, it's still a beautiful song."

Of course, a second party in the band's writing process is Steven's English counterpart, Stephen Duffy. Duffy and Steven cowrote three songs on *Stunt:* "I'll Be That Girl," "Alcohol," and "Call and Answer." "I had a rather dreary idea called 'Angela,'" Duffy recalls. "In a second it was a song called 'Alcohol' that knew where it was going. I love 'If I Had a Gun' [Author's note: I believe Duffy is referring to "I'll Be That Girl"] and 'Call and Answer' as well. The last two we started in Chelsea one afternoon in the summer of '96."

Duffy says that there is a like-mindedness, or kindred spirit, in Steven that makes their collaborations enjoyable to both writers. "I think we write songs in the same way," says Duffy. "We aim for simplicity and clarity, although you wouldn't know that from some of the lyrics. We both listened to the first solo McCartney album too much as kids and worshipped Leonard Cohen too much as adults. We have the same musical goals as writers; we like the same records in general."

178

Duffy recalls that a song called "The Girl on Christopher Street," the very first song that the two wrote together, was not considered for Barenaked Ladies' set. "It wasn't very good, apparently," admits Duffy hesitantly. "But then we wrote 'Alternative Girlfriend,' 'Trust Me,' 'The Wrong Man Was Convicted,' 'Everything Old Is New Again,' 'Jane,' and 'I Live with It Every Day.' That was October, November, maybe even a bit of December '93. At times I felt like I'd never leave. Toronto does feel like a second home because of it."

And of the all the songs they've written together, does Duffy have a favorite? "I love 'Jane,'" Duffy admits to me online, "mainly because of the line 'Jane doesn't think a man could ever be faithful.' It was also the first great song we wrote." And of the Barenaked Ladies songs that he didn't have a hand in, does Duffy favor one in particular? "'In the Car,'" he responds, but jokingly adds, "although I'm pretty sure I did write it (ho, ho)."

Most suprisingly, for Duffy anyway, was just how much the English art-pop maven stood to learn from a precocious Canadian upstart by the name of Steven Page. "He's influenced me in many ways," admits Duffy of Steven. "I'm probably more ambitious now than I was over the last few years. I share songs with people now, rather than keeping them all for myself. I'm not as inward-looking as I was before."

Of course, having their songs recorded and played in concert by Barenaked Ladies was a big help in sharing them with the millions of people Duffy might not have otherwise reached from his niche in the U.K. underground. The "bed-sit angst" of Leonard Cohen's sad-young-man style is a far cry from McCartney's silly love songs. Yet remarkably, the pair manage to take their personal maelstrom and make it mainstream. Once again, Duffy thanks Steven for turning potential obscurity into pop sensibility: "He makes songs that mean nothing to anyone but me speak to others," says Duffy of Steven. Then he adds, "It's rather astonishing for an eccentric old English cult artiste to hear tens of thousands of North Americans bellowing his poesy."

Is Stephen "Tin Tin" Duffy's status as an English cult artiste ever threatened by his association with a dreadful American Top-40 band such as the multiplatinum Barenaked Ladies? While certain associates have raised an eyebrow over his street cred–threatening partnership, Duffy maintains that attending just a single BNL concert is usually all it takes to get the skeptics to come around to his way of seeing things. "People are surprised that I work with BNL," says Duffy. "But then you only need to see one show to be won over and understand. They are more outside than the outsiders. And they've taken the most difficult route to success, going out and entertaining people every night for over eight years. I've learned a lot from them. Like you don't make it by sitting around in your bedroom being fey. Although I tried my very best."

Yes, "the Two Steves" certainly do have a way with words. And some of the words they've gotten away with defy the predictable pop-song fodder. Steven says that "I'll Be That Girl," was "deceptively difficult to write." "I'd written it and thought I was finished, but when we went to record it, I realized, 'This doesn't make any sense!' Saying what you want to say in a three-minute pop song is really difficult sometimes, but I love the challenge. And I love songs that have lyrics that surprise people, especially in a song like that—so poppy and melodious. Hinting at things like autoerotic asphyxiation and suicide are pretty unexpected in that kind of music."

In *Launch*, a CD-ROM magazine, Steven discusses the latter subject, and his approach in general, with executive editor Dave DiMartino. "Harry Nilsson was a big hero, Leonard Cohen—these are writers with a great breadth of subject matter. Humor and darkness. Wordplay. A lot of what they do is about language," Steven offers. DiMartino then zeroes in on "I'll Be That Girl," and Steven is forthcoming on the subject. "I wanted to write a song about desperation and how a man would do anything to get the gratification that he thought he wanted, deserved, needed," Steven told *Launch*. "And if that meant hurting himself or inducing others to hurt themselves, that's what he would do. It's kind of a French movie in three minutes."

While admitting that he hadn't tried autoerotic asphyxiation himself, Steven does admit to loving the fact that "people will go to any extreme to make themselves feel . . . good? strongly?— even for a brief period of time, and risk either death or humiliation to do it. I think the worst thing would be hanging and to still be alive. Can you imagine someone walking in, and you're naked, genitals in hand?"

In the same *Launch* feature, Ed discusses some of his own lyrical directions on *Stunt*, particularly on the Grammy-nominated single, "One Week." "'One Week' is pretty indicative of what we do live all the time," Ed told DiMartino. "We will always just make up songs, improvise music, and most of the time it's freestyle rap stuff. That's really fun music to improvise. The band lays down a groove, and we just lay down a rap on top of it. It's never reared its ugly head on a record before, though. When we were working on this, I had this idea. I was going for horribly complex, well-crafted shit about a relationship. Steven said, just go home and freestyle, and keep the good stuff. I tried to write it for three months, and then I wrote it in five minutes."

Freestyling, as if I need to explain, is a cornerstone of modern music, not only in rap and Jamaican dancehall music, but in the songwriting process of artists as diverse as Paul McCartney, David Byrne, and Anthony Kiedis from Red Hot Chili Peppers. McCartney, as it is widely told in songwriting circles, wrote the first set of lyrics for his song "Yesterday" as a gibberish rhyme about scrambled eggs. He later replaced the lyrics, but artists like Byrne and Kiedis have been known to leave the initial stream-of-consciousness words in the final song.

Try this at home, take a melody—either one that you've come up with or the melody of your favorite song or commercial jingle. If you have a tape recorder lying about, record yourself singing that melody with your own new words, words that you make up on the spot. Try not to think about whether the words make any sense; in fact, try not to think at all. Just pretend that you're a really great songwriter and that anything that comes out of your mouth, save for excessive amounts of saliva, is great art. Blurt it out. Anything you say is the right thing to say. Do this for a while until you get tired or the tape runs out. Then rewind the tape. Ten to one, you'll have at least three or four lines, sometimes more, out of the many you blurt out, that are actually kind of cool. Try it. Go on.

Ed and Steven, after a few years of uncertainty, really got back together when writing some of the songs on *Stunt*, a fact that was emphasized in the record company's band bio, issued to announce the release of the new album. "Steven and I write so well together," Ed declares. "When I get a song started, I always know that, no matter what happens, together we can finish it and we'll have a great song. A lot of the time—because we've been working together so long and we've known each other for twice as long as that—we know right away where the other person is going. I certainly hear a confidence in our writing and playing on this album, but I think that stems from natural growth. I think we're all growing naturally, as writers and musicians." "It took me awhile to get used to it [*Stunt*], but I love it," Steven adds. "It's our most consistently good record. It has the least amount of what I like to call 'fast-forward songs.' In fact, I don't think this album has any."

One key to understanding Ed's songwriting is in the work of the enigmatic so-called country artist Lyle Lovett. When I accompanied the band on the *Stunt* tour, Ed told me to race out and get Lovett's album *Joshua Judges Ruth*. And I did. The stoic, often melancholy, yet incredibly sardonic lyrics and confessional tone of Lovett's music has clearly sent a message to Ed that can be heard in some of his songs for *Stunt*, including "Light Up My Room," "Told You So," and "Leave." On "Leave," Ed returns to one particularly grave subject matter: the death of his older brother, Doug.

On "Leave," Ed was not merely discussing the loss, he was discussing a side effect of the tragedy not often explored in song.

The sort of haunting that often bears down so hard on the living family members that it threatens the quality of their lives. One person dies, yet no one is really living anymore. Some become resentful or angry toward the ghost and demand that it step aside in the name of life itself. "How can I miss you," the saying goes, "if you won't go away?" Ed, though he may never "get over" it, felt it was definitely time to "get on with it" and rejoin the living.

The album had now reached the (drumroll, please) final-mix stage. Having had just enough time to complete all the band tracks and most of the lead vocals, Rogers handed off the tapes to Leonard, who beefed up the tracks during a whirlwind two-week period at Phase One in Scarborough. Rogers points to Leonard's layering expertise, in particular his knowledge of what she refers to as "heavy, distorted electric guitar" sounds, for the songs final heaviosity. "My main contribution," Leonard determines, "was to put more noise and grit into the tracks and to mix it with that edge. There's a lot of levity in their music, so I thought adding a bit of angst to the tones would be a good combination to give it some bite."

Back at Phase One, Leonard led the band through the overdubs of what he calls the "colors and sprinkles." These were things like additional background and harmony vocals, a whole lot of percussion, assorted synthesizers, and, of course, all of those big electric guitars. "Ed did all the loud guitars on the choruses," Leonard remembers. "I asked him to play things that were a little more aggressive than what was already on the tracks. That made the choruses hit louder and have more dynamics. We experimented quite a lot. I had him detune the guitar, which enabled me to put the guitars under, or over, the track in a mix. To Ed's credit, he figured out the voicings in all these weird tunings."

The final stage in the album's evolution began when Leonard took the tapes to mix at East Iris Studios in Nashville. There he did a few cool things to the final sound, like process the lead vocals on "One Week" through an amplifier designed for guitars, thus making them sound louder than they are. After he'd finish mixing a song, Leonard would listen to a DAT tape of it, patched through the radio of his truck.

In the following months, all Leonard had to do to hear the band was turn on the real radio. With their first number-one hit single, first platinum album, and their first Grammy nomination, 1998 was a year of firsts for Barenaked Ladies.

Stuntman

During the recording of *Stunt* in Austin, Kevin's health began, as he puts it, "a rapid demise." At first, his symptoms seemed relatively innocuous: a cough that didn't go away, general weight loss, and loss of appetite. But as his symptoms increased and his health deteriorated, he started to realize that something much worse was happening to him. "Eventually," he recalls, he developed "bad pains due to an enlarged spleen, night sweats, ghostly pale skin, and bloody noses."

Craig Finley (a.k.a. "Fin"), with the intuitive powers of both a tour manager and a den mother, knew that Kevin would have to fly home ASAP to have a doctor check him out. The band, committed to a year of impending tour dates, reluctantly but realistically kicked around contingency plans in the event that Kevin would have to miss a few shows. Kevin, as it turned out, would definitely have to miss a few shows: He had leukemia.

And so, in what was to be the biggest year for Kevin and the entire Barenaked Ladies organization, he would be benched indefinitely. In fact, if he didn't get a stem-cell transplant—and soon—it would be a permanent situation. The *Penguin English Dictionary* defines *stunt* as a "remarkable feat of physical skill entailing danger." That pretty much summed up the coming year in the life of Kevin Hearn.

Was he scared? Was he bitter? Probably. But mostly, Kevin was pissed off at having to sit out the victory lap that what was rightfully his. It was, he tells me, "a fucking drag!"

What follows is his own description of just how he felt: "How about . . . the girl of your dreams approaches you, tells you she loves you, then kicks you so hard in the nuts that you can't get up for a week. In the meantime, she models lingerie for you."

The *Penguin English Dictionary* defines *stuntman* as "a person paid to perform dangerous acrobatic tricks, feats of strength, etc., esp. as stand-in for a cinema actor." Enter the stuntman Chris Brown. Not merely an arbitrary sideman, Chris had been there for many of the major events in BNL history. He'd played on their debut album, *Gordon,* and had played some parts on *Born on a Pirate Ship* after Andy left. And, of course, he'd been one-third of Tyler Stewart's one-off project, *Don't Talk Dance,* along with guitarist Gordie Johnson.

"He was a natural first choice," states Jim. "I think Ed really wanted him to be in the band because of his attachment and relationship to the history of the band. Ed was really set on getting him." Jim, who'd formed a friendship with Chris while living in New York, wasn't sure if having a friend come into the band was going to work out. "I knew he would have to sacrifice his own shit," says Jim.

Chris and band mate Kate Fenner, both formerly of Toronto's Bourbon Tabernacle Choir (referenced, as we now know, in the Suburban Tabernacle Choir on *Gordon*'s credits) were now living in New York, playing and recording their own quite excellent songs. Having just released their independent CD *Other People's Heavens,* the pair were on the road in Edmonton when Chris got the fateful phone call from Tyler.

"Tyler had actually phoned my family in Toronto," remembers Chris, "because he was so anxious to get in touch with me. Then we continued the tour, and when I was in Massachusetts, where we played with Ani [DiFranco], I called them back and we had this long talk. I said I wanted to conference and talk to everybody and tell them what I was after if I was going to do it, because I wanted very straight terms, and I wanted to be sure that the lines of communication were very open and that my relationship with them was very defined."

Chris was very aware that Barenaked Ladies' breakout tour would be all-consuming and that this would require a serious commitment to the band. So he and the band all agreed, and everyone in Barenaked Ladies' camp bent over backward to accommodate his minor conditions. But at the end of the day, Chris says it was compassion more than compensation that influenced his decision to put his own career virtually on hold for Kevin. "I just kind of did it," recalls Chris. "When the guys first asked me, Kevin's situation was pretty serious, so I felt a bit petty talking about my own shit. I was like, 'I'll do anything for you, fill in or anything, but I can't do that.' Then I just kind of figured it out.

"It was very delicate in terms of Kevin. He's the keyboard player in that band. I made sure everybody knew I was just pinch-hitting for him, for a number of reasons, not the least of which [was] it's not really fair to Kevin to be struck by this illness and then to have to question his position in the band. That was just never really a question." So rather than try to replicate every single nuance and synthesizer patch that Hearn had played on *Stunt*, Chris chose to translate the spirit of the parts into his own setup of Hammond organ and Hohner Clavinet.

"Well," admits Chris, "I couldn't play what Kevin plays. He's a really strong personality with these really wild clips. He's got a distinctive thing. The fortunate thing was that I wasn't a stranger to them. They knew what I did, and they were hiring me for this, and they allowed me to bring an organ, which is what I feel at home on." Chris, the band, and the audience were more than satisfied with his sonic contributions, dotted with various musical detours, to Barenaked Ladies' live set. "I felt I had something to offer," says the keyboardist, "and that I could play inside the music."

Fans on the *Stunt* tour also noticed, and frequently thanked him for, the presence of Hugo, the little bald guy from Kevin's

186

keyboard setup, who represented Kevin from atop Chris's Hammond organ. Hugo just happened to be around during rehearsals for the tour, so why not bring him along? "It just made sense," declares Chris in hindsight. "Why wouldn't we? He's always there. A lot of people asked about him in interviews, but the real fans knew exactly what it was, and what it meant."

Much later in the year, when the recovering Kevin was just well enough to play a reduced role in some of the shows, Chris says it was even more fun to share the keyboard duties.

"There were a few shows in England," recalls Chris, "a couple in New York, a couple just down the road down south. And we did *Saturday Night Live* together like that."

While joining the Ladies' tour may have been his own personal sacrifice, taking time away from his own music, his actions had a direct impact on his band mate Fenner. "It was harder for her because I was the one who was busy," remarks Chris, "but it wasn't that I took the job as a great opportunity. I took it because I really felt a sense of duty. It did end up being a real extraordinary year for us actually, but it was definitely hard for the two of us to balance that out."

As a result, during the *Stunt* year, Chris and Kate only played a few shows in New York City, basically whenever the Barenaked Ladies tour was on a break. And so it was a case of hitting two birds with one stone when they opened for Barenaked Ladies at a few shows. Chris says that, while the music that he and Fenner make is sometimes at odds with the Barenaked Ladies audience's taste, they nonetheless made a host of new friends by opening these shows.

"Their audience," says Chris of BNL's loyal fan base, "is definitely more response-based, whereas some of our music is a bit of a slow burn. But it was challenging, and in the end, it worked great. We have a big mailing list from down south now, which is really cool. It was really good and it was kind of fun for me being on the road to just sound check, gig, sound check, gig every night. Fill it all up with music."

And the steady paycheck didn't hurt when it came time to record Kate and Chris's second CD, *Geronimo*. "For sure," Chris concurs, adding that it was educational to be "experiencing the industry at that level, safe within the confines of people you trust. You're there with a very defined reason and purpose. It allowed me to view that whole world from a kind of safe place. Initially, I was worried that the bigness they're involved in might consume or abrogate my smallness. But it wasn't like that. In fact, it was quite the opposite. The crew and everybody were like real homeboys, very straight up. That's the kind of environment I want to be involved in, all the time. It was very comfortable."

In fact, the *Stunt* tour keyboardist singled out one man as a kind of role model and teacher. By the time he left the school bus, he'd learned much from Fin, the tour professor. "Fin's a remarkable human being," declares Chris of the road scholar. "His level of commitment and self-discipline is an intense spiritual education to hang out with. He's so focused and committed. I really took cues from him this whole year. He really inspired me to work hard on my shit."

Having played a role in the early career of the band, Chris has seen BNL handle Canadian superstar status and the inevitable domestic backlash. As such, he's uniquely equipped to speculate about the aftereffects of the victorious *Stunt* tour into which he was drafted. So-called overnight success, he feels, isn't likely to spoil them. Not this time around, anyway. "I guess because they've already gone up and down a couple of times, they're more acclimatized to the weather. I'd say that they approach things with less drama but with an equal amount of enthusiasm, if not more so, because when that happens you also realize how blessed you are to be involved in something that maybe as a kid you just dreamed about doing. There's that sense of real joy, which is definitely there. I'd say that their appreciation of that joy has probably increased. It may be a little easier for them this time around."

Chris, however, suspects that there may be other things in the personal lives of Barenaked Ladies that are much harder now. World tours, for instance, when three of the guys have at least one young child, can't be easy. "There's the prospect of being farther away, being busier," proposes Chris, "and having a world market to look at rather than just the country. And putting your personal stuff on hold because the seeming momentum of the whole machine is much bigger than any one person."

A year later, Kevin was out on the road again but not out of the woods. He'd kicked cancer's behind, but there were still miles to go before he was back to normal. I spoke with him, prior to an open-air concert south of San Francisco, on the Midsummer Night's *Stunt* Tour in 1999. Although his medications were clearly limiting his ability to be sharp and to concentrate, I thought he was doing an admirable job just by being out of bed. And his playing didn't seem to be all that affected by the fact that he was now the bearer of a whole new immune system. "My problem," he told me at the time, "is that my new immune system is attacking my liver, so I'm taking steroids to strengthen my liver, and I'm taking other immune suppressants so that my new immune system isn't as strong in attacking my liver. But it also means that I have a weakened immune system, so I can't go out and do as many meet 'n' greets and shake hands. Because I get sick easy."

At this point Kevin had to raise his voice, with much discomfort, over the sound of opening act Semisonic. "I like Semisonic, they're a good band," he said as an aside before detailing a litany of the joys of the road life that were still tantalizingly out of reach to him. "I can't eat sushi, I can't go swimming, I can't be in the sun," he bemoaned understandably. "It's a drag."

While it wasn't exactly an ideal scenario for Kevin's comeback tour, it was still a far better deal than he could have hoped for only a year earlier. "I just think back, and, you know, it's better than it was," he admitted. "A year ago I was locked in a room for thirty days or whatever." And that wasn't the worst of it. "A year ago I couldn't eat because my mouth was so full of sores," Kev recalled in detail. "I was bald. I could barely get up and have a shower. I had a tube coming out of my chest, so I couldn't roll over when I was sleeping. When I wanted to have a shower I had to cover my whole chest in Saran Wrap—so I'm enjoying the little pleasures."

Kevin also admitted to suffering from sporadic moments of mental confusion, a side effect of his medication that tended to make him a bit dopey at times. "I have to go really slowly, and I think slower," he explained with admirable frankness. "We play the same set every night, so I have my marks set out; definitely my concentration is affected by the drugs. My hands shake, so I'm not up to par yet, but the music's uplifting, and the fans are singing along and stuff, so it's got a lot of power."

In fact, he said, the fans' adulation and support played a huge part in his recovery and increased his morale to fight the disease. And while he was obviously very tired at the end of the night, he still tried to meet and greet the fans every now and then. "The fans have been really great," Kevin raved above the din of the opening act. "I receive e-mails and still go back to meet them, but mostly I can't go to the business things like radio stations and industry functions, so I'm limited a little."

Sensing a need to change the subject, I switched gears and asked Kevin what he felt was the main difference between Steven and Ed, as far as their songwriting was concerned. "Steven writes with his fingers, and Ed writes with his hands" was Kevin's rather cryptic reply. So cryptic, in fact, that I asked him to elaborate a little. "Ed is often more subtle lyrically, slightly veiling his meaning or his point," Kevin explained. "Steve tends toward the 'in-your-face' approach, I find. In their lyrics, Ed's humor is usually genuine fun, as in 'One Week,' whereas Steve employs, and enjoys, dark humor, often twisting cliché lines or themes, such as in 'Break Your Heart.' Between the two, I think that there's a healthy balance achieved."

Fittingly, *Stunt* was the first Barenaked Ladies studio album to feature the prolific input of Kevin, who'd previously only appeared on the live album. Something that may surprise casual listeners or those who don't read album credits or those who frankly don't read at all is that while Kevin does in fact play the keyboards in Barenaked Ladies, he is also a very gifted guitarist. And he got to play a lot of guitar on his very first studio album with the band. "I play lead guitar on, like, half of *Stunt*," Kevin admitted when we discussed his guitar prowess.

On "One Week" Kevin plays at least three different guitar parts, including the solo and the vaguely African-sounding parts. "I'm a big fan of the African musicians like King Sunny Ade and stuff like that," Kevin confessed, adding that "all the harmonic stuff is me." And that's Kevin playing the Duane Eddyfied guitar on Steven's song, "In the Car." "I played that surf-guitar solo on this Yamaha Tennessean guitar," he says. "It's sort of a copy of a Gretsch Country Gentleman. I grew up playing classical and then bluegrass, so I never really use a pick."

Producer David Leonard picks Kevin out as an exceptional all-around musician. "Kevin is just phenomenal," says Leonard. "He has a lot of clever little sparkles and ear candy and things that really make a mix fun. He did some wonderful work on sounds with keyboards but also with guitars. He's got a whole sampler full of crazy little homemade things."

Kevin may have been phenomenal, but so was *Stunt*. After it's July 7 release, it entered the prestigious *Billboard* 200 at number three and sold an impressive 145,000 units in its first week, going platinum by the fourth week. It was all coming true, the second coming of *Gordon*-mania, only in USA-sized portions. This time, however, it was a personal triumph that BNL felt, not just a professional one. "It's not something we need for validation," says Ed, "because we know what it's like to be that appreciated. We made a great record, and that in itself is validation."

And the band seemed at last ready to enjoy it.

19

Stunt Tour
Burbank, 1998

Backstage at "enormo-domes," many unseen people do many unseen activities, most of which have to do with keeping unwanted visitors out of the secured area. Clinging to my coveted "All Access" credentials, I'm led through many corridors past many doors and still more people, until I get to the production office. This is the War Room—a cramped little alcove, stuffed with cell phones, laptop computers, and filing cabinets on wheels that travel with the show from city to city. At each venue they plug in this circus of circuitry, making it home base for all operations. After the show everything's unplugged, packed into road cases, and shipped to the next city where they'll do it all over again.

It's here among the road cases that I first make contact with three road cases themselves. Seattle's own Shannon Reddy—whose job title is tour accountant, but like everyone here, does so much more than that—hands me my very own copy of the tour phone book, often called a "Tour Bible," which bears the appropriate title *Barenaked Ladies Stunt Show '98*. I'm introduced to Winnipeg-based Dean Roney, production manager, although to say that anyone in this organization is "based" anywhere is misleading. Reddy gets on her radio to attempt to pin down the man who carries the whole thing—the guy who puts the *man* back in tour manager, Mr. Craig Finley. You can call him Fin. Why not? Everybody else does. And they call him constantly. He's the man who made the calls to make the travel arrangements that made my arrival here happen. And he makes it look easy.

"Hi, Paul. Flight okay?" asks Fin, cradling a cell phone in one hand while extending his free hand to shake. He may be splitting his attention, but the sincerity of his concern is obvious. The guy cares. Period. With my new tour book in my hands and various passes around my neck, I'm beginning to feel like this is my first day at a new school. The tour book itself is a three-hundred page photocopied tome containing the names of every band member, crew member, promoter, record-company representative, manager, travel agent, bus driver, hotel, and venue. There are day-by-day breakdowns of where the tour will be and when. There are seating capacities and accommodation arrangements for every stop on the tour. There are designated travel days, show days, and even the rare day off, which are few for budgetary reasons but necessary for sanity reasons.

Like a prayer book, a playbook from the NFL, or a *Playboy* hidden from your parents, the tour book is sacred and to be guarded with one's life. "This is your tour book, soldier. There are many like it, but only this one is yours. Don't lose it, or there'll be hell, and Fin, to pay." Clutching my copy of this precious document, I decide it's time to pay a visit to the band, and let them know, or perhaps warn them, that I'm here.

It's now about two P.M. and the tour's security director, Joe Self, an amiable Texan from Austin, leads me to Barenaked Ladies' dressing room. Self has been on many a Barenaked Ladies tour in addition to working with Willie Nelson. Upon hearing this fact, I begin to wonder just how incongruous these two worlds, Willie's and BNL's, would be. They say you don't mess with Texas, and frankly, I wouldn't mess with Joe, either. But hey, play fair with him, stay out of the areas he's guarding, and there isn't a warmer, gentler person this side of the Rio Grande.

Since no one's really around, I'm left alone in the dressing room, which resembles a kind of living room complete with couches, a television, a stereo and a bar fridge stocked with various soft drinks and bottles of water. I also notice that this dressing room features a rather large grand piano, on which I plunk a few haphazard notes. Hmmm, it's in tune, I think, and scan around the room for other treats. Along a countertop lies a selection of herbal teas, a large fruit basket, a few unopened bottles of wine, and a plate of really expensive- and fattening-looking cookies.

But when Tyler ducks his head around the corner and invites me to lunch, I opt for a real meal and head with him to Catering. Ah, yes, the wonderful catering room. Every show day, starting as early as 8:30 A.M., the caterers have the all-important responsibility of producing three meals a day for everyone associated with the entire tour.

Since the rigging crew—who rigs up all the lighting trusses, builds the set, and loads out the speakers and amplifiers—starts work at 9 A.M. on show days, breakfast is of great importance around here. Food is available pretty much all day, served buffet-style in the catering room, or Catering, as it's known. Today at the Universal Amphitheater, Catering seems to be an actual cafeteria, but from venue to venue, Catering's room size and location changes drastically. In some places, Catering will commandeer what appears to be a janitor's office and stuff it full of steam tables, Styrofoam coolers, coffee urns, and food: cereals, breads, hot entrées, ice cream, yogurt, fruit, pastries, the whole shebang. At other places, the secure area to the side of the stage is the only space large enough to accommodate this movable feast.

Later, between the 4 P.M. sound check and showtime at 8 P.M., the band and crew will get together for a 5 o'clock dinner. Unlike with some other bands, there's no band or crew hierar-

PAUL MYERS

195

chy. Crew and band mix freely—heck, these guys are friends. The band may be the center of attention, and the employers of this whole circus, but there's a genuine mutual respect for every talented person in this organization. Most are specialists in their given fields—some are the best, in fact—and since many of these skilled people have been with BNL for many years now, the band's recent success belongs to the entire organization. It's somewhat reassuring, though not in the least surprising, that BNL has not gone "rock star" on us. To be honest, if any of them did get a swelled head, there would be plenty of people around here who would gladly chip in to straighten him out.

Back in the dressing room, the band members have returned to the nest, and each greets me in his own way. Perhaps predictably, *Stunt* tour keyboardist Chris has discovered the grand piano and is currently lost on Planet Ivory. He looks up and nods a greeting as if to say, Hey, don't mind me. I'm not really here, anyway.

Tyler has located a VHS tape of Steven's recent guest appearance on ABC's *Politically Incorrect with Bill Maher.* Steven's always struck me as a very aware guy, knowledgeable on world politics and possessed with a snappy wit. Just the kind of thing you would expect to see on the show, a kind of symposium where celebrities pose as pundits. Unfortunately for him, and perhaps for us all, Steven must share the panel with Vicki Lawrence, best known as Mama from the old *Carol Burnett Show,* who was also a one-hit wonder back in the '70s, having sung "The Night the Lights Went Out in Georgia." Ms. Lawrence, as it turns out, has brought her own prop in an effort to elicit one very cheap and easy laugh: a cigar as a "comment" on the then-recent Clinton-Lewinsky scandal. You do the math:

> Bill Clinton
> + Cigar
> + Monica Lewinsky
> ——————————
> = Howls of laughter from Bill Maher
>   and the studio audience

There goes the symposium. Steven didn't have a chance. Oh well, the show must go on.

Even when you're being pelted with food from well-meaning fans.

Much to Barenaked Ladies' collective chagrin, the ritual throwing of macaroni during "If I Had $1,000,000" has become as predictable as ants at a picnic. Not that it's always a picnic for band and crew, mind you. But, still, it could be worse. What if "$1,000,000" contained references to anvils or Shaolin death stars? Now that could really be a hazard.

Barenaked Ladies now post this sign at the entrances to all shows:

Macaroni & Cheese
Hurts
When you get it in the head.
BNL would appreciate donations
to the food bank instead.
Thank You

Tonight, regardless of the polite signage, there is indeed a mild pelting of the uncooked elbow pasta during "If I Had $1,000,000." The band really does appreciate the love, but hard, uncooked pasta really does hurt. And don't cook it first, either; it gums up the instruments and ruins them. Besides, food banks really do need the food. And Barenaked Ladies really do thank you.

The show is, by this stage of the tour, a real tour de force. Early hits like "Brian Wilson," "Straw Hat and Old Dirty Hank," and "The Old Apartment" elicit cheers of recognition, and newer songs like "It's All Been Done," "Call and Answer," and the inevitable "One Week" drive the crowd into fits of sing-along energy. This is a real rock spectacle, I assure you. When the flashing BNL sign, with its thousand points of white light, drops down during "Alcohol," Barenaked Ladies could be Kiss (without the high heels and Kabuki makeup, of course). And the

197

stripped-down, unplugged take on "Some Fantastic" really is, well, fantastic.

Chris plays his own versions of Kevin's parts, as opposed to just aping his sound, and this makes these shows unique. The band is firing on all cylinders. A bass solo, a dangerous idea in the hands of many musicians, is a musical treat when played by Jim. Tyler drops the beats, but picks 'em all up at just the right time. He's both dope and fly. I'd forgotten just what a great guitar player Ed is, and I'm happily reacquainted with his nimble finger work. And when did Steven become opera's newest star? Sure, he may be having a laugh by closing with "Touch Me" from *Cats*, but you have to admit, he's really got the voice to carry it off. And off they go.

Phoenix, Mesa Amphitheater, 1998

It's sound-check time out in the Mesa Amphitheater near Phoenix, and the band is understandably a little uncomfortable. For one thing, this outdoor stage gets very hot in the Arizona sun, and at 3:30 in the afternoon that Arizona sun is aiming perfectly into the eyes of the band as they go through a few songs. On top of that, Ed's brand-new guitar seems to be acting up and his guitar technician, Tim Blunt, wants to have a little extra time to fix whatever the problem is. For some time now, both Ed and Steve have used wireless guitar systems that send a specific radio frequency to little antennae atop their amplifiers instead of snaking long guitar cables around the stage. Fancy, you say, but if you can imagine what havoc would ensue onstage as the guys run over one another's guitar cords, wireless is the way to go, for the safety of the band if nothing else.

With my security passes dangling around my neck, I opt to take a walk around the amphitheater to get a fan's-eye view of the show. After being backstage for most of the L.A. show and missing a key stunt from drum tech Rob "Tiny" Menegoni, I'm eager to be among the paying customers tonight. These outdoor amphitheaters, which the industry calls "sheds," are built to maximize profit and minimize frills like padded seating. And more often than not, outdoor venues, such as Shoreline Amphitheater in Mountainview, California, where Neil Young holds his annual Bridge School Benefits, or Kingswood Music Theatre, north of Toronto, where young Steven once held a summer job, are 50 percent seatless. This is a promoter issue, and the band has little control over the fact that you've paid good money to get grass stains on your khakis. The amusement industry, as it is sometimes called, may be amused, but as a paying customer, I am not. Still, I'm in my thirties and therefore well past the age when the pain-vs.-fun continuum makes lawn seating a realistic option for a concertgoer.

Speaking of pain, dry uncooked macaroni is, by itself, one thing, but later on during the show, a misguided, or drunk, fan figures it would be clever to bring the accompanying cheese sauce. So while pasta reigns supreme, a liquid stream of molten processed-cheese food has landed on, and in, the keys of Chris's vintage Hohner Clavinet. This is not cool. Chris is not happy. This is not love, it is vandalism. Gooey, sticky, hard-to-clean vandalism. Before most of us even know what has transpired, I'm once again impressed with security guy Joe Self, who's already identified the culprit in the crowd. Alerting the house security, the so-called fan is escorted out, but not before being taken to Chris. Chris wants the guy to see just what he did, and confront the human being affected by those actions. It seems to me that this is far more meaningful than just having the guy tossed. But the rest of the show at Mesa is a mess o' fun.

After the show, the band assembles in the hotel bar for a little winding down before heading back to their rooms. I end up talking with Chris, not about the cheese-sauce issue, but about *The Tibetan Book of the Dead*. And he's not just surfacing; it seems he's really read the book. I'm now beginning to see what makes him tick, if only a little glimpse. He's a stoic, but gentle, soul. He's also a strong survivor who knows when he's being messed with.

In the midst of a traveling circus, I feel for a brief moment like I'm at a Buddhist retreat. Thank you, Chris.

Suddenly, it's very late and we all trudge off to the hotel to get a bit of sleep. Tomorrow is a travel day, and we're flying to Dallas.

Dallas, 1998

Let's not forget what built this city. Oil that is. Black gold. Texas tea. Well, the first thing you know, I'm on the shuttle bus from Dallas/Fort Worth International Airport, a sprawling multiterminal hub that services millions of flights a day. Just getting out of the airport proper is a journey in itself. The shuttle, I learn, must stop at every post at all four terminals, each a block or two away from each other, before heading onto the interstate and into downtown Dallas.

I check into Le Meridien Hotel and flop onto the couch. Nice couch. Nice hotel room. After enjoying a hot shower, I make my first attempts at contact with anyone from the tour. Problem one: I don't have the coded names of the guys and can't find Fin. And without knowing their code names, I can't find their room numbers. This wasn't in the mighty tour book, was it? After frantically flipping through the pages, I'm no closer to learning the codes. I decide to go to the lobby and see if anyone's kicking around. There, several rock-and-roll people, dressed all in black with dyed black hair, are going through black binders with black Sharpie markers. It's another tour: the Antichrist himself, Marilyn Manson. Tonight, the dope showman is booked into the same Bronco Bowl that Barenaked Ladies will play tomorrow night. If it's still standing, that is.

Finally I find Steven, who invites me to a movie. It's a night off, so why not do something normal? We take a cab into a university neighborhood, where we find an art-house cinema. There are two features playing, and since we've just missed the first twenty minutes of the reissued Orson Welles noir *A Touch of Evil*, it's a pretty simple choice to see *Happiness*, a dark comedy from director Todd Solondz, who also made *Welcome to the Dollhouse*. *Happiness* is one of the best films I've ever seen, I decide, but it's also one of the sickest and bleakest comedies ever committed to the screen.

The movie elicits some strong discussion over drinks and not surprisingly, I discover that Steven, with kids of his own, is quite opinionated on the subject of child welfare. We agree, after all is said and done, that *Happiness* is a great film about really bad things.

Dallas, Bronco Bowl

NOVEMBER 6, 1998

They say you "don't mess with Texas," but they don't warn you about messy Texans. As the crew sets up for tonight's show, the floor of the Bronco Bowl is still sticky from the previous night's black celebration with Marilyn Manson. Just what this sticky substance could be is anyone's grisly guess. Blood? Maybe. Something far worse? It's likely. I'd rather not speculate. Anyway, by the end of the night there will be a layer of uncooked macaroni mixed in with whatever the hell is already there.

Besides being pelted with the relatively harmless pale yellow projectiles here and there, there's been the odd, so-called fan who, oblivious to the old FTD credo "say it with flowers," insists on saying it with flour-based products, throwing full boxes of Kraft Macaroni Dinner stageward.

But out in the middle of a packed Bronco Bowl, we're well into another of the many sold-out shows on this tour. Critics will attribute this "overnight success" to the fact that *Stunt*, the band's fifth release in ten years, is double platinum in the United States, and "One Week" has virtually become the official theme song of summer '98. But the more than three thousand fans in attendance tonight seem to know better. Sure there are the recent converts, the "stunties," in the house, but there are just as many die-hard, long-term fans. As the band strikes the opening chords to "If I Had $1,000,000," an air of anticipation and recognition sweeps over the audience. And Robin Billinton, throwing a protective sheet over his mixing board, knows all too well what's about to happen next. It's time to duck and cover! Battle stations! Everyone prepare for incoming pasta barrage! But thankfully, the pasta rain is light tonight.

Tonight, these vociferous BNL fans have come to praise the band rather than bury them in uncooked Kraft dinner. Indeed, many of them will follow the band to the next shows in Austin and Houston. And while I'll be leaving the tour after Houston, many of these loyal fans will in fact stay on their trail all the way through New Orleans, Birmingham, Charlotte, Fort Lauderdale, Orlando, Atlanta, Nashville, Indianapolis, St. Louis, Minneapolis, Chicago, and Cincinnati before the band closes the tour with another sold-out show back home at Toronto's Massey Hall.

Austin, Texas

SATURDAY, NOVEMBER 7, 1998

Nashville may be more ostentatious, but nothing compares to Austin, Texas. This is a real music town, and to prove it, Austin is the home of one of the finest music festivals in the business, South by Southwest. Every year musicians flock to Austin for great bands, great bars, and great barbecues. Barenaked Ladies are especially psyched to be back in town, playing to three thousand fans at the Music Hall. And let's not forget that *Stunt* was recorded here at Willie Nelson's Arlyn Studios. And speaking of Willie, Austin is the hometown of Nelson's erstwhile employee Joe Self. Tonight, Self will bring his wife and kids out to the show.

The concert is one more in a series of great shows. This is the fourth night I've watched BNL, and I'm impressed with how consistent, yet improvisational, they are night after night. But hey, the night is still young. And this is no ordinary young night; this is Austin, Texas, Saturday night! There's music to hear and drinks to order.

Once the band has chatted with after-show guest Tom Arnold, yet another celebrity fan, we bolt over to a nearby club to see New Orleans–based Cowboy Mouth. Barenaked Ladies became friendly with them when Cowboy Mouth opened up for some BNL shows awhile back. The two bands clearly have a mutual respect for each other, and it's a treat for BNL to be able to catch the band's set here in Austin, again, on Saturday night!

Houston, We Have a "Tiny" Problem

NOVEMBER 8, 1998

Talk about saving the best for last. The last stop on my one-week tour, although the band will continue on to New Orleans and beyond, is Houston, Texas—the Houston that's referenced in *Apollo 13* with the line "Houston, we have a problem." But I had no problem with being included as the guys accepted an invitation to tour NASA's celebrated Johnson Space Center. Driving along the interstate and out of downtown Houston, I look around the van and see the faces of the band members. They're barely concealing a childlike sense of anticipation. "I'm goin' to the space place" is the phrase written across their collective faces. For all the nice things that happen to the band—singing national anthems at sports events, getting to meet movie stars and the like—it's not every day you get to go to such a poignant symbol of the late twentieth century as Mission Control.

The old Mission Control, the Mission Control of my youth, has a decidedly greenish-yellow tint to it. Like an old hospital wing. When CapCom was built, it transpires, NASA rightfully declared the old Mission Control room a historical site. And it is.

This is the room that the world watched when *Apollo 13* "had a problem." This is the room from which NASA made it possible for the world to witness, on July 23, 1969, Neil A. Armstrong stepping onto the moon and flubbing his first lines there. (History note: Armstrong actually planned to say, "This is one small step for a man, one giant leap for mankind," but in the excitement of the moment, and broadcasting live to the whole world, he left out the *a* and said, "This is one small step for man, one giant leap for mankind.")

Since the likelihood of finding a nice, clean service station out in space is next to nil, the good folks at NASA have devised a rather elaborate device, which we'll call the space toilet. Steven, being Steven, elects to simulate a space dump for the camera of an eager Warner Bros. rep who's accompanied us on the tour (although in hindsight one would wonder just how useful such a photo-op could be). The picture is snapped, and just as the rep is promising to send a copy to the band, something very cool goes down. Joe Self, and let's remember his role is security, has wisely realized that this roll of film is not something that should be allowed to go to the local Fotomat, where it's only a scan away from the Internet. In that spirit, he diplomatically seizes the camera and promises that the band will send the reps the picture of our Steve's simulated space dump. That's the mark of a smart-thinking team member.

It's getting late, and we have to get back in the minivan or the guys will be late for sound check. We bid our astronaut guide adieu and motor back to the city.

When bands tour together, there's a tradition of playing practical jokes on one another, usually on the last night of the tour. Now, I'm not in the band, but I am leaving the tour tonight, so I've been trying to decide what I could do that wouldn't really screw them up (they've been so nice to me all week). Then it occurs to me.

Every night on the tour, Rob "Tiny" Menegoni doubles as a side-stage percussionist for various songs. A big figure in a western shirt and cowboy hat, Tiny makes one such cameo every night during the song "Crazy." Before the show, Tiny and I plot how I will become him. The show is going great. Ed's had the security guard join the band for a rousing romp through Lenny Kravitz's "Are You Gonna Go My Way?" The fans are pumped and appreciative. There's a lot of love in the room, as they say. But unbeknownst to the band, I've swapped clothes with Mr. Menegoni and have donned the Tiny one's western duds, and am now hidden from view with a tambourine in my hand. A song ends. The group kicks off the first bars of "Crazy," just like every night. But tonight, there's a tiny difference, or shall we say a different Tiny. Houston, we are a go for launch, and I leap onto the stage. Liftoff. No time to think better of it, I tell myself. At first no one seems to notice, but as the cheers rise up (not necessarily for me—the mere fact that there was an entrance triggers the already adrenalized crowd), Steven turns back to see what's going on, and Tyler shakes his head, laughing. Mission accomplished.

The guys give me curious looks, which I interpret as "What the hell are you doing, Myers?" mixed with "I can't believe you actually did this." I have to say that as I became one with Barenaked Ladies and felt the exhilaration of the fans' energy, I could see very clearly why they do what they do, traveling miles for months on end, away from their loved ones and the comforts of home. To quote the words of Kevin's song "What Is Life?": This is it / this is it!"

And that was it.

20

Marooned at Sunset and Gordon
2000

Man, I'm having a déjà vu. All over again.

It's just over two years since I went to meet the guys over on the Rock—that's Alcatraz—in San Francisco Bay. Back then, I was about to hear tracks from *Stunt* for the very first time. And it's almost two years since I flew into Burbank to meet up with the *Stunt* tour and witness firsthand one week in the life of a very busy band of musicians. Now in June, in the summer of 2000, I'm back at Burbank Airport to hook up once again with the Ladies. Only this time, I'm in an air-conditioned rental car and heading for a recording studio. And this time, it's only for one night as opposed to one week—just in time to hear the songs that comprise the band's first new album since the hurricane that was *Stunt*.

This will be the first new Barenaked Ladies album since Kevin's brush with death at the hands of his own blood cells. It is also the first new Barenaked Ladies album since Tyler married his sweetheart, Jill, in an outdoor ceremony in her hometown, Ottawa. And it is also the first new Barenaked Ladies album since the births of three more Barenaked Babies. Newlyweds Tyler and Jill welcomed a daughter, Milagro, a.k.a. Millie; Steven and Carolyn welcomed Benjamin, baby brother to Isaac; Ed and Natalie became the proud parents of Lyle, baby brother to Hannah.

Meanwhile, the rest of the world welcomed (I guess it depends on whom you ask) a new millennium. And, in the dawning of that new millennium, the Ladies' new recording, *Maroon*, is being produced by the one and only Don Was. Was is the man who, among other things, produced the definitive Brian Wilson documentary *I Just Wasn't Made for These Times* and its soundtrack. So it was especially interesting when Brian Wilson himself dropped in on Barenaked Ladies to personally play them his own recent recording of, you guessed it, "Brian Wilson."

"This whole 'Brian Wilson' experience has been incredibly strange," Steven says. "'Brian Wilson' is a song I wrote when I was nineteen or twenty. It had a life on both *The Yellow Tape* and on *Gordon* before being resurrected and having its biggest success in 1998, just before *Stunt* came out. I think there are at least three videos for it, and four released recordings by us, and now it's become the first song of ours to be covered by another artist. Meeting him [Brian] was a thrill," Steven says, "but also as anticlimactic as one might expect: He's painfully shy and seems incredibly childlike, but I get the sense that he's finally surrounded himself with people who truly love him."

The song BNL played for Wilson was *Maroon*'s tragic but romantic "Tonight Is the Night I Fell Asleep at the Wheel," which the band had just finished recording when Wilson arrived. "His response," reports Steven, "was 'Hmmm . . . different.'" Wilson then played a few cuts from his recent *Live at the Roxy* album, including his version of the song that bears his name. "It was so blindingly exciting," says Steven. "I can't even remember what it sounded like. We had our photos taken together, and then he left, saying, 'Remember guys, don't eat too much!'" Such are the pearls of wisdom that wash up on the beach now and again.

And now, I'm again struck by a million cosmic convergences: For instance, it dawns on me as I see the retro-futurist

Capitol Records Building in the distance that the Beach Boys themselves may have put their little Hondas into first gear along this very strip back in 1965. Think of that. I'm driving to work, just like Brian Wilson did. Manager Pierre Tremblay told me that Cello Studio was located at the corner of Sunset and Gower, but as I pull up to it and begin looking for a parking spot, it occurs to me that Cello is actually at the corner of Sunset and Gordon. I couldn't make that up if I tried. I wouldn't even believe me if I did. But here we are at the convergence of two street signs. Signs from the heavens, perhaps? (No, they're from the Los Angeles Department of Traffic.)

Still, I choose to see it as a Hollywood sign.

Entering the building, I stumble on the biggest of today's convergences. Cello Studio wasn't always called Cello Studio. Formerly known as Ocean Way Studio, this is where Brian Wilson recorded a little album called *Pet Sounds*. A smiley smile curls up onto my lips as I become aware that, years after driving downtown in the rain to buy Brian Wilson's recorded history, Barenaked Ladies are making their own history in his room. I enter the doors and try to imagine Ocean Way the way it used to be. Suddenly, I'm distracted by the sounds coming from the control room. The sounds of Don Was, who is and has been producing this record, ably assisted by Jim Scott, a man who puts the ears into *engineer*.

Don Was is a soul man on every level. As a musician in Detroit, Michigan—before Was (Not Was), when Don Was was Don Fagenson—Don grooved on R&B, soul, and rock and roll in countless bar bands. He developed his chops as a bass player and multi-instrumentalist before teaming up with David Weiss to form Was (Not Was). Both accomplished musicians, their collaboration encompassed the whole gamut of human emotion, yet many music listeners seem to remember only their funnier stuff. Don Was tells me in his little office at Cello that Was (Not Was) could be dead serious one minute and highly satirical the next. They took the music very seriously, but not themselves. So it should be no surprise that he felt an affinity with Barenaked Ladies, who tread the same line—or blur it—in everything they do. He told me that, from his own experience, it can be a frustrating thing to pull off in the mind of the public at large, simply because standards tend to be a little more strict when it comes to those who create the soundtracks to our lives.

"It's weird," Was begins. "Everyone knows that the same companies that own the movie studios also own all the record companies. And yet, when E.T. flies a bike across the moon, no one screams, 'Hey, that alien didn't really fly across the moon!' But, God forbid, a couple of people should sing for Milli Vanilli and you've got an international incident." According to the veteran producer, music serves a distinctly different function in the lives of most people. "Films," he says, "are an escape. Pop music articulates personal feelings that transcend conversational language. And people use it because it actually expresses your feelings in a more eloquent way."

The be-dreadlocked Was is summoned back to the control room by engineer Jim Scott. Scott has been assembling a mix for the song "Go Home" and is now ready for Was's input on the final balance. Was takes a seat in his swivel chair and stares forward in complete concentration. This is the man who can speak intellectually but with a bluesman's sense of passion, the man who has the job of producing the follow-up to the most successful Barenaked Ladies album ever. But Was isn't worried. He understands Barenaked Ladies. He feels their message. In fact, he believes they have that rare ability to communicate on a personal level to thousands of people at one time. "Anybody" he says, "who can fill Madison Square Garden is communicating on some level."

Over a year or so ago at the Garden (as Jason Priestley's *Barenaked in America*'s camera crew hovered over the proceedings), Pierre Tremblay was struck with the unmistakable feeling that the Ladies had arrived. "That was the day it hit me like a ton of bricks," he says. "One Week" had become a summer anthem, and high MTV and VH1 visibility had helped it become Barenaked Ladies' first-ever *Billboard* number-one record. "That's a big, big day," declares Tremblay, with mild understatement. "Sometimes, when you're in there and working really hard, you don't take those things in. I rarely take those things in. But that day just really hit me, big time. Wow, we really accomplished something."

Big-time pop music is, apparently, a "Jung man's game." At least it seems that way in Don Was's office and mind. Was is attempting to employ the archetypes laid down by Carl Gustav Jung to determine what mythic role Barenaked Ladies provide in today's society. "I'm not sure," Professor Was admits, "what their mythic role is in terms of Jungian archetypes. I'd really have to read through the archetypes again; their role may not necessarily be 'the Hero,' maybe it's 'the Jester Who Provokes Thought.'"

I'm brought back to the present by the energetic track playing on the master tape. As the song finishes, we await the master's take on the take. Pushing his ever-present sunglasses back on his nose, he listens intently to each sound as the song booms out of the studio's huge professional speakers. The song ends. The tape stops. Turning his swivel chair around, the producer is smiling like a proud papa. "I think this is the best record that they've ever made," he proudly declares. "Their songwriting and their playing [have] hit another plateau." And this is high praise, indeed, coming from the Grammy Award–winning producer who has himself earned the respect and admiration of high-profile clients such as the Rolling Stones, the B-52's, Bonnie Raitt, and Bob Dylan.

And let's not forget, folks, Was's production on *Suicaine Gratifaction*, the third solo disc from former Replacements leader, Paul Westerberg, or the two records that Was made with everybody's favorite self-mutilatin' crooner Iggy Pop. Iggy Pop and Paul Westerberg were part of the reason that Steven wanted to work with Was. In addition, Was has the distinction of being responsible for taking great artists, often late in their careers, and drawing out their true nature.

And now ladies and gentlemen, welcome to the world of *Maroon*. This time, it's the real world. And this time, it's personal. Lyrically, the songs speak frankly about the life and times of the band, while musically, the band appears to be having the time of their lives. The band comes out swinging on "Pinch Me," the infectious first single that Ed sings. According to Was, "Pinch Me" could just as easily have been called "What's the Meaning of Life?" "It goes to the core of the most intense metaphysical and philosophical issues facing man," Was remarks. "That's pretty heavy turf, you know? Yet it sounds like a happy-go-lucky, almost superficial little song. Looking through the lens of the mundane, at the simple everyday things, it becomes metaphorical and the song makes its point—that in simple things lie the most valuable things."

A remarkably upbeat album musically, for all its thematic weight lyrically, *Maroon* investigates and celebrates the events, both good and bad, that make life worth living. Was loves the duality of the record, claiming it's a lot like life itself. "You put this record on," Was says, "and sonically, groovewise, it's upbeat. It makes you feel good. It's stuff you'd play at a barbecue, yet lyrically they're dealing with more grown-up subject matter." Was can't say enough about the band's ability to write songs that help people come to terms with complex feelings or emotions that they couldn't verbalize for themselves. "They're communicating," the veteran producer says once again. "They're actually getting through to people. If these guys are the torchbearers of the light side of the human psyche, then on this album the torchbearers are acknowledging that you can still live a joyful life and be a good and happy person, but that you'll mess up sometimes. You'll think of heavy things. And they've done it in a way that isn't a downer to listen to. Now, I think that's brilliant songwriting."

Songs like "Pinch Me," "Sell, Sell, Sell," "Helicopters," and the dramatic album closer, "Tonight Is the Night I Fell Asleep at the Wheel," are emotionally direct and politically aware. But Steven made it abundantly clear that this is not a "Barenaked Ladies political record." He also disagreed with Was's belief that *Maroon* may well be the darkest album they've ever made. "I think all our albums are dark," Steven assures me. "I think he's just shocked by it."

With "Helicopters," Steven and Ed say that it's better to actually try to make a difference, even if nobody knows how to accept your actions at face value. Discussing the topic, Steven explained how the challenges facing today's popular artists are unique to our age. "Let's just say it's about a musician or whatever who goes into a place where there's a conflict," Steven told me at Cello Studios. "It could be Serbia, or it could be Columbine High School. It's that idea of 'Let's get the famous musician to come' and things like World Vision or Sting's rain-forest thing. They come in there and they're shaken to the core by it." Steven continues, "It's saying that Sting, for instance, gets made fun of or becomes an ironic icon for being involved in a cause. The world loses sight of the fact that he wasn't doing this for self-aggrandizement; he's thinking 'What can I do to help?' But two stages down the road, that gets lost."

Steven says that "Helicopters" is part of trying to understand the phenomenon of being asked to do charity events, and the marketing trade-off implicit in these events. "Whenever you attract cameras to some event where you're speaking of an issue," he explains, "like 'millions of children are dying of tooth decay' or something, then you're also helping to sell some of your own records."

In other words, to paraphrase George Lucas's *THX* slogan, the audience is doing more than just listening. They are actively dissecting the star-making machinery. As a result, says Steven, the audience is way too cynical. "Unfortunately," he says, "we live in a world now where ten-year-olds know what a movie's gross was on its opening weekend. So people are all thinking, 'What's his

213

angle?' or 'What's his spin?' and they stop thinking about what the actual message is. We're so media-savvy nowadays that we train our kids to look for the ulterior motives all the time." As Steven sees it, the first casualty of media sophistication is the ability to accept idealism.

"Now there's no room for the protest singer," the singer protests, "because it's just too sincere or straightforward." Along those lines, a uniquely present-day dilemma presented itself to the band, in the wake of the horrific massacre at Columbine High School in Colorado. The band turned down a request by a third party to go to the school and play in a feel-good media event. The decision, Steven tells me, was not an easy one to make, and he and the band spent a long time asking themselves just what it was that made them say no. Upon deeper reflection, however, there turned out to be many reasons.

"We were asked by *Teen People* to do it," Steven recalls, "not by the students themselves. If the kids of Columbine had all written us a petition saying that it would be helpful for us to play for them, then we absolutely would have gone. No question. In fact, that was one of the reasons we didn't do it. It wasn't coming from them."

The band didn't fully understand the magazine's true motives for staging the highly visible, newsworthy, and topical event. Perhaps, I offer, it was because their readership is the same age as the kids who were killed and the magazine wants this to be a gift to the community. "Well," Steven says, "I like that idea, but meanwhile what you're also doing is selling magazines, and whatever products are being sold in those magazines by doing it. And what are you actually doing for those families? How is my concert really helping them?"

Ed points out that, as a Canadian, he felt that the overt gun-control issues surrounding the tragedy were inappropriate for the band to comment on without presuming some sort of moral high ground. "I felt that it would be difficult for us to just go down and entertain without being 'the Crusaders from the Land of No Guns,'" Ed admits. "There's a danger of appearing to be self-righteously moralizing. I felt that it would be difficult to comment on the situation as an outsider."

Steven points out that *Maroon* has a few common themes running through it. For starters, those old faithful themes of exploitation, celebrity, and the exploitation of celebrity rear their ugly heads in "Sell, Sell, Sell." "It's basically about an actor this time, who finds out too late that he's a mouthpiece for government propaganda," says Steven of the album's mildly operatic centerpiece. "It's kind of story I just made up, but it's based on something I remember hearing, during the Gulf War, that the two largest U.S. exports were arms and entertainment. So it's based on the theory that one fuels the other. The Cold War ended, and what happened to Stallone?"

"It's about an artist who's really good," Steven explains, "but his talents get wasted. Eventually he becomes a huge star with his movies, but he doesn't realize that what he's doing is really fueling this other stuff. It also comes partially from me knowing that I'm part of this huge Time Warner AOL conglomerate, you know. I'm a little tiny thing, but what I'm doing is fueling the bottom line for this huge company.[1]

The album opener, "Too Little Too Late," features an edgy, distorted guitar figure, the urgency of which should be a clue to the biting tone of the rest of the album. I had a unique experience—in the studio lounge—listening in as the guys decided on the running order of the songs on *Maroon*. This is where you whittle down the list of songs (in this case sixteen to twelve) and decide on the order of the final sequence. This can be an arduous process for one person, but in a group such as Barenaked Ladies, comprised of very diverse and distinct personalities, it can often

---

[1] Not surprisingly, Barenaked Ladies' music is released through Reprise Records, a subsidiary of the AOL Time Warner Company. Most record companies today are owned by huge conglomerates. Very few media outlets are not in some way connected with either AOL Time Warner, Disney, Sony, Philips, or Rupert Murdoch.

resemble the Middle East peace talks. A journey of a thousand miles begins with a single set list.

Although each member of the band weighed each choice, the steering wheel seemed to pass most frequently between Ed and Steven. I had the distinct impression that whenever any one person took control it was out of a need to instigate a lively debate, one in which all were welcome to participate. And from where I was sitting, it seemed that Ed's sequences were based more on musical and dynamic flow, such as, if a song had a loud major-chord ending, should the next song be one that opens with an acoustic guitar in a minor key? Steven clearly seemed to favor the lyrical flow for his choices. For instance, does the subject matter in one song set up the subject matter in the next?

Once Ed or Steve had a list of songs, each would pitch the sequence to the others, just as advertising executives would pitch slogans. In the course of this pitching, the various players, and even the producer, effectively explained most of the songs on the album. At one point, Steven toyed around with the idea of making *Maroon* into a loosely defined concept album, where each song tells another part of a larger story.

"'Too Little Too Late' is the introduction," Steven begins. "It says, 'Here's what's going to happen.' The character has made some mistakes in his life. Is it too little too late? I don't know, but we're gonna find out over the course of this record, folks. It's just the preface. On the second song, 'Never Do Anything,' we're introduced to the main character of the piece, the Willy Loman to *Maroon*'s *Death of a Salesman*." Steven then proposes that the third song and first single, "Pinch Me," is where our story actually begins in earnest.

"We've got this bored guy," Steven continues with his pitch. "He's just living his life sleepwalking. He can dream about big ambitions, but he's a bit of a jerk. It's not entirely clear, but after the cautionary and highly hummable 'Go Home,' you get the feeling that in his boredom our hero has been sleepwalking around, straying from his domestic responsibilities. The song is like a best friend who reminds him of his priorities. Not to mention how lucky he is to have a home to go to in the first place.

"I originally had 'Go Home' on my sequence second last," Steven remarks, mulling it over. "I think, maybe thinking of the way '$1,000,000' goes into 'Crazy' at the end of *Gordon*. That really worked well, although it might get buried. Still, I love a good feeling at the end of the record."

As Steven's concept album begins to unravel, it becomes clear that the protagonist of *Maroon* is not a superhero but a normal, nice guy who makes some dumb choices and screws up his life. Through the album's songs the only truly constant themes are temptation and sin and their consequences, which are followed by regret and, finally, attempts at redemption. Throughout the album, our hero is cast into the slippery arms of temptation, only to slip and fall flat on his face.

Ed says that falling flat is not something to be afraid of, that Barenaked Ladies thrive on their ability to take risks. "I think that the strength of the band is that we're not afraid to fail," Ed says. "We're not afraid to just go for it. The thought of something being lame is not enough to stop us from trying it [laughs]. And it never is. It can be a very liberating experience to fuck up and feel it and learn from it as opposed to being dysfunctional and just getting past it." Was says that songs like "Falling for the First Time" celebrate human mistakes, and that nice guys sometimes do bad things and have to pay for those mistakes. This is what makes Barenaked Ladies important.

In "Conventioneers," our hero, that lovable *Maroon*, is once more tempted by heavy things, namely, the pleasures of the flesh. The mellow ballad, which was recorded with the working title of "Senior Citizens in Love," provides a blow-by-blow narration that's convention-fevered, interoffice-affair, from the predictable cat-and-mouse of flirtation and the inevitable flights of passion to the inescapable shy apologies and polite regrets of the morning after. "That title had to change to 'Conventioneers,'" Steven confesses, "because it's not really what the song's about. You don't

217

want to wave your arms around and say, 'Look at the title!'"

And since our crumpled hero still has to go back to work on Monday, where he must face his conquest's cubicle, the song ends with a rhyming couplet that Shakespeare himself would have signed off on:

> *It'd be great,*
> *If you transferred out of state*
> —from "Conventioneers" by Steven Page
> and Ed Robertson.

Our hero is also tempted in "Sell, Sell, Sell," this time by the two-headed lure of vanity and celebrity. Steven may profess to loving a good-feeling song at the end of the record, but that doesn't explain the fact that the song they eventually chose to close *Maroon* bears the not-so-feel-good title "Tonight Is the Night I Fell Asleep at the Wheel."

"Metaphorically," Ed explains, "that song is about living without knowing what is precious to you. And the twist of the lyric is even, in fact, articulating that it's not precious to you. Going out of your way to say, 'You were the last thing on my mind.' I'm like coming home from work and you're the last thing on my mind. Then when everything crashes and falls apart, that's when he says, 'You were the last thing on my mind.'" "I fell asleep at the wheel," adds Steven. "I wasn't paying attention to what I was doing. I forgot the most important thing in my life."

"I like the wry smile in 'Asleep at the Wheel,'" Ed admits. "What I was trying to explain to Don the other night, the thing that it's not about is laughing in the face of death; it's not about fear of death; it's not about the responsibility of death. It's about the surreal couple of seconds when you realize you're dying." For Ed, this was the moment he thought about most when his brother Doug died on his motorcycle. "I thought when he died, he was asleep," Ed explains. "And he was probably awakened by the absolute violence and chaos of an accident, and probably for a split second went, 'I'm gonna be all right [looks around him]. Ooops. No. I'm dying!' Your body must flood with endorphins to make the pain go away, and for a second you're lucid. For a couple of seconds you think, 'I can't believe I'm okay,' but then you realize you're not okay."

In the song, our hero reaches the same fatal conclusion, only he's in a mangled car. "This guy wakes up to the violence of a car crash and thinks, 'Wow, I can't believe I—'" Just then, Don Was walks in and joins the discussion, giving the guys some commonsense advice.

> **Don Was:** Can I give you my philosophy on this? Pick the best twelve. Make the best record you can make. Don't worry about what you're gonna do with the other stuff. What's the difference between *Sgt. Pepper* and *Rubber Soul*? We're in agreement about all the major stuff. You don't have to sell any song to me. There's no song that I'm not happy to put on the album, and the stuff that we're talking about leaving off, I could leave any one of them off.
>
> **Steven:** (*Throwing up his arms in mock protest.*) You hate them all, I'm not listening. . . .
>
> **Don Was:** I have no condition about these last couple of songs; they're all okay. It's really that we've got to start assembling what feels good. I think "Sell, Sell, Sell," man, it's a brilliant fucking thing. You're getting to a point that's over here, and you start driving in this direction. And you take everybody with you, thinking, "What's going to happen to this actor?" Whoa, it's not about the actor at all. It's fucking amazing, the dynamic to the storytelling is genius.
>
> **Tyler:** It's true. (*Smiles.*) It's fucking true, man.

(*Starts to laugh.*) He's telling the truth. (*Becomes excited.*) That song is a mindblower. (*Smiling, practically yelling.*) It's a total mindblower.

Steven: I'm with Don on "Sell." I think it's one of our most interesting achievements and one of our best achievements as far as writing.

Don Was: But compare that to "Conventioneers," they're both not rock-and-roll songs, so to me they're kind of interchangeable. But I think there are great laughs and the payoff; it's a major fucking song, man. Just in terms of poetry, it's probably your best poetry on the record. And "Asleep at the Wheel" is also really metaphorical; it could be about anything that you think you got away with but you didn't.

When the incense had cleared, this was the final running order:

"Too Little Too Late"
"Never Do Anything"
"Pinch Me"
"Go Home"
"Falling for the First Time"
"Conventioneers"
"Sell, Sell, Sell"
"Humour of the Situation"
"Baby Seat"
"Off the Hook"
"Helicopters"
"Tonight Is the Night I Fell Asleep at the Wheel"

Mind you, these weren't the only songs that were recorded for *Maroon*. The casualties, songs that were recorded but cut from *Maroon*, include "Half a Heart," sung by Ed; "Powder Blue," a dark cinema-noir piece reminiscent of *Spike*-era Elvis Costello, sung by Steven; and "In Line Bow Line," a surprisingly alterna-rock sing-along written and sung by Jim.

There were also two Kevin Hearn songs recorded. "Born Human, Raised by Wolves" is a whimsical, lighthearted song that Kevin wrote just as he was being welcomed back into the fold after his hiatus in hell. "I was writing a lot of songs that reflected on what I'd been through for the last two years," Kevin says. "And as I started playing again, I thought, 'I just want to do a song that's not based on personal experience. Not based on anything.' Initially, I played that one first, and then I put in 'Hidden Sun.'"

Kevin wrote the powerfully haunting "Hidden Sun" while he was still a patient at Princess Margaret Hospital in Toronto. "I was going through heavy cancer treatment and a bone-marrow transplant," he recalls. "I was reading a lot of *Rolling Stone* magazines, and other musical rags. I was kind of opening my eyes and seeing who the kids' heroes are today, you know? Guys like Marilyn Manson, Trent Reznor, Tommy Lee, and Mike Tyson were all in the same column, you know, like at this party doing this, or that. I was thinking, 'Why is this being reported? Who cares?' When all around me in the hospital, I was seeing a lot of people working hard on the night shift, taking care of people in pain. And I was thinking, 'These are the real heroes in life.' Those heroes in *Rolling Stone* are gonna need these heroes when they get sick."

After much eleventh-hour deliberating, however, the song was cut from the final sequence of *Maroon*. Although everyone really liked it, it just didn't flow with the rest of the set. "They took it from a very fast song, which I think was my way of kind of hiding the theme of it," Kevin recalls, "and brought it down to minimal instrumentation, and really brought the lyrics out."

Yet the album's explicit references to life, death, and all the baggage in the middle ultimately become an affirmation of life itself. And Steven isn't kidding when he says there's been a lot of life in the lives of Barenaked Ladies recently. Now, finally, and thankfully, Kevin takes his own personal victory lap around the twelve tracks that make up *Maroon*. All over the record, the multitalented Kevin is heard on piano, Clavinet, organ, guitar, glockenspiel, Melodica, accordion, synthesizer, vocoder, and digital sampler.

And when Jim isn't slapping or bowing the double bass, he can be heard strapping on his electric bass in addition to his textural work on viola, violin, and baritone guitar. Jim's groove is once more pinned down by Tyler's elastic and funktastic drumming—he even gets busy on castanets, tambourines and the odd timpani. While the lead vocals are shared between Ed and Steven, Ed does most of the guitar work while Steven, playing the occasional acoustic guitar, flute, or recorder, concentrates for the most part on his vocal skills. The result is the acoustic-electric eclecticism that defines Barenaked Ladies' fifth studio album and their sixth album in general.

Was feels that one of the reasons for Barenaked Ladies' phenomenal success is their ability to really communicate with their live audience and to send out a genuinely good vibe in concert. It's that vibe that Was sought to capture on *Maroon*. "I was looking at the smile on Ed's face," Was remembers of a recent performance. "It never leaves his face for the entire show. He's Mother Teresa, man, for that alone. If you're going to stand up there and smile and have fun for two hours and show people that there can be joy in life, you really can affect other people by example. There's no greater thing you can do than to demonstrate how happy you can be, to that many people, night after night. That's a fantastic service to perform."

Both Was and Barenaked Ladies are quick to credit Jim Scott, who engineered and mixed *Maroon*, for his unique approach to studio decoration and vibe control. According to Ed, Scott, an accomplished producer and a musician in his own right, came to embody the very soul of this record. Scott's studio environment could well be described as "Sixties Hippie Chic." Picture this: Hung high on the wall between the main speakers, a black-velvet painting of Elvis gazes down regally. Persian rugs double as wall hangings and acoustic reinforcements. The green and red blinking lights of the studio electronics are augmented by Scott's multicolored Christmas-tree lights, as wisps of smoke from patchouli-scented incense billow up through Scott's own beaded curtains.

"Jim Scott has great ears," Steven declares. "He listens to everything very closely, even when my ears are tired and I've lost concentration after a million takes. He's amazingly relaxed; he's always up. He never gets tense about anything, no matter what happens. When we were getting a bit tired, Jim would play us back the tape and spontaneously start dancing or playing along on air guitar."

"I'll tell you something," says Was. "There's only two kinds of music: It's either up or it's down. You're either holding your hands up and you're offering something good to the universe, and the down is just self-indulgent, noncommunicative, ego crap. The other day, I went up and down the radio dial, and you could tell in a second who was giving out something good. It made me feel good about what I do for a living.

"What I enjoy about the job of producing is that you get into the artist's head. You basically have to be a surrogate for the artist for when they lose their objectivity. So you really have to understand them, and get to know someone really well in a short period of time. And when I make a suggestion about something, I'm making a suggestion thinking like them, that if they had my objectivity, then this is what they would probably do with their song. And if it's not—if they say, 'No, here's what I want to do,' then that's what I want. I want that reaction."

And Was reports that, from what he's seen, today's Barenaked Ladies have an exemplary interpersonal relationship. "Most bands have pretty much the same DNA code," says the veteran musician. "Ultimately, they fight like an army to conquer the world and once they've achieved their dreams the two principals turn on each other. And the tensions that exist in the biggest rock-and-roll bands in the world also exist in garage bands of twelve-year-olds. I don't know if they went through that earlier, but these guys really get on well together. There's not been a tense moment in the whole making of this record. And that's not only rare in this business, it's unheard of."

Was heaps praise and respect on the band in an almost fatherly way. "A producer named Jimmy Iovine told me years ago, 'Never produce anybody that you mind losing an argument to.'" So when the red light came on, how was the band? "I've never ever worked with a band who had better basic tracks than Barenaked Ladies," says Was. "It's never happened before.

"It's like actors—the best ones are the ones who listen to the other and are in the moment; they're not thinking, 'Oh what's my next line?' Don't think about yourself; react to them, feed them something new to play off of. A couple of times we had a hard time selecting which take to use—a couple times we cut up composites of two different takes, but for the most part, really, the barometer was the vocal. If the guy's telling the story right, then everyone must be setting him up to tell the story right. So when the vocal rings true, STOP—you've got it."

Afterword:

Thanks, This Was Fun . . .

Well, dear reader, since I last made an entry in my notes in November 2000, much has changed in the world of Barenaked Ladies and the world at large. What happened to them after those sessions for *Maroon*? you ask. And how's Kev?

Well, some happy news first. Kevin Hearn is back in fine health and continues to reclaim his life, finally enjoying the spoils of the Ladies' success and realizing his own parallel creative goals to boot. Kevin and his band, Thin Buckle, toured in support of the keyboardist's *H Wing*, which was picked up for distribution by Nettwerk America. A highlight of the Thin Buckle tour, opening for the Rheostatics, was Kevin's rendition of the old Black Sabbath chestnut "War Pigs." The assistance of Kev's cousin, comedian Harland Williams, in the guise of "Flamehead," made the Sabbath classic seem as relevant for our time as it did back in the '70's, when the idea of Ozzy Osbourne having a hit television show would have seemed outrageous.

But there was more outrageousness to be found as the Barenaked Ladies toured the world to promote the *Maroon* album and the subsequent greatest-hits release. After the success of "Pinch Me," the band released two follow-up singles: "Too Little Too Late" and "Falling for the First Time." Although neither of these reached "Pinch Me" heights, at least "Falling" was another hit in Canada, where a video (featuring Cousin Harland again) was well received.

Still, it was the road that beckoned the Ladies. Sitting down with me in October 2002, Tyler Stewart recalls the past couple of years, those days on the *Maroon* tour and especially having Kevin back on the keys.

"The *Stunt* tour was quite successful," says Tyler. "It was our biggest production to date. We had video [projection] and everything, but then *Maroon* became, by far, the biggest production we have ever undertaken. We had a great crew of people and the big stage set with this big blow-up head, and all these floating caricatures from the *Maroon* album artwork."

And of course, Kev was back.

"That was a big factor," recalls Tyler. "We felt complete and whole again. Having Kev back in the fold for the full *Maroon* tour made us realize just how much we all went through that whole experience with him. So for him to hear us tell stories about how we were feeling while he was going through his own ordeal was very therapeutic, for everyone"

And of course, anyone who attended the *Maroon* shows recalls hearing a K-Tel–inspired medley of every single song BNL has ever played. As they went from hook to hook, song to song, a scrolling list of titles appeared in rear projection behind them. Tyler said the medley was partly born of necessity and partly just a hoot to perform.

"It was a very fun thing," he tells me. "Fans are always asking us to play old stuff. But some songs you just can't play anymore, for whatever reason. Maybe you don't relate to the time you wrote it in, or instrumentally your headspace just isn't there. For instance, I always find that at the end of 'Enid,' which is kind of really frenetic and skippy, I'm like, 'Whoo!' I mean, that's some high-energy music."

But for BNL to entertain a full range of fans, Tyler tells me the band finds it necessary to broaden its focus when choosing set lists.

"What we've learned is that although we have quite a lot of hard-core fans, and not to discount them, there's just not that many of them compared to your average concertgoer. I think it's our responsibility to our whole audience to play the best show possible. And even that's going to be debated. I mean, to a hard-core fan who has everything you've ever recorded, the best show possible has to include the most obscure songs possible. And fandom like that is great, don't get me wrong, but it's also a relatively small group of people."

Nonetheless, Tyler recalls the *Maroon* tour set list frequently dipping into what are sometimes called "album tracks." Thus, on alternate nights the Ladies would pepper the set with either "Sell, Sell, Sell" or "Tonight Is the Night I Fell Asleep at the Wheel."

"'Tonight Is the Night,' says Tyler, "was a really interesting moment in the show for us. I think that Steven really gets across this idea that a car crash is in this kind of weird netherworld. It really worked, and we really enjoyed playing it. A friend of ours, Wynn Klosky, said that the first time she heard us do it live, it felt like the whole audience was holding their breath while listening to it. The story is so compelling, and the music is so loopy and strange that she said that by the end of it she heard the whole audience exhale. There's this light-headed feeling to the whole experience."

The only *Maroon* single to really chart, "Pinch Me," was nominated for a Grammy, and the high-rotation video featured a cameo appearance by fellow Canadian Eric McCormack, star of NBC's hit-com *Will & Grace* (he plays Will, by the way). Hey, Ty, how'd you get that "Will" guy in that video anyway?

"Eric McCormack," Tyler reports, "was a huge fan of the band. He's from Toronto, and he used to come see us all the time. The great thing about the cameo is that it's so subtle. He's just

227

one of the guys in the restaurant dressed in identical stripe shirts."

What, I inquire, was the deal with those stripes?

"Steve Page came up with the concept of that video," Tyler tells me, "and it's so great, just so trippy and laden with meaning. Everybody is dressed sort of like that Steve guy from *Blue's Clues*. If you don't have kids and watch kids' TV, you might not know that Steve from *Blue's Clues* dresses like that. The concept, I guess, is that this Burger World in the video is the new community center, the new meeting place. I think that, to a certain degree, the song and the video observe a kind of assembly-line feel to life. The song's about waking up from that and actually participating in life. At the end of the video, in the burger place, both the disgruntled employee, played by Ed, and the regular, happy burger-eatin' people get jolted out of their moribund roles, everyday lives to do a dance number. Steven expressed it as 'Once in a while, you just gotta dance.' There's this concentration of happy people and sad people, and the video asks the question 'Can't we all just get along, and dance?' It's really a kind of a Busby Berkeley[1] type of thing."

The *Maroon* album represented a kind of full-circle, complete walkabout for BNL. As I mentioned in an earlier chapter, BNL had gone from *Gordon* to the corner of Sunset and Gordon. And as the sun set on that chapter of their career, the timing felt right to commemorate this milestone with a greatest-hits package, taking the band one step closer to what all bands aspire to: the Great Box Set in the Sky. *Disc One: All Their Greatest Hits 1991–2001*, gets its title from BNL's song "Box Set," which, you may have noticed, I quoted in the intro to the chapter on the recording sessions for *Gordon*. In addition to the two new tracks, "It's Only Me (The Wizard of Magicland)" and "Thanks, That

---

[1]Busby Berkeley (1895–1976) was an American choreographer and film director noted for lavish, synchronized dance routines in films such as *42nd Street* (1933).

Was Fun," the band has included a couple of tracks that have appeared elsewhere but never on an official Barenaked Ladies release. "Lovers in a Dangerous Time" is actually a cover of a Bruce Cockburn song. For those of you who may not have heard of him, Cockburn (pronounced "COE-burn") is a legendary Canadian songwriter whose passionate and sometimes politically charged songs are well known to Canadians. "Lovers" was one of his more accessible hits in Canada, and when the Ladies recorded it, before *Gordon,* it became not only their first hit single but their first-ever video as well, costing the equivalent of seven thousand U.S. dollars to make. Also included on *Disc One* was BNL's contribution to the *King of the Hill* TV soundtrack, "Get in Line." If you resisted buying that soundtrack then, you'll be happy to know the song has surfaced on the greatest-hits volume. I asked Ty about the new songs recorded especially for the hits compilation.

They recorded "It's Only Me (The Wizard of Magicland)" and "Thanks, That Was Fun" with Jim Scott at Phase One in Toronto. (Scott had been the engineer and did most of the mix on *Maroon.*) "Steven and Ed wrote those two new songs in four days," recalls Tyler, "because we were going into the studio to record this stuff in between the *Maroon* tours.

"When Kev first the heard the main riff of 'It's Only Me,'" recalls Tyler, "he just started singing, 'I am the wizard of Magicland.' We loved that. So we just put it into the title as a tribute to that. Now the song was just called 'It's Only Me,' but we wanted to confuse our manager, Terry, by telling him that it was called 'The Wizard of Magicland.' We just enjoyed hearing our manager say, 'The Wizard of Magicland.' We were all sitting around in this control room, and we had a conference call on a speakerphone. Terry asked what the new song was called. We told him, 'The Wizard of Magicland,' so he said it back to us, '"The Wizard of Magicland"?' We were, like, 'What was that, Terry?' He said, '"The Wizard of Magicland"' again. Then he asked, 'Do you have bad connection or something?' We said,

229

'No, we just wanted to hear you say "The Wizard of Magicland" over and over.'"

According to Tyler, Steven Page's lyrics to the song are about, and I quote directly here, "whacking off."

'Nuff said, really.

Another bonus on the hits compilation is a retrospective and somewhat melancholy song entitled "Thanks, That Was Fun." While it was a bona fide hit in Canada, it was not even released as a single in the United States. "We did a video in Canada," Tyler reveals. "It ended up being a kind of pastiche of all of our previous videos, but it was digitally altered to look like Ed was singing the new song. One of our managers, Pierre Tremblay, came up with that idea"

Tyler admits that while the Ladies were "under pressure" from their managers to have a new single on the collection, the unanimous reaction from the U.S. record company was that there was, as they say in the biz, "no single." "We had the 'we-don't-hear-a-single' chat," Tyler remembers. "So that's why there wasn't one released in the United States. At any rate, the record came out and still quietly went gold. So we were happy with that."

Tyler also announced, exclusively for this book, an unreleased gem in the vaults, one that might represent a possible new direction for the band. "There is," he told me, "this unreleased track called "I Can, I Will and I Do." It's sort of a slow funk number that we recorded at one in the morning. Maybe it'll surface one day; you never know."

And speaking of retrospectives, the Barenaked Ladies also took the time to catalog and release *Barelaked Nadies* (you read that right), an interactive DVD compilation of their greatest, and in some cases, cheapest videos. Released through Reprise Records on November 5, 2002, the disc features seventeen BNL music videos, plus seven songs from a live Ladies gig in New York City. All in glorious 5.1 surround sound (optional).

Not only does the DVD feature audio commentary from the

band, but you can also choose to view a video-commentary track that enables you to watch them watch themselves. Very postmodern of them, don't you think?

Additionally, the disc's groundbreaking ReVoice Studio feature allows you to interact and sing along karaoke-style with the "One Week" clip. *Barelaked Nadies* was the very first long-form music DVD to feature this technology.

Tyler says the experience of assembling and watching the clips was illuminating to all involved. They began with the very first video the band ever made. "'Lovers in a Dangerous Time'," recalls Tyler, "was our first hit in Canada, and our cheapest video ever. It cost only eleven thousand dollars Canadian, which is like seven thousand dollars American, maybe. Compare that with five hundred thousand dollars U.S. [for the] 'Too Little Too Late' video. You know, for some reason, 'Too Little Too Late' didn't do anything as a single. I mean, it's a crowd favorite, and I personally think the song has some magic."

Tyler admits that the DVD was not only a trip down memory lane for the guys; at times it was just trippy. "It was good to look back and see how horrendous our clothes and hairstyles were before we had stylists," offers Tyler. "We comment on that on the DVD as well. We did it in July 2002, at the Four Seasons Hotel in Toronto. It turns out that it was actually a star-studded day at the Four Seasons because at the same time, the Rolling Stones were also staying there. Later, I saw tennis star Pete Sampras in the elevator and Steve Yzerman of the Detroit Red Wings in the lobby."

These stars did not, however, join Barenaked Ladies back at their suite. The task of providing audio and video commentary fell to the Ladies themselves. "We all sat on a bed in this hotel room," says Tyler, "and they filmed us watching the videos and chatting. So now you have the option of just having the audio commentary while you're watching the videos or having a split-screen image of us sitting watching them and eating chips."

• • •

Also newly released during the last couple of years were three more Barenaked Babies. Yes, Ed, Steven, and Tyler have all reproduced yet again (each with his own respective partner, of course). Tyler and Jill had their second child, Hazel, on the exact same day that Steven and Carolyn had their third child, Jonah— April 16, 2001. Meanwhile, on August 7, 2002, Ed and Natalie released Arden, their third baby.

In lieu of making babies, the Brothers Creeggan gave birth to a record called *Sleepyhead*, their fourth (see "Appendix A: Serious Moonlighting"). I know I mentioned Kevin Hearn's *H Wing* disc, but what I didn't tell you is that at press time, he was busy readying yet another solo album that should be available by the time you read this.

And the Barenaked Ladies were the amiable hosts of the Canadian equivalent of the Grammy Awards show, the Juno Awards, a live TV special which was broadcast from St. John's, Newfoundland and seen across Canada. BNL performed original material and satirical songs written especially for the show, winning them a Gemini Award (like a Canadian Emmy) for their efforts.

Various other activities included Ed playing solo, accompanying skater Kurt Browning's *Gotta Dance* show in Vancouver, British Columbia, while elsewhere, solo Steven took part in the fifth annual White Ribbon Concert at the Phoenix Club in Toronto. Steven was one of many who helped raise money and awareness about men's violence against women. On that evening Steven joined legendary Canadian songwriter Bruce Cockburn (the man who wrote and first recorded "Lovers in a Dangerous Time") for an impromptu cover of the Beatles' "Don't Let Me Down." Additionally, Steven out-LeBonned himself with a characteristically irreverent version of Duran Duran's "Rio."

"With our stature," says Tyler proudly, "we've been able to do some really good things for charities in the last couple of years." One such charity event was the Barenaked Circus. Held at Molson Amphitheatre in Toronto on June 8, 2002, the circus featured Barenaked Ladies along with all their affiliated off-shoots: Thin Buckle, the Brothers Creeggan, and Matthew Page (Steven's brother) with his excellent band, Boyce's Road. The event was a benefit for an organization called Serve Canada, a youth-oriented community-service organization. The organization takes young people from diverse socioeconomic and ethnic backgrounds, divides them into teams, and then sends them out to do community service. "Through this work in team building," says Tyler proudly, "[Young people can] gain meaning in their lives and learn more about themselves."

While Kevin may be out of the woods with his leukemia, that doesn't mean that cancer is out of his life forever. As a cancer survivor, Kevin has been drafted by the disease, so to speak, to be a spokesman. Tyler is aware of the emotional toll this can take on his band mate. "I mean, Kev has to relive it every day, because people come up to him and kind of just start talking about their own experiences with cancer. Kevin becomes like an empath—a receptacle for people's feelings about cancer—and it's a tough role. Now it's such a hard-core part of his identity. Sometimes I see how it exhausts him, and I see him just go 'whoa' after hearing a harrowing story of survival, or even death. But even if he's a reluctant spokesman, I think he's really taken on the role eloquently. He does a great job of being an inspiration to people."

On October 9, 2002, Barenaked Ladies appeared at the British Columbia Cancer Society Benefit at GM Place in Vancouver. It was a memorial concert for Michelle Bourbonnais, who had succumbed to cancer a year earlier. "Michelle," Tyler explains, "was the wife of Clear Channel's Shane Bourbonnais, who is one of our promoters in Vancouver. Michelle had passed away really suddenly, at age thirty-one, and her dying wish was that there be a fund-raising concert to try and beat this thing."

At the concert, Barenaked Ladies joined Bryan Adams, Sarah McLachlan, Jann Arden, and Chantal Kreviazuk to raise $1.5 million (Canadian). Kevin, naturally, was an essential part of the event. "There is hope in finding a cure," Kevin told the Canadian

Press. "Twenty years ago, I certainly would have died, but thanks to research and the money that funds research, [I] and a lot of other people like me have been very lucky and are still alive."

"Shane had come to Kevin about the concert," Tyler explains, "and really opened [up] to him about his own situation. Our version of 'Close to You,' which we did with Burt Bacharach, had been [Shane and Michelle's] wedding song. It was a song very close to their hearts. When we performed the song at the show, Kevin introduced it and explained its significance. There wasn't a dry eye in the house."

One of the great side benefits for me in writing this book (and believe me, there have been many) has been meeting and working with so many inspiring and inspired people, as when yours truly was invited to speak at the Barenaked Bash in Toronto on June 22, 2002. I met many of the Ladies' fans and signed copies of the Canadian edition of this book. By the way, if you were among the many American fans in attendance and I signed your copy, please lovingly transfer my signature and any other scribblings that I may have made to this new version. And, hey, don't think of it as having bought the "same" book twice. No, no, no. Tell your friends, "I even have the rare Canadian edition *and* the more up-to-date U.S. edition." Add to this "I'm so cool, etc." and you're on your way.

Yes; that was Barenaked Ladies at the 2002 Superbowl Pregame Show in New Orleans and again in Salt Lake City for a triumphant appearance at the 2002 Winter Olympics. Partially broadcast on NBC's *Tonight Show with Jay Leno*, the boys went for the gold, with Ed donning his speed-skating one-piece as controversial Canadian skating medallists Jamie Sale and David Pelletier joined in the chorus.

Indeed, there has been much to rejoice in over the last couple of years. But it would be impossible to speak of these last years

A
F
T
E
R
W
O
R
D

without mentioning the ominous and omnipresent tragedy that occurred in New York, Washington, D.C., and rural Pennsylvania on September 11, 2001. Ask anyone from World War II– or Vietnam-era America: It's never easy living through history, especially life-altering, nasty, and downright frightening history in your own backyard. When the world changed that fall, the Barenaked Ladies paused like so many others, to reflect on family, friends, and what matters in life. But as Tyler Stewart explains here, for the first time in print, the politically aware Ladies were also moved to speak out in the wake of the tragedy.

Politics aside, I spoke with Tyler about the personal toll that 9/11 took on the band members' lives. "Immediately following September 11," Tyler recalls, "I didn't want to travel anywhere. We were supposed to play a show in Boston, a week later, and I just canceled it. Essentially, I wasn't going to leave my family. I was at home, but Jim was on his way to New York, driving from Boston to a gig with the Brothers Creeggan. My first thought was 'Was Jim down there?' plus we have a lot of friends in New York. Luckily, Jim was safe. But I essentially fled to the cottage with Jill and the kids, and absolutely realized just how important my family was to me."

Incredibly, the band had just flown from Boston's Logan Airport only three days before the eleventh. "We had just done a corporate show," Tyler recalls, "actually, for S.G. Cowan, which was, sadly, one of the firms that ended up losing people in the Trade Center collapse. We were on those early-morning flights all the time, and as far as I was concerned, I could have been on one of those planes. So it really, really freaked me out on a lot of levels. I didn't want to go back to the States, and I didn't want to leave my family right then. I didn't know if it was safe to fly. I mean, this was a big show in Boston. The Mix in Boston has been very supportive of us, and we were one of the headliners. I think they were thinking that 'the show must go on,' that it would be good for their listeners to help people through what had happened."

According to Tyler, Steven and Ed felt it was their duty to see that the show went on. Tyler, however, was not going to leave the cottage just yet. "I needed time to reflect. The world needed time to reflect. This was a human catastrophe, and I was feeling sick about it, mentally at least. And when people are sick, they take time off work. I thought everyone felt that way. Conversely, Ed felt it was his job to go and entertain and make people feel good. I couldn't do that, so we didn't go. At least my family was really happy that I didn't go. It was the first time in my life that I felt 'I can't do anything with this band right now; I need to be with my family.'"

Tyler admits that Jill had lost a former boyfriend in the Twin Towers. The tragedy that touched millions touched each one in different and personal ways. The Barenaked Ladies, while clearly a Canadian band, had spent a substantial part of their career in the United States, and as the crisis unfolded, there was no questioning the band's empathy for the Americans who had embraced them unconditionally for so many years.

"We're not American," Tyler explains, "but we've made our living there [the United States] for the better part of ten years. You know, right after 9/11 we missed an opportunity to reflect fully on what just happened. Immediately, perhaps, there was a necessary pause where we could take a look at ourselves, and maybe think about why this happened. America does a lot of good in the world, and yet there's been a lot of questionable foreign policy over the years." I point out that a lot of Americans I know feel just as bad about those things themselves. Nodding in agreement, Tyler points out that much of the best criticism he's read was written and published in America by Americans. "I've learned a lot by reading the writings of Noam Chomsky and reading publications like *Harper's* or [by checking out] Michael Moore in his films like *Canadian Bacon* and *Bowling for Columbine* or reading his book *Stupid White Men*."

One of the Barenaked Ladies responses to the inevitable bombing of Afghanistan was their involvement in a charity concert in Toronto, held just weeks after the attacks. They joined Nelly Furtado, Shaggy, Sarah McLachlan, SUM 41, and others in a concert that raised more than money; it raised questions and awareness.

Music Without Borders was an event to raise money for Afghan refugees displaced after their country was bombarded. Tyler says the concert was not motivated by any anti-American sentiment. It was merely a humanitarian response to the unfortunate side effects of the war on terrorism. "That still didn't stop the *Toronto Sun* from calling us apologists and cowards," Tyler admits. "They thought we should have been raising money for the Trade Center victims instead of the three million people who were facing starvation in the winter of 2001–2002. Since there was already quite a lot being done for the New York tragedy, [Music Without Borders] thought, 'How about helping elsewhere in the world?'

"Mr. Bush's immediate reaction," Tyler asserts, "was to bomb the poorest country on earth to 'root out the evildoers.' Granted, the guy who they thought did it was supposedly living there. They didn't get him, but they bombed the living crap out of the place looking. So we just thought about those victims, too. We want to try and save some lives and we'll use our musical voice to present alternatives. We raised $750,000 for food and medical aid, all of which was airlifted into Afghanistan."

According to the Red Cross and UNESCO, a lot of the funds reached the people who needed it. But besides raising money, the band chooses to use their media profile to raise awareness for a variety of causes. As a case in point, the Barenaked Ladies contributed a song to the *GasCD* (Governments Accountable to Society and Citizens = Democracy), an agitprop compilation put together by their friend and associate Chris Brown. The proceeds from the disc were to help promote awareness of the social and environmental impact of corporate globalization.

According to the *GasCD* website (www.gascd.com), "Funds generated [would] assist activist[s] and organizations who are

doing this important work, often in the face of severe repression."
The website explains that the project was inspired by the events
at the Summit of the Americas held in Quebec City in April 2001.
Tens of thousands of people from all over the Americas gathered
there to protest the FTAA (the Free Trade Area of the Americas)
and "the dominance of transnational corporations over local
communities, and to demand that our governments be accountable to the people they're supposed to represent."

The *GasCD* was released on the unfortunate date of September
11, 2001. Not the most media-friendly day in history to release anything with a dissenting social slant, although certainly a poignant
one. The album features politically charged spoken-word contributions from a wide array of academics and social commentators
as well as musical offerings from the likes of Ani DiFranco,
Spearhead's Michael Franti, and, of course, Barenaked Ladies. I
asked Tyler what motivated them to contribute a song to the affair.

"The *GasCD* was Chris Brown's baby. Chris has been so helpful to us over the years, and he really enlightened us to a lot the
stuff that went down at the Quebec Summit [of the Americas]. I
really supported the thrust of the *GasCD*, which was to raise
money for the legal defense of people who were arrested and
detained for the mere act of protesting in a democracy [Quebec
City, Canada], which is supposed to be our right. The amount of
force that was used, the excessive violence of the police was
really shocking to us. So we thought, 'If we can't express ourselves and voice dissent, then what is democracy?'"

Tyler says that the band was compelled to uphold freedom
of speech, one of the basic tenets of a democracy. "So we contributed 'Sell, Sell, Sell' to the *GasCD*, the band played at a concert, and Jim Creeggan did a [small tour] with Chris Brown."

But at the end of the day, Tyler said it best with the title of his
side project: *Don't Talk Dance*. For Barenaked Ladies is first and
foremost about making music and entertaining people. And as
we went to press, Barenaked Ladies began writing a new album,

which should already be in the stores by the time you read this. I don't know much about the titles or what the songs sound like, but Tyler did share something with me about the writing process. A new way of working has emerged for them. In the past, Steven or Ed would do the lion's share of the songwriting; maybe get together to demo the songs and then bring them to band rehearsal pretty much finished. This is great if you don't like writing songs and just want to play. But for the other guys, particularly Jim and Kevin, the old approach excluded them from the songwriting process and left them to their respective solo careers as solace for their hungry muses. All that has changed, as the band entered the writing sessions for the first time entirely as a collective. Tyler says that it's more of a statement of maturity in the band, after years of getting to know one another.

"I think everybody in the band now knows that we all own the group," Tyler explains. "We've all matured so much over the years of this band. That's why we wrote the new album as a group. It was all new for us as a band."

I asked Tyler to describe a typical writing session. So he did. "Basically, the band would set up in a rehearsal studio with all our gear and crew. Then, it's like, 'Anyone got any ideas?' So Jim might say, 'Yeah, I have one.' Then he might start playing or singing a line, and we'd respond with one. Then it's pad-and-paper time, going line by line, working it out. It's been really good, I feel, for Jim and Kevin who are fairly prolific songwriters outside the band. I think they wanted a change from Steven and Ed coming in with demos that are nearly finished. In the past, by the time they heard [the demos], the imprint of the song was so burned into our skulls that it was hard to find any variations from it. I think it was just time to tap into the full resources, and it's a good thing for Jim and Kevin. And it's great for me. I just get to play all kinds of interesting music. I don't even like to put myself deep into the foray. I see my job as support and seeing everything through. On *Maroon* it really came home to me that I'm just the drummer. I think over the years, I had this delusion that I was going to one day write songs. Any minute I'd just come up with one. But oddly enough, it was only on *Maroon*, five albums into our recording career, I let go and fully became *the drummer*. Not being a songwriter, I feel I'm kind of like a cheerleader for all the songs. I love them all. Now the writing process is more equal, but I still think there's a lot things we all have to consider, though. Ed had a valid point when he said that in the past our stuff wasn't presented equally. Ed and Steven would get together and write, and their songs would be developed really seriously before the demos were presented to the band. Whereas Jim or Kev might just play them to us on a piano or an acoustic guitar, so it was never presented equally. Steven has to become comfortable singing other people's songs, or having people adding to his songs. And likewise, Steven and Ed have to become more like Jim and Kev. But Jim and Kev, I think, have to become more like Steve and Ed and assume some of their responsibilities, in terms of the writing. It's a trade-off. It's a nice challenge."

What, then, does the future hold for Barenaked Ladies? What will be on *Disc Two*, the second disc in the Great Box Set in the Sky (my guess for the title, not theirs), to be released presumably in ten years' time? Will there even be a Barenaked Ladies? Perhaps Tyler's closing comment provides the answer.

"You know, when we hosted the Juno awards in St. John's, we had to come up [with] all this material off the top of our heads in no time at all. We just hunkered down and did it. It worked. And I thought, right there, 'I just signed on for another ten years in this band.'"

Appendix A

Serious Moonlighting:
Solo Stunts Featuring Various Ladies

At various times during BNL's career, certain band members, in their desire to satisfy their muse, have taken to moonlighting on projects outside the city limits of Barenaked Town.

The Brothers Creeggan

Andy and Jim have long realized their sixth sense, or intuitive connection, as brothers. Over the years, this chemistry has evolved into a repertoire of original material. Four full-length CDs, *The Brothers Creeggan*, *The Brothers Creeggan II*, *Trunks*, and recently, *Sleepyhead*, have all been released independently, originally distributed by Naida Creeggan. With every CD delivered, there was a personalized note from Mom.

Jim says that he and his brother had visions of their own special groove and simply went to track it down. "We'd been making recordings since high school. It was a perfect time to explore the brother thing a little further."

The Brothers Creeggan

The Brothers Creeggan (released on Warner Music Canada, CDW 46091) was recorded between Barenaked Ladies obligations and just before Andy left the band. Although it represents a departure from Barenaked Ladies' sound, it was actually produced by Michael Phillip Wojewoda, producer of *Gordon*, *Born on a Pirate Ship*, and *Rock Spectacle*. Andy plays piano, percussion, accordion, hammer dulcimer, and steel pan in addition to singing some lead vocals. Jim plays his trusty bass but also plays guitar, tap-dances, and sings. He even plays piano on "Fallin'."

Various friends help out on the record, such as singer John Millard on "Clown Song." Erica Buss sings soprano, while Moxy Fruvous's singer, Dave Matheson, loans his distinctive tenor to "Bienvenue." Parents Naida and Burn Creeggan sing on the old family favorite "Shantytown," on top of which Dad plays piano. And *The Brothers Creeggan* also features a cameo by one particular invited guest whose voice you oughta know. Yes, that is *the* Alanis Morissette scatting and cooing on "Places."

The Brothers Creeggan II

The website describes it best: "1995 was a year of big changes (Andy left Barenaked Ladies), however we managed to get into the studio for album number two. It was done in little bits with friend Rick Kilburn at his home studio in Vancouver between the fall of that year and the following summer. Like the first album there was a lot of writing done right in the studio but unlike the first, we produced it ourselves. Despite the short duration of *Brothers Creeggan II*, there was a lot of material to be experimented with. In fact there was too much, so we concentrated on the 'ditties' and left the more experimental instrumental ideas for another time (some still lie in wait, but Andy went ahead and recorded most of his ideas in May and July '96 in Toronto with Wojewoda for *Andiwork*)."

Trunks

The sibling revelry continues with the release of *Trunks*, the first Creeggan project with an actual title. Andy, deep into a music-composition program at Montreal's prestigious McGill

University, managed to tear himself away long enough to join up with equally free time–challenged Jim, and knock out eleven more slices of Creegganism. This time, the boys pulled even more toys out of their collective musical trunks. In addition to his trusty piano, Andy plays accordion, guitar, Peruvian box percussion, and hammer dulcimer. While it's a no-brainer that Jim plays his double bass, he also stretches on the viola, guitar, piano, and tap dancing.

Their album bio says, "*Trunks* reflects a mélange of styles borne out across its eleven songs, from the ringing melodicism of 'Stuck' to the jazzy, Bacharach-style pop of 'Fondly Yours,' the slippery Latin tinge of 'John's in the Fridge' and the rootsy jangle of 'Lila' (pronounced Lee-la). Skewed, jagged piano lines slice through 'Kitchen Dancing,' while 'She Married a Cowboy' and 'There's a Melody' are gentler, marked by subtle touches such as polyrhythms and melancholy whistles."

Trunks sounds like a house, or a home rather, inhabited by a very musical family. Drummer Ian MacLauchlan moves into the guest room, so to speak, to play drums throughout, while Kevin Hearn stops by to lend his guitar skills to "John's in the Fridge" and Vancouver singer-songwriter Veda Hille lends a neighborly accordion to "Lila." Despite these house guests, *Trunks* is very much a family affair, with much of the lyrical content dwelling on what Jim calls "Creeggans lore."

Author's note: In January 2000, just prior to Jim's beginning work on *Maroon*, the Brothers Creeggan pulled off an impressive forty-city tour of North America that reached, as they say, "every major U.S. and Canadian market."

Sleepyhead

For their fourth album, the original "band of brothers," Jim and Andy Creeggan, along with third "brother" Ian McLauchlan, decamped to an "old stone house on a windy patch of land" to record the dreamily titled *Sleepyhead*. The first song on the album, "You Will Be Adored," is a kind of hello-good-bye song filled with the trials and tribulations of love and loss. The lovely and talented Sarah Harmer (a familiar Barenaked Ladies opening artist) makes a pivotal appearance on a plaintive little tune called "Anna on the Moon," which also features the lovely and talented Ed Robertson. In the bio for the album, Jim told Anna Hill about the song's central idea. "As a constant traveler," Jim explained, "I often wonder if home is a person, place, or symbol. In the song, I realize that home is where the heart is."

Other songs include "Vote for Beauty" (a song for which Andy claimed musical inspiration from the work of former Eric's Trip member Julie Doiron), "Coastline," and "Ali Baba's," the latter being actually a tribute to a Toronto falafel shop frequented by the Creeggans. With it's allusions to Middle Eastern cuisine, one might assume that it was written in some way as a post–9/11 reaction to a growing consciousness of Arab perspectives and culture. Not so, says Jim. "I wrote 'Ali Baba's' before September 11," Jim told Anna Hill, "and now, when issues in the Arab world are so weighted, the simple celebration of what this family brings to my neighborhood is that much more valuable."

The ephemeral nature of joy and the inevitability of sadness coexist on *Sleepyhead* as it delves into the subconscious mind of the listener; its sound is kind of like that of the sound asleep. The dream theme runs through tracks like "Long and Slow," "Sometimes," and "Grey." "Bye Song" attempts to convey Andy's feelings about the death of his mother-in-law, in musical as well as verbal terms.

The Brothers Creeggan toured in support of *Sleepyhead*, as they continue to do whenever Barenaked Ladies are dormant. Additionally, Andy Creeggan has been seen preparing *Andiwork II*, the sequel to, um, *Andiwork*.

Andy and Jim's Other Excellent Adventures

Honor the Earth (a tribute CD)

Jim and Andy backed up renowned songwriter Jane Siberry on a tune called "My Mother Is Not the White Dove."

Just Andy

Andiwork

Andy's solo album, produced by Michael Phillip Wojewoda.

Pet-Kout-Koy-ek, Songs for a River

A benefit CD for the Petitcodiac river in Moncton, New Brunswick. The last track on the disc, which includes many east coast artists, is another collaboration between Andy on piano and percussionist Jean Surette on marimba.

Just Jim

Surfacing (Sarah McLachlan)

Jim Creeggan's upright and outright bass appears in four songs: "Do What You Have to Do," "Witness," "Angel," and "Last Dance."

Angel Food for Thought (Meryn Cadell)

Jim plays bass on "Confide" and "I Say."

With Love and Squalor (Mia Sheard)

Andy plays a "little tiny bit" of piano on "Call Me." The album was coproduced by Michael Phillip Wojewoda.

Tyler Stewart

Don't Talk Dance

Now a hard-to-find collectible release, *DTD* was actually a funky, improvised collaboration between Tyler, guitarist Gordie Johnson from the band Big Sugar, and erstwhile Barenaked Ladies keyboard player Chris Brown, then a member of the Bourbon Tabernacle Choir and now one-half of Fenner and Brown.

The album has a good beat and is easy to dance to. Chris, however, recently recalled the whole thing as a "total joke" that went too far. "We used to have these New Year's parties at the Bourbons' house at Dundas and Sherbourne in Toronto," he says. "There would be, like, three hundred people there in this big old Victorian mansion, with a huge backyard and a fifteen-hundred-square-foot basement, and we'd have these parties that were so great, especially the New Year's parties, because people would start showing up around two or three A.M., after their own gigs, you know. We'd have big breakfasts and everything."

But, according to Chris, it was literally an underground music scene. "The basement was where we all played and made music," he says, "so those parties would always have these weird musical conglomerations of different people playing different shit. Gordie and Ty and I would just end up as the rhythm section.

"'Hey,' someone said, 'let's book a gig and play this stuff for paying customers!' All *Don't Talk Dance* was," deadpans Chris, "was us shamelessly taking that to the stage and then shamelessly making a record. Which Warner Music Canada shamelessly released." *Gordon*mania was still in full swing back then, so logically *Don't Talk Dance* was marketed (if you could call it that) as a "Tyler Stewart Solo Project."

The *Don't Talk Dance* album has become a collector's item to Barenaked Ladies fans. It's a fun record, even though, as Brown admits, it sounds like it was slapped together a little hastily. "It was mainly done over the course of one night doing these live gigs at Ultrasound, and we just recorded them. Then we went into Presence Studios in Toronto and did a bunch of overdubbing. It was just a total joke that went too far. We just played live and recorded the whole thing."

Vostok 6 (Kurt Swinghammer)

Tyler makes a vocal appearance on *Vostok 6*, an electronic space odyssey by Toronto multimedia composer Kurt Swinghammer. *Vostok 6* is a concept album about "space travel, the Cold War, feminism, and unrequited love," inspired by the Soviet space mission that launched cosmonaut Valentina Tereshkova, the first woman in outer space. *Vostok 6*, described as "sixty minutes of songs, soundscapes and spoken-word vignettes blended into one seamless musical statement," has recently been rereleased by Ani DiFranco's label, Righteous Babe Records.

Tyler plays MC Squared, a late-night radio DJ sending shouts out to Bob Moog and Leo Theremin, inventors of some of the electronic instruments employed by Swinghammer. The mix was done by Wojewoda.

Kevin Hearn

The Look People (various recordings)

Kevin made several albums with the Look People before joining Barenaked Ladies. These wacky, off-the-wall records are packed with examples of musical virtuosity and manual dexterity. Think Frank Zappa, then stop thinking Frank Zappa and think Barnum & Bailey Circus. Here are the albums: *More Songs about Hats and Chickens; Small Fish, Big Pond;* and *Boogazm and Crazy Eggs.*

Mothball Mint (Kevin Hearn's first solo album)

"It's too scary to think that people are listening to songs about me, you know?" Kevin says. "I guess *Mothball Mint* is the songs I wrote to counterbalance the comedy world I was in. While I was singing it, I started realizing what the songs were about. It was hard, but I'm glad I did it. I sometimes felt guilty that I hadn't done it sooner. Making *Mothball Mint* was something I always wanted to do. Most of these songs were written in the last few years of the Look People. My other bands were always kinda kooky and fun, so to balance that out, I would write sadder or more serious songs.

"I got Jim on bass, Great Bob Scott [from the Look People] on drums, and Martin Tielli [from the Rheostatics] played some guitar on it. It was all my favorite people." He adds, "It got me excited, but I was also kind of scared about the responsibility. I remember thinking, 'Well, I'm paying for this, so I can do whatever the heck I want!'" Kevin recorded the album at Toronto's Rogue Studio; Wojewoda produced.

H Wing (Kevin Hearn and Thin Buckle)

Kevin wrote a lot of dark songs to reflect his dark times while confined to the hospital during his recovery. Much of this writing became the basis of his second solo album, *H Wing*. "I wrote the whole thing while I was in isolation," he says. "There's the darkness of the situation but also a lot of lyrics about hope and transcending the situation and the challenges, and some humor, too."

When not off touring with Barenaked Ladies, Kevin's Toronto-based band, Thin Buckle, affords him yet another outlet for his tragicomic muse. The band is comprised of some of Kevin's favorite players, from bands like the Rheostatics and his old band, the Look People.

"It's three guys from the Look People," Kevin explains. "We've got Derek Orford, and there's Chris Gartner on the bass, and they're joined by Great Bob Scott, who plays quite tastefully on the drums. And then there's Martin Tielli on guitar." One song, originally intended for Thin Buckle, was recorded by Barenaked Ladies for *Maroon*. Although it didn't quite fit in the final running order and was relegated to a bonus track on the initial pressings of *Maroon*, "Hidden Sun" is one of the most arrestingly humble and beautiful songs I've ever heard. I hope you get to hear it, too.

It's not surprising that Kevin would hook up with the Rheostatics' Tielli, who also played on *Mothball Mint*. Kevin is a key player on at least two of the Rheos' most serious works.

Music Inspired by the Group of Seven (the Rheostatics)

Dave Bidini of the Rheostatics says that his band had long been admirers of Kevin Hearn. So when they made their tribute to the Canadian painter's collective known as the Group of Seven, they brought him in on keyboards. "We'd always thought about recruiting him for the Rheos," Bidini admits, "but, like a lot of things, could never decide how or when. So when we did 'G7' [*Music Inspired by the Group of Seven*], it was something we'd all thought about for a few years."

Bidini notes that Kevin brought what he termed a "real tenderness" to the project. "Especially a song like 'Kevin's Waltz,'" he says, "which immediately became our favorite, more than any of our own compositions." Kevin performed the G7 song cycle with the Rheostatics at Toronto's Danforth Music Hall, shortly before he was to enter the hospital for his cancer treatment. Bidini remembers how everyone was touched by this poignant performance. "When he sang [the phrase], '. . . and then lie down,'" Bidini remembers, "I think we all felt this terrible beautiful charge in our hearts. It was quite emotional. None of [us] knew what the future held, and I think the thought crossed our minds that it could potentially be the last time we ever played this way together. We did about five songs from G7 that night, and the audience just dropped their chins to the floor. It worked so well. Page was there, showing his support, and so was Tyler, who, in fact, appeared dressed as a bumblebee onstage."

The Story of Harmelodia (the Rheostatics)

The Story of Harmelodia is ostensibly a children's record with an accompanying storybook. The Rheostatics' core lineup of Don Kerr, Dave Bidini, Tim Vesely, and Martin Tielli is augmented by Michael Phillip Wojewoda and Kevin Hearn. Kevin not only played keyboards and guitar, but he also wrote and sang lead vocals on "Monkeybird," "Dot Tries the Wingophone," and "Wingophone." Over the course of its twenty songs and thirty illustrated glossy pages of text, *The Story of Harmelodia* describes the adventures of Dot and her brother, Bug, in the land of Harmelodia. Filled with memorable characters such as the Monkeybird and a dude named Drumstein, this cautionary song cycle peddles a progressive-rock-concept-album theme previously employed by countrymen Rush for their *2112* in the '70s. But, in the steps of Harry Nilsson's *The Point!* and the lesser-known *Mount Vernon and Fairway* (a recording by Brian Wilson and the Beach Boys, based on an obscure but recently rediscovered bedtime story), the heavy message is cleverly wrapped up in a children's story. And the CD's storybook packaging takes the concept all the way home; it even comes complete with a "This book belongs to" page, so your little brother doesn't take your copy to school by accident.

Reptilian (Mia Sheard)

Kevin plays keyboards (tracks not specified on CD) on Sheard's second album, once again produced by Michael Phillip Wojewoda. By odd coincidence, original Barenaked Ladies keyboard player Andy Creeggan performed on Mia's first album, *With Love and Squalor.* Kind of makes you think, eh?

Steven Page

Thomas and the Magic Railroad: Original Motion Picture Soundtrack

Steven sings the song "Really Useful Engine" on this soundtrack album to the big-screen adaptation of the popular kid's television program that starred Alec Baldwin and Peter Fonda.

Borrowed Tunes: Out of the Black, into the Blue (Choclatey)

Chips off the old block, Steven, Tyler, and honorary Ladie Stephen Duffy appear as Choclatey on this Sony Canada tribute to the songs of Neil Young. Appropriately enough, the trio performs a Neil Young song called "Burned." Released only in Canada, it's a hard-to-find prize.

Ed Robertson

Shakespearean Fish (Melanie Doane)

You'll hear Ed's backup vocals on Doane's first CD, in the song "Tell You Stories."

The Waltons

Ed produced two tracks, one of which appeared on the *Friends 2* soundtrack.

Andy Kim

This is a not-yet-released cowrite produced by Ed.

Yap (A Canadian indie hip-hop band)

Rapping on a song called "Comin' at Ya from the Suburbs."

Barenaked Ladies with Rheostatics

Whale Music

Long before Kevin joined either of these two bands, the original five Barenaked Ladies provided the "ooohs" on the Rheostatics epic "California Dreamline." In the same spirit of *nom de disque* accreditation that saw the Suburban Tabernacle Choir make an appearance on *Gordon*, the Ladies returned the favor under the cover of an easy-to-guess-who-it-really-is alias, "The Scarborough Naked Youth Choir."

According to Dave Bidini, *Whale Music* was a product of the collaborative era of the Toronto music scene. "It was a sweet time," says Bidini. "The spirit of the times was 'Let's everybody play on each other's records!' It still exists to a point, at least with some bands." But back in the times of *Gordon*, what Michael Phillip Wojewoda once called "cross-pollination" of the bands was more common.

According to the way Bidini remembers it, this sharing of talent was largely due to a general sense of cocky optimism that pervaded the local scene. "Everyone was emerging and very confident, if not competitive," Bidini admits, "and we all felt good enough about what lay ahead to assert ourselves in each other's domain."

But there's always been something more pronounced in the camaraderie and history between Barenaked Ladies and the Rheostatics. The connection runs onto many levels, throughout many years and across countless miles of cold, cold road. That road initially stretched from Toronto to the nation's capital, Ottawa, and to Café Deluxe, then managed by Pierre Tremblay, future member of the Barenaked Ladies' management team. The Rheostatics were headliners, but they brought along their recent acquaintances Barenaked Ladies in the support slot. The rest is Bidini's story.

"Café Deluxe," Bidini recalls, "was a great night—very hot and sticky, and the jamming stretched as far as the summer sky. As I recall, things went on a bit and we had a big 'Horses' ending with both bands going at it atop speakers and stuff. I believe there were about twelve people in the audience."

An earlier New Year's Eve show that they'd shared was Bidini's first brush with Barenakedness. And the catalyst for him even being there was a local rock-journalist-turned-band-manager (and wicked slide guitarist) named Howard Druckman. "Howard Druckman had talked them up an awful lot," says

Bidini, adding, "I think he's the true source of their local popularity—[he was] Fan Number One—and I was curious. First, they were great guys: warm, hilarious, obviously very close. Page wore this great sparkly blue Treat Baker blazer and had such a powerful voice. They were as quick and funny as their songs."

However, the bonding wasn't all mutual appreciation and back-patting. The two bands were also bluntly honest with each other about what they'd expected their bands to be like. "I remember Ed telling me that he thought the Rheos were gonna be all cornball C&W 'cause all he'd heard was 'The Ballad of Wendel Clark,'" Bidini recalls. "I told him that I thought the BNL would be just goofy novelty tunes. We proved each other wrong and had a pretty close relationship, as bands, for the next couple of years.

"We shared managers, offices, and labels with BNL [Rheostatics were signed briefly to Sire Records], but that wasn't really the root of it," Bidini says. "It was this breakout Toronto sound that I think we've gone on to explore in our own ways. I mean, jeez, Change of Heart's *Smile*, *Whale Music*, and *Gordon* were all made by the same producer in the same studio and came out within a year of each other. There was great synergy, and it's reflected on those records."

The place was Reaction Studios, where the ubiquitous Michael Phillip Wojewoda usually worked, and a studio that the Rheostatics considered "sacred ground." In fact, says Bidini, he was a little overwhelmed by the crowd that had gathered to sing on "If I Had $1,000,000" that day. "The *Gordon* sing-along freaked me out a little," admits Bidini, "because I wasn't sure why so many people had been invited to Reaction. It had been a sacred place for us."

Bidini is credited on that session as "Veteran Warhorse," which always seemed appropriate yet curious to me. So I asked him if there was any great back-story behind the equine alias. "It was just a name Dave Bookman gave me," he says, "so it stuck."

Bidini told me a bit about opening some shows for the Ladies and the subsequent jams that occurred. "Calgary was the best show," he reflects. "Page joined us onstage and sang 'Rock Death America.' He freaked us out 'cause we didn't think he knew the words. Jim jammed in 'What's Going On.' Tyler was up all the time, of course. I remember seeing the BNL stage, which had all this blue-and-white bunting on it, and Tyler saying, 'It looks like the fuckin' Democratic convention.' There was something unimpeachable about the vibe there, and at Ontario Place (we opened that show, too), when the crowd sang 'Brian Wilson,' Page stepped back from the mic as if he'd been shot. The astonishment was clearly written on his face: the crowd just opening up and letting go. It was really moving and sweet, and the song never sounded better. I heard that Brian Wilson recently sang that song, but I don't think any version could match that evening's."

Barenaked Ladies with Tom Jones

Reload ("Little Green Bag")

This is Steven Page in a sort of duet with the Welsh belter Tom Jones on the retro classic "Little Green Bag," which some of you might remember from Quentin Tarantino's film *Reservoir Dogs*. On the heels of *Stunt,* it's likely that Tom's "people" had the excellent idea of inviting the guys to sing on his duet album, which also includes British stars like Robbie Williams, Cerys Matthews (from Catatonia), and Australian popstress Natalie Imbruglia.

"It's kind of an all-star British lineup, for the most part, but we're there," says Tyler. "He [Jones] was only there on the first night, and his voice was blown out. He was wearing a mesh-singlet, really loose-weave angora sweater, and he blew in and said, 'My voice is fucked.' His voice may have been blown out, but he still sang like a motherfucka."

"I think he had bronchitis or something," says Steven, "but he still blew everyone away. But he really did have to cancel a few dates after that session, and he had to go back later and re-

A
P
P
E
N
D
I
X

A

254

record his vocal parts on it. We recorded it in this studio that UB40 have in Birmingham—it's a bit of a shithole—then we went back to London to rerecord it."

"Tom was amazing," says Ed. "He's got this big, rockin' voice [does booming impression of Tom Jones singing first line of "Little Green Bag]."

"Steve sings his ass off too, though," declares Tyler. "That's the thing. It's a totally even duet." Ed warned me in advance about the mix, which I assume he didn't approve of. "Wait," he cautioned, "till you hear the totally English, reverb-crazy production, though."

In addition to meeting the man who sang "Delilah," Kevin was even allowed to take home a tiny lock of digital Tom in his trusty sampler for future use. "I thought Tom Jones was a great guy," Kevin raved. "It was inspiring to meet someone like him. I got permission to use some samples of his solo vocal track, got some great stuff. I use it in the show."

Barenaked Ladies with Burt Bacharach

One Amazing Night

In 1998 the band was asked to appear with legendary pop composer Burt Bacharach for a concert that paid tribute to his many great pop songs. Bacharach and his lyricist, Hal David, were responsible for many classics, including "Walk on By," "I Say a Little Prayer," and "Do You Know the Way to San José." On the heels of Bacharach's collaboration with Elvis Costello, *Painted from Memory*, an assortment of great artists was assembled. These included Costello, who performed "God Give Me Strength," Sheryl Crow, who performed "One Less Bell to Answer," and Ben Folds Five, who hammered out "Raindrops Keep Fallin' on My Head."

Barenaked Ladies prepared their own version of the Carpenters' hit "Close to You," but according to Tyler, Burt had his own ideas about the arrangement. "He wanted us to do a different song, and then he said, 'It's too much of a tribute to Karen Carpenter.' We were like, 'What's up with that?' I think it was because he wasn't playing with us or something. So we sat with him and rearranged it. "I was playing guitar all along," adds Kevin. "We were trying to take it away from the kind of traditional versions of the song; that's what we understood that they wanted.

"They said it was a Burt Bacharach tribute concert," Kevin continues, "but when we showed up, it had turned into just a Burt Bacharach concert. I also don't think that he liked the fact that we changed the music. It'd become something different—he said he liked what we did, but we didn't get to do it."

And yes, folks, Mike Myers, the comedian, actor, and cultural icon whose show-stopping rendition of the Bacharach classic, "What's New, Pussycat?" is a highlight of the soundtrack album, also hails from Scarborough, Ontario. Just like the Ladies. And myself.

The show is also available on videocassette.

Barenaked Ladies with the Lilac Time

lilac6

Three fifths of BNL unite with Stephen Duffy's band, the Lilac Time, on their *lilac6* album. Steven Page, Tyler Stewart, and Kevin Hearn appear, in various roles, on the songs "Jeans in the Summer," "Entourage," (cowritten with Page), "Foglights," "Forest Brown," and "Dance out of the Shadows."

Steven Page also reports that the Japanese version includes a bonus disc with "Dance out of the Shadows," "Kiss Me," "The Girl Who Waves at Trains," and "Looking for a Day in the Night," featuring an uncredited BNL as the backing band, recorded live in 2000 at the Royal Albert Hall in London, at the culmination of the Lilac Time's support tour for BNL.

Barenaked Ladies with Various Artists

Listen to What the Man Said (Oglio Records)

Subtitled *Popular Artists Pay Tribute to the Music of Paul McCartney*, Ladies Kevin Hearn and Steven Page join their old mate Stephen Duffy and bow to "Macca" on their version of "Junk," originally on the Cute One's eponymous solo debut. In addition to Top 40–charters and former BNL tour mates Semisonic, who perform "Jet," the album also features fine interpretations of solo McCartney songs by a diverse range of so-called alternative artists—hence, the respectful presence of Matthew Sweet, They Might Be Giants, Robyn Hitchcock, Sloan, the Finn Brothers (Neil and Tim), and, of course, Karl Wallinger's "band on the run" World Party, for whom this McCartney-themed project must have seemed like a busman's holiday.

For the Kids ("La La La")

Having conquered the legendary Burt Bacharach, the Ladies next pondered the importance of being Ernie and Bert, as they took on the Sesame Street classic "La La La," brought to you by the letter *L*.

For the Kids was released by Nettwerk on November 5, 2002, to benefit the Sarah McLachlan Music Outreach. On the CD, Barenaked Ladies are joined by contributors Five for Fighting, Dan Wilson, and Wilco. Proceeds go to Sarah's venture with Arts Umbrella, in the form of a unique school offering free music education to inner-city youth in her home of Vancouver, British Columbia. Stateside, Nettwerk America has teamed with VH1's Save the Music as part of an ongoing campaign to restore and nurture music-education programs in the U.S. public-school system and to raise awareness about the importance of music programs for children. A portion of the proceeds from the U.S. release of *For the Kids* will be donated to Save the Music, which is a nonprofit organization.

Barenaked Ladies Album Cut
for Movie Soundtrack

At Any Cost: Original TV Movie Soundtrack

This VH1 original movie for television is about a fictional band looking for their big break and a chance at platinum, at any cost. Predictably, their story turns grisly as the band members, their girlfriends, and their manager all sell their various and collective souls. One band member dies of an overdose. The manager cuts a deal with a record label that will result in blue-chip stock options for himself at the expense of his trusting client. Bullets are fired, people fall from spiral staircases to their death. Think *This Is Spinal Tap* meets *Faust*, blend in the earnest melodrama of *Party of Five*, add a dash of *Melrose Place*'s glamorous L.A. nightlife, and you've got the idea. While the Ladies are on the soundtrack with "Pinch Me," the movie really has nothing to do with anything in the career of Barenaked Ladies. So stop asking, okay? Several original songs were written and performed for the fictitious band to mime along with on camera. But Barenaked Ladies' song "Pinch Me" is not one of them, and Barenaked Ladies do not appear in the movie at any time. The first single from *Maroon* was merely added to the soundtrack album, along with a new song by Eagle Eye Cherry, to lend a little real value to what would have been a hard sell otherwise. It also provided the Ladies with a prerelease teaser that would be advertised on the music channel a month before the September 12 street date of *Maroon*.

Barenaked Ladies Single-Song Exclusives

What follows are some of Barenaked Ladies' recordings of songs that haven't been released, for one reason or another, on actual Barenaked Ladies albums, as well as secret tracks found on *Rock Spectacle*. In the studio, a band will often record more songs than they can actually use in order to have more songs to choose from in the final sequencing of the finished album. Early on, Barenaked Ladies found that these tracks could be incredibly handy as exclusive offerings to supervisors of soundtrack albums and other specialized projects. Perhaps one day there will be an official Barenaked Ladies compilation of all of these stray tracks, but until that day, you'll just have to go hunting for these rarities.

Coneheads: Music from the Original Motion Picture Soundtrack ("Fight the Power")

Contains a remake of Barenaked Ladies' version of Public Enemy's "Fight the Power." The original had been the only cover on *The Yellow Tape*, yet this version was recorded by Michael Phillip Wojewoda during the sessions for *Gordon*. It was left off of *Gordon* in favor of an all-original set list.

Disney's Music from the Park ("Grim Grinning Ghosts")

Barenaked Ladies perform "Grim Grinning Ghosts" on a 1996 Disney album called *Music from the Park* with various artists performing Disney songs. Steven reports that this was "Kevin's first studio venture with us."

King of the Hill: Original TV Soundtrack ("Get in Line")

Barenaked Ladies perform "Get in Line" on this soundtrack to the popular Fox Network animated series from *The Beavis & Butt-Head Show* creator, Mike Judge.

The Grinch: Original Motion Picture Soundtrack ("Green Christmas")

During the *Maroon* sessions, the guys were approached by Ron Howard to contribute to the holiday fantasy film *The Grinch*, starring Jim Carrey. At the time, they were jokingly referring to Carrey's next movie as *Liar Liar 2: Pants on Fire*, even describing the French version as *Pantalon au Feu*. Ed cooked up "Green Christmas" after the band had watched a prerelease video of the finished film. In two days, the band wrote and recorded the track, an upbeat song that Kevin described as "from the Grinch's perspective—but with a twist."

Grinch me.

Christmas Songs: The Nettwerk Christmas ("God Rest Ye Merry Gentlemen")

Originally recorded on a portable DAT player backstage at the Palace of Auburn Hills in 1997, Little Drummer Guy Tyler Stewart had only a suitcase for a drum (pah-rum-pah-pum-pum). This version of "God Rest Ye Merry Gentleman," a duet with Nettwerkmate Sarah McLachlan, is one of many interesting and delightful holiday offerings on this late-November 2000 release.

Barenaked Ladies: Rock Spectacle

The 1996 live album includes the uncredited, hidden gems "Sweetest Woman" and "Uncle Elwyn" at the very end of track eleven, "If I Had $1,000,000."

Barenaked Ladies Hits Compilation

Disc One: All Their Greatest Hits 1991–2001

Don't be fooled. This is not just a clever title; this is the real deal. A complete retrospective of the Barenaked Ladies first ten years as a group, *Disc One* takes it's title from the first verse of "Box Set," from the band's seminal debut album, *Gordon*. When Steven Page wrote the lyrics for that song, the idea of a box set seemed rather unlikely for a band at the start of their career. But funny things happen when a group stays together for more than a decade. And this is one of those things. True to form and formula, this compilation does indeed contain all BNL's greatest hits with the obligatory "unreleased" and "hard-to-find" tracks. But in addition to obvious tracks like "One Week," "Brian Wilson," and "If I Had $1,000,000," there were two new tracks recorded especially for this release: "It's Only Me (The Wizard of Magicland)—see Tyler's discussion of, page 229—and "Thanks, That Was Fun."

A kind of thank-you note left on the dresser of life, "Thanks, That Was Fun" is a mildly melancholic stagger down memory lane. The solemnity of the tune brings to mind an earlier Ed Robertson song, "When I Fall," while the lyrical refrain of "Don't forget / No regrets" makes a quantum leap into something resembling a band philosophy. This was a hit in Canada, by the way, where it was released with a fascinating video that employed digitally altered retrospective footage (apparently the brainchild of Pierre Tremblay).

Disc One also includes "Get in Line," which previously appeared only on the *King of the Hill* soundtrack, and "Lovers in a Dangerous Time," a song by fellow countryman Bruce Cockburn, which appeared on a Cockburn tribute album, released only in Canada, entitled *Kick at the Darkness.* The low-budget clip for this song, featuring members of other bands like Skydiggers and the Rheostatics, was the very first video Barenaked Ladies ever made, and it shows.

Appendix B

Roadside Diversions

And now, Ladies—and friends of Ladies—a little light entertainment.

Hearn's Index

Number of times I change my shirt before a Barenaked Ladies show: 4

Number of times the other band members change shirts before a show: 1

Number of times I change my shirt during a Barenaked Ladies show: 3

Number of times the other band members change shirts during a show: 0

Number of seconds after walking offstage that I have a piece of chocolate cake in my mouth: 27

Number of portable CD players Jim has: 0

Number of portable CD players I have that belong to Jim: 1

Pairs of headphones Gary has: 0

Pairs of headphones I have that belong to Gary: 1

Number of bars in the intro of "Great Provider" before I join the band: 4

Number of bars in the intro after I join the band: 48

Number of group activities I've attended this year (2000): 237

Percentage of group activities that I've slipped away from early without anybody noticing: 96 percent

Number of keyboards I've had that don't work: 4

Ratio of the number of times I told Andrew Creeggan that I would return his accordion to the number of times I actually returned it: 1:0

Ratio of the number of shows attended by Pat Hearn (my dad) to the number of shows attended by all other fathers of the remaining four band members combined: 15:1

Number of days, before Barenaked Ladies fired their former manager, that he asked me if I "needed any help with my keyboards": 10

Number of times since Barenaked Ladies fired their former manager that I have needed help with my keyboards: 16

Rank of Marilyn Manson among the weakest stomachs in rock and roll: 3,058

Rank of me among the weakest stomachs in rock and roll: 1

Number of times I've puked after removing a frozen rotten turkey from Brown's freezer: 1

Number of times I've sat and made rhymes with my friend . . . *Maroon*: 28

Number of shows the Waltons opened for Barenaked Ladies in the summer of '95: 26

Number of times I asked Jason Plumb if it was "hot up there" before we went onstage: 26

Number of times the tour bus has pulled away without me on it: 1

Number of girls I've kissed since joining Barenaked Ladies: I can't remember, to be perfectly honest.

Ten Famous Gordons

(Cue: Drumroll)

Flash Gordon: Retro-futuristic, mildly homoerotic space wanderer of '50s B sci-fi movies. Years later, Mr. Gordon was immortalized on record by Queen, the retro-futuristic, operatically inclined British group led by the extremely homoerotic singer Freddie Mercury.

Gordon Gano: Songwriter and lead singer for the seminal '80s group Violent Femmes. Steven Page first heard the Femmes in 1983 and was impressed with how they managed to get a punk-rock sound out of acoustic guitars and their voices on songs like "Blister in the Sun" and "Add It Up." Later, Steven would be surprised to learn that Gano was only seventeen when he recorded those songs. "I'd always thought he was just pretending to be a teenager in those songs," says Steven, adding that "in many ways he was one of the Gordons in *Gordon*."

Gordon "Gord" Downie: Canadian rock singer, poet warrior, and iconic front man of the Tragically Hip. The Hip, as they are known to Canadian fans, are not that well known in the United States, despite their rootsy rock sound and song titles like "Last American Exit" and "New Orleans Is Sinking." The latter is not to be confused with "If Venice Is Sinking" by Spirit of the West, another Canadian group and an early influence on Ed and Steve.

Gordon Sumner: Better known as Sting, Sumner is the tantrically hip former front man of the Police and erstwhile rainforest activist name-checked by Ed Robertson in "One Week" between Harrison Ford and Snickers.

Gordon Gekko: Fictional character in Oliver Stone's film *Wall Street* whose motto, "Greed is good," spoke to a generation of coke-fueled capitalists. Portrayed by Michael Douglas, Gekko was a slimy lounge lizard and all-around bad-karma chameleon.

Gordon Lightfoot: Archetypal Canadian folksinger known for his popular hits such as "Sundown" and "Early Morning Rain," in addition to the mariner's lament "The Wreck of the Edmund Fitzgerald." The Rheostatics, art-rockin' pals of Barenaked Ladies, went on to cover the latter, which was produced by Michael Phillip Wojewoda, who also cotton-swabbed the tape decks on *Gordon*.

Gordon's Gin: Alcohol, so goes the song, is a party-time necessity, and in the song "Alcohol," Steven Page is heard to request "a G&T for me." The *G*, of course, stands for *gin*, the clear alcoholic beverage of which Gordon's is a popular brand. The *T*, however, stands for *tonic*, a clear, tasteless mixer. Not to be confused with Tonic, a tastily and clearly mixed band from L.A.

Gordon Jump: Although his name sounds more like a direct order than a proper noun, this actor played Mr. Carlson on the sitcom *WKRP in Cincinnati*. Later he would replace Ed White as the "lonely repairman" in ads for appliance manufacturer Maytag.

Gordon "Gordie" Howe: Number 9 on the Detroit Red Wings but Number 1 in the hearts of a generation of NHL fans, including a young Wayne Gretzky, who chose to wear the number 99 by way of tribute to his hero. The owner of the most celebrated elbows in the league made history in his post-NHL career by becoming the first father to play on a line with both his sons, Mark and Marty Howe, in the short-lived World Hockey Association.

Gordon Sinclair: Canadians, of a certain age anyway, will recall this veteran radio broadcaster and regular panelist on CBC's long running current-affairs game show *Front Page Challenge*. Americans of a similar age may or may not recall that in the '70s, an editorial by Sinclair about the American Red Cross's financial woes was set to music. "The Americans," a jingoistic flag-waving novelty single, was quite popular for at least a few days.

So, as I'm sure you've guessed, the guys sometimes have plenty of time on their hands as "the wheels on the bus go round and round." As a result, they've invented their own favorite ways of breaking the boredom. In short, they play games.

Slint

"One of the games," Ed reveals, "is called Slint. It's a musical variation on the cities game where you name one city and then the next person has to name a city that starts with the letter that the former city ended in."

Have we lost anyone yet? What Ed is saying is that if someone says the city name *Toronto*, then the next player has to take the last letter, which is *O*, and come up with a different city name that begins with *O*, such as *Oakland*. Then the next player's city has to start with a *D*, and so on. But that's the cities game, and Ed says that Slint is more music-oriented. "We play it with band names, instead of city names," he explains. "The first player starts with 'A,' so he might start with 'Anthrax.' Then the next person might say 'XTC,' and then the following person would say 'Cream,' then 'Matchbox 20,' and so on. If there are numbers in the name, like 'Matchbox 20,' for instance, then you use the letters for the number, so it would be 'twenty,' and the next name would have to start with a 'Y.'"

Bonus: According to Ed, a player might get bonus hoots and hollers for a double answer, i.e., *Steeleye Span*, with the repeating *S*. But that's not all. You can also get the bonus hoots and their respective hollers for a band or artist name that is deemed current. "For example," Ed says, "right now, if someone busted off a 'Christina Aguilera' then everyone might go 'oh, current.'" Another rule is that all band names must be as they would be filed in a record store, i.e., the Beatles would be under *B* for *Beatles*. So Christina Aguilera would be considered *Aguilera, Christina*, which is under *A*. It ends in *A*, so it's a double.

"We call this game Slint," says Ed, "because once, after playing this for a very long time on a van ride, from Vail to Denver, 'S' passed to Tyler. There was a long, long pause (during which we all faked snoring and falling asleep) while Tyler tried to come up with an 'S' name. We had been playing for a long while, and many 'S' names had already passed. So after many miles of driving in silence and jeers from the other band members, Tyler came up with 'Slint.'

"We all laughed uproariously, me the hardest," Ed continues. "Tyler went on to say, 'No, they're like, a seminal Chicago "noise band," and they've got a Korean bass player,' which I thought was one of the most lyingly innocuous things to cite about a band to give them some validity. I thought, 'What could be a more ridiculously mundane thing to point out about a band to justify its existence?' I thought he was being a total ass wipe, and I don't think we allowed it. I think we made him struggle and find another 'S' band.

"Then the next day, when I got to sound check, there was a Slint disc on my monitor, along with a note from Tyler that read, 'Lick my hairy asshole—Slint exists!' Apparently, he went to the record store that day, found it, and yelled out loud in the record store. That's why Slint [is] in fact thanked on the *Stunt* liner notes. Forever after, that travel-pastime band-name game has been known as Slint. We tend to play it every time the whole band is riding in a van, and usually Craig Finley is involved and several other crew members. Once there was a crew member who refused to play. He's no longer with the organization."

Whaddya Like Better?

"It's a game that we played for a long time," says Ed. "Its origins, I think, are from a time when I just asked Steve, as a joke, 'What do you like better, salt or pepper?' And he just answered, 'Spinderella.'"

Now, with this game, the first point of contention is that one would never refer to the game's name itself. For example, you would never ask someone, "Do you want to play Whaddya Like Better?" "It just starts," says Ed, "by saying to someone, 'What do you like better . . . ?'"

Got it so far? Good, because here's Ed to explain away any semblance of understanding you may have about it. Keep in mind that kids who went to schools for exceptional students devised this game. Special Ed continues: "This is a bit hard to explain, but I think you'll get it. Essentially, what it is, is listing two things that have a similarity, but you leave out the similarity."

Okay, here comes the algebra. Ed illustrates the basic equation of the game. "You ask, 'What do you like better? "A-B" or "A-C"?'

APPENDIX B

267

But when you ask the question, you don't actually say the 'A' part. The person being asked then has to come up with something that conforms to 'A-D.'" Come on, Ed, we need examples.

"Okay, an example would be 'What do you like better? "Sabbath" (the B part) or "Grape" (the C part)?' Again leaving out the 'A' part. Now, what they have in common, or the 'A' part, is the word 'Black,' i.e., 'Black Sabbath' or 'Black Grape' (both bands from the U.K.). Then the answer could be: 'I think I like "Frank," as in "Frank Black," the former Pixies leader.'" Recapping, here's how that round would go:

Question: What do you like better? Sabbath or Grape?
Answer: I think I'd have to say I like Frank.

The idea is to show that you know the unmentioned word that is common to both choices and then to come up with a third choice that works with the previously assigned format. I told you these guys went to special schools.

"It can get really obtuse," Ed admits. "Like Steve said recently, 'Ed, what do you like better? "Edley" or "o wrestlers"?' And I replied, 'I'd have to say I like golly golly.' So the missing thing was 'sum,' as in, 'sum-o wrestlers,' 'Sum-edley,' or 'Sue Medley,' and then 'Sum Golly Golly.' Often the last one is a little off the beaten path or a bit of a stretch, but it's more fun that way."

Road Story

New Orleans: I Can't, I'm Workin

First, a little background: Barenaked Ladies' initial foray into the United States saw the neophyte band driving all night in a straight haul from Toronto, Ontario, down to Austin, Texas, for an appearance at the popular South by Southwest music festival. Ed says that it was a very cool thing, indeed, and the mini-tour did produce some wonderful highlights.

In Austin, the band performed alongside the Rheostatics for

a Canadian-themed showcase night. During the festival, Ed sat next to the Rheostatics' Dave Bidini. "I told him how much his band excited me," Ed recalls, "and how they reminded me of the spirit of Max Webster."

Max Webster, for the millions of you who may have never heard of them, was a great Canadian cult-rock band. Led by Kim Mitchell, who later had a mild U.S. hit as a solo artist with his sobriety anthem "Go for Soda," Webster was sort of a bar band, but with Frank Zappa–like arrangements and a decidedly cosmic lyrical bent, courtesy of the whacked-out poetry of non–band member Pye Dubois. Growing up in southern Ontario in the '70s and '80s, Max Webster was the missing link between progressive rock and good-time-boogie party music. And besides, they were pals and label mates with Rush! So you had to love 'em.

"I was probably insulting him," Ed worried, "but I think not. I was probably nineteen or twenty at the time, I didn't know jack shit."

He needn't have worried, for the Rheostatics have more than once been compared to Max Webster for their own skew on progressively arranged rock with a unique lyrical outlook.

The Ladies and the Rheos bonded, and the festival was a huge success all around. That was a highlight. But there were some lowlights as well.

A funny thing happened on the way back from Austin. Nigel Best thought it would be prudent to stop in New Orleans on the way home to Toronto. Not exactly a straight-line stop. Anyway, they went to New Orleans to meet up with Jocelyn Lanois, U2 producer Daniel Lanois's sister. Best was good friends with her, allegedly. The guys waited in a restaurant for two hours; she totally blew them off. Best swore she'd be there any minute. She never showed. So the band never went to Daniel Lanois's studio, and there they were—in New Orleans.

"We arrive [in] New Orleans at two in the morning," Ed says. "We pull into this real dive, a two-story motel, and we check in and get our keys. We've all got luggage, and we're all

A
P
P
E
N
D
I
X

B

269

dead tired and just wanting some sleep. Just then, we're met by this big, tall security guard. He's this mildly disheveled-looking black man, a big burly guy with this huge goiter on his neck. 'You boys best take the stairs,' he says to us. 'No,' we tell him, 'we're really tired, and we're just gonna take the elevator.' So he says, 'Ah-yate, then, I'll go wiss ya.' (Translation: 'All right, then, I'll go with you.')

"So this big guy just hauls off into the cramped little elevator with us," Ed continues. "Meanwhile, we're all just totally bagged and silent, so tired that we don't even question why we he wanted us to take the stairs and not the elevator, not to mention the fact that this means he obviously has to ride the elevator with us. The doors close.

"'You boys a little early,' he suddenly announces, then adds, 'About three, three-thirty in the morning, that's when all the pussy come out to the pool.' We're still just totally silent, not even looking at each other. Then he starts into his story: 'Yeah,' the big man begins, 'I remember one night, I was out by the pool. There was some ladies skinny-dipping in the pool. As I walked by, they called out to me. "You wanna join us?" they said. So I told 'em, "I can't. I'm workin'." Then she bend over, open up her ass, and do one of them dives into the pool.'"

Ed continues: "Then the doors open on the elevator, so he stops telling the story. I mean, the story had to be directly out of a *Penthouse* magazine or something. I'm sure that this never, ever, really happened to him. Regardless, he just cut the story off right there.

"'Ah-yate,' he says, 'you boys have a nice night.' And we got out of the elevator. We moved silently down the hall; once again, we were just dead tired at this point. We get back to our rooms. I think, at this point in our career, it was Ty, Steve, and me sharing a room, and Nigel, Jim, and Andy in another. We take all our luggage off and kind of sit down on the beds. Still, no one is speaking at all. We turn on some lights. Someone goes to the bathroom and comes back. Then Tyler looks over at us and goes, 'She bend over, open up her ass, and do one of them dives into the pool.' And we all just broke out laughing and couldn't stop laughing for about twenty minutes. We talked at length about how often a giant, disheveled, goiter-necked security guard gets beautiful women bending over and, quote, 'opening up their ass,' whatever that is, and doing, quote, 'one of them dives into the pool.' What is that, 'one of them newfangled dive things'? And what exactly did he mean by 'open up her ass?'

"So that became a very long-running joke with us. When we'd be in a school, we'd say, 'Ah, you boys a little early. You see, about three-thirty, four in the afternoon, that's when all the teachers come into the hallways. I remember one time this teacher came in and said, "You want to join me in the class-room?" We said, "We can't. We're workin'." Then she bend over, open up the class. . . .' We would basically substitute anything that rhymed with 'ass.' You know, 'Joe Strummer bent over and opened up the Clash. . . .'"

Roadside Story

Raleigh: The Duck Story

Duck: the word is simultaneously the name of a quasi-amphibious bird and a potentially life-saving instruction. As in, "Duck! There's a low-flying duck heading right for you!" But we won't get into that right now. Instead, we present another road-side distraction, one with a decidedly ducky quality to it.

It all began innocently enough at a cozy little restaurant inside a cozy little mall just outside Raleigh, North Carolina. The band had just finished eating, and as Jim recalls it, the whole thing was pretty uneventful until they stepped out of the mall and into the parking lot. While they waited for a cab, the guys noticed something that was causing quite a commotion.

"A panic-stricken duck," says Jim, "was waddling aimlessly over in the main flow of traffic." Onlookers were stymied as to what to make of this web-footed wanderer. And the guys, as Jim tells it, found themselves equally confused by the daffy little duck. "The mallard seemed plumb out of its quacking head," reasons Jim.

Upon closer inspection, however, it became clear that this wayward waterfowl had good reason to be freaked. She was distinctly postnatal. In layman's terms, she'd just hatched a whole nest of baby ducks. "On a nearby parking-lot island," Jim remembers, "there was a nest full of freshly hatched baby ducklings. Poor place to put a nest, one might say, but how's a duck to know? The heavy noonday traffic must have been keeping the mother from taking the youngsters to feed, or whatever mother ducks do with their kids just after egg break."

A variety of rescue solutions sprang up from the impromptu audience of assembled onlookers. "Someone tried calling Wild Animal Control," Jim reports, "but they couldn't get through. The flailing mother duck flew off in the meantime. It seemed as though it might just leave its little ones. Trauma! So now we're left with some helpless baby ducks and some helpless humans."

Jim says that the guys discovered a pond, just behind the mall, that was frequented by most of the other ducks in the area. "Somebody from the restaurant brought out a box that we could at least put the ducklings in," continues Jim. The box, it was believed, would keep them from scattering onto the road. One problem solved, then. But there was yet another dilemma awaiting our boys: "Do we leave them here in this hostile environment," Jim asked, "and just hope that the mother duck would eventually return? Or do we take them to the safety of the pond but risk the mother never finding them?"

After much deliberation, they decided the latter was the best option. So the ducklings were gently placed under the shelter of some bushes along the edge of the pond. "Now," says Jim, "comes the tough part: How was Mom going to find these guys? Last we saw of her, she was going off in a huff to who knows where."

They were secretly hoping that ducks might, in fact, possess some sort of innate tracking device. "We waited many minutes, hoping she would magically fly in." The band was also going to be late for a local radio-station visit where they were scheduled to perform live on the air. So the pressure was on. "It came to the point where we thought we had made a bad call in moving the babies."

Then, Jim recalls, just when all hope was lost, Ed came up with a brilliant idea: attempt to attract the mother by placing bread crumbs near the ducklings. "So we kicked into high gear," remembers Jim, "and threw enough bread around to bring on the entire migratory flock of the great Newfoundlandian puffin."

Turns out the puffin was a no-show, but Jim says that the idea was indeed popular with the duck population. "Sure enough, it was a duck party, all right. A particularly frenzied flier came barreling in, and we had a hunch that she just might be the mom. So we created a trail to the sheltering bush in hopes of luring her over to where the ducklings were. The once-frantic duck curiously gobbled bread along the trail and disappeared under the bush."

Several anxious moments passed as the guys waited, wondering just what the duck was going on under there. Then, a beak-through [sic]! "Within moments," recalls Jim, "to our cheers, the mother duck emerged from the bush with a proud waddle, leading every last duckling behind her in single file."

Ah, justice.